CHRISTOCENTRIC COMMENTARY SERIES

A COMMENTARY ON THE EPISTLE TO THE

GALATIANS

The Gospel *versus* Religion

James A. Fowler

PUBLISHING
P.O. Box 1822
FALLBROOK, CALIFORNIA 92088-1822

A COMMENTARY ON THE EPISTLE TO THE GALATIANS

The Gospel *versus* Religion

~ Christocentric Commentary Series ~

Copyright ©2006 by James A. Fowler

ISBN-10 – 1-929541-10-4
ISBN-13 – 978-1-929541-10-2

All rights reserved. No part of this publication may be reproduced, stored in a retrieval system, or transmitted in any form or by any means (including photocopyings, recording, electronic transmission) without the prior written permission of the author, except for brief quotations embodied in critical articles or book reviews. For information contact the author at C.I.Y. Publishing.

Published by **C.I.Y.** Publishing
P.O. Box 1822
Fallbrook, California 92088-1822

Printed in the United States of America

Scriptural quotations are primarily original translations from the Greek text of the New Testament, but otherwise from the New American Standard Bible, copyrights 1960, 1962, 1963, 1968, 1971, 1972, 1973, 1975, 1977, 1995 by the Lockman Foundation, LaHabra, California.

CHRISTOCENTRIC COMMENTARY SERIES

Cognizant that there are a plethora of New Testament Commentary series available on the market, the question might legitimately be asked, "Why another series of New Testament commentaries?" Although many capable commentators with varying theological perspectives have exegeted the text of the New Testament over the years, seldom do they bring with them into their studies a Christocentric understanding that the Christian gospel is solely comprised and singularly centered in the Person of the risen and living Lord Jesus Christ. The *Christocentric Commentary Series* will exegete and comment on the text of the New Testament from the perspective that the totality of what Jesus came to bring to the world of mankind is Himself – nothing more, nothing less. Having historically died on the cross and risen from the dead, He is not confined to the parameters of the "Historical Jesus," but as the Spirit of Christ He continues to live as He spiritually indwells those who are receptive to Him by faith. This recognition of the contemporary experiential dynamic of Christ's life in the Christian will form the distinctive of the *Christocentric Commentary Series,* bearing out Paul's Christ-centered declaration, "I have been crucified with Christ; it is no longer I who live, but Christ lives in me; and the life I now live in the flesh I live by faith in the Son of God, who loved me and gave Himself up for me" (Gal. 2:20).

All legitimate exegesis of the scriptures must pay close attention to the context in which the texts were originally written. The historical context of a text's *sitz im leben*, the "setting in life" of the author and recipients, is particularly important, for otherwise the interpretation will simply read into the text the presuppositions of the commentator and become *eisegesis* instead of *exegesis*. The *CCS* will carefully consider the historical context as well as the textual context of the scriptures.

Whereas the *CCS* is not intended to be a devotional commentary series or a detailed technical commentary citing all contemporary scholarship, our intent is to steer a middle course that maintains non-technical explanation that is academically viable. Although reference will be made to words from the Hebrew and Greek languages, those words will be converted to Roman lettering, allowing those who do not know the original languages to pronounce them. Citations, quotations, and endnotes will be kept to a minimum.

A diversity of interpretive formats will be utilized in the *CCS*. Some volumes will employ a verse-by-verse exegetical format (cf. *Hebrews* and *Galatians*), whereas others will provide comment on contextual passages (cf. *The Four Gospels* and *Revelation*). Regardless of the interpretive format, the *CCS* will render a "literal interpretation" of the scripture text, that is, in accord with the intended literary genre of the author.

As most biblical commentaries are utilized by pastors and teachers, or studious Christians seeking to understand the scriptures in depth in order to share with others, we join the Apostle Paul in the desire to "entrust these to faithful men (and women) who will be able to teach others also" (II Tim. 2:2). In so doing, may you "do all to the glory of God" (I Cor. 10:31).

TABLE OF CONTENTS

Introduction 1

Galatians 1:1-5
   Grace Greeting 9
Galatians 1:6-10
   Distorting the Gospel 27
Galatians 1:11 – 2:10
   Defending the Christocentric Gospel 43
Galatians 2:11-21
   Straightforward About the Gospel 65
Galatians 3:1-14
   God's Blessing Received by Faith 89
Galatians 3:15-29
   The Precedence of God's Promises 113
Galatians 4:1-20
   The Privilege of Sons 141
Galatians 4:21-31
   Sons of Promise 167
Galatians 5:1-12
   Stand Firm in Freedom 193
Galatians 5:13-26
   Freedom to Love by the Spirit 217
Galatians 6:1-10
   The Community of the Concerned 247
Galatians 6:11-18
   The Completeness of the Gospel of Grace 267

Addendum 283
   Maps 285
   Bibliography 289

Introduction

If I were to write a letter which began with the greeting, "Dear Frenchmen," to whom do you think I would be writing? Would I be addressing the citizens or residents of the nation of France? Would this be a broad greeting to all peoples of French ethnicity or ancestry? Would I be addressing only ethnic French males? Or perhaps it would be written to all peoples who speak the French language, whether in Quebec, New Orleans, Sierra Leone, Madagascar, Polynesia, etc. By the way, the words "*Francaise*" and the Anglicized word "French" are etymologically derived from the Germanic word for "free-man"; a fact that has no doubt long galled the French in their intense desire for ethnic and national distinction.

I employ this introduction to reveal one of the major issues of consideration concerning this letter – the identification of the recipients – which, in turn, reflects on its dating and the interpretation of its theological content. To whom was this letter written? Who were the original recipients, and what was the context that necessitated such correspondence?

Internal evidence within the epistle adequately reveals that it was written to the "Galatians" (1:2; 3:1). But who were these Galatians, and where did they reside? These have long been issues of differing opinion by biblical commentators.

Some historical background is necessitated. The designation "Galatians" refers to "Gaul-peoples," or "the persons of Gaul." When we look back in history, we note that Celtic people had settled in the central part of the territory now known as France

Introduction

at least by the sixth or seventh century B.C. They came to be known as the Gauls (Latin: *Galli*), and the territory they inhabited was designated as Gaul (Latin: *Gallia*), although some referred to the region as Galatia.

In the third century (approximately 280 B.C.) the Gauls invaded Rome and were ultimately repulsed in Greece. Apparently it was a contingent of these Gallic invaders who migrated in the middle of the third century B.C. into the north-central part of Asia Minor (aka Anatolia) south of the Black Sea, in what is now known as the nation of Turkey (cf. map #1). Known as fiercely independent peoples, they conquered the indigenous peoples of that region and established their own independent kingdom. The Romans eventually defeated these Galatians, and in 64 B.C. the Galatian kingdom was recognized as a subsidiary client-kingdom under the jurisdiction of Rome, but allowed to maintain their own king. By 50 B.C. Roman Emperor, Julius Caesar, had also captured the entire territory of Gaul in western Europe, which he referred to as *Gallia Transalpina* (Gaul across the Alps), noting in his *Commentaries* that the *Galli* or *Celtae* peoples inhabited the central portion of the territory, while the *Belgae* were in the north, and the *Aquitani* people resided in the south. When the king of the Galatian sub-kingdom in Asia Minor died in 25 B.C., the Romans used the occasion to change Galatia from an ethnically designated kingdom into a political province of the empire with borders that extended in a narrow band down towards the Mediterranean Sea (cf. map #2). This province was called "Galatia," and was so designated during the first century A.D. when the New Testament literature was written. It is also worthy of note that a portion of the Galatian political province was removed and added to Cilicia in A.D. 137, while another portion was removed and added to Pisidia in the third century, leaving only the northern portion of what was roughly the original Galatian ethnic region identified as the Roman province of Galatia (cf. map #3). The importance of this later provincial restructuring is apparent when we note that early Christian commentators of the second and third centuries A.D. tended to identify the recipients of Paul's letter to the Galatians as residents of the northern area which was the geographical area of the province so designated in their time. Based upon their early determinations, this became the prevailing understanding in Christian interpretation for many centuries.

Now the reader can begin to see why Paul's addressing of this letter to the "Galatians" raises questions whether the recipients are to be regarded as primarily ethnically designated, or whether this was a political and provincial designation, which in the middle of the first century A.D. would have included southern regions and cities into which Paul is known to have visited and ministered on his first missionary journey (cf. Acts 13,14) with Barnabas (who is mentioned by name in 2:1,9,13 as an individual with whom the readers would have been acquainted).

Recent biblical scholarship in the nineteenth and twentieth centuries A.D. has overwhelmingly advocated that the original recipients of Paul's letter to the Galatians were citizens of such cities as Lystra, Iconium and Derbe where Paul had established churches on his first missionary journey. This has come to be known as the "south Galatian" interpretation, as contrasted with the "north Galatian" interpretation which had prevailed for so many centuries in Christian thought, based on the comments of early Christian writers. Evidence that bolsters the "south Galatian" view includes the fact that Paul had founded these churches (1:8,11; 4:19,20), and there is no explicit record, in Acts or elsewhere, of his founding any churches in the northern region. Also, the readers were apparently acquainted with Barnabas (2:1,9,13), who accompanied Paul only on the first missionary journey into the southern cities.

What difference does it make whether the original recipients are accurately identified as from the north or the south? Not a lot! The content and message of this Galatian letter remains of value despite the specificity of its recipients. But there are some other issues which connect with the identification of

Introduction

the first readers. The first is the attempted reconstruction of the context of the situation that necessitated this correspondence, which is sketchy, at best. The second issue is the attempted dating of the writing of this letter. If the letter was written to the Christians in the southern cities of the first-century political province of Galatia not long after the first missionary journey, then it could have been written as early as A.D. 48 to 50, making it the earliest extant letter of the Apostle Paul. If the letter was written to Christians in the northern region of Galatia, then it could have been written as late as A.D. 56 to 58. Again, this does not greatly affect the value of the letter's content, but it does have some theological implications in the interpretation of the entire corpus of Pauline literature.

If Galatians is the earliest of Paul's epistles, then it could and should serve as the rudimentary and germinal thought of Paul's nascent theology. These incipient and inaugural thoughts might be regarded as foundational to the interpretation of all the rest of Paul's writings. If Paul's striking conversion on the road to Damascus is dated in A.D. 34 or 35, then Paul obviously had sufficient time in fourteen to fifteen years to be taught of the Spirit and to develop a well-formed Christian theological understanding that was radically and diametrically different from his previous Judaic theological training. Here in this early Galatian epistle Paul makes a heated polemical defense of the gospel of God's grace in Jesus Christ, features of which must be brought to bear on the interpretation of theological and eschatological statements in the remainder of Paul's writings. It can safely be said that all Pauline interpretation must reference his initial and inceptual expression in the epistle to the Galatians, drafted as it was in an unmitigated and unattenuated, straightforward defense of the gospel.

Mention has already been made to the "sketchy" information available about the contextual situation that prompted this letter. Paul had obviously planted these churches (1:8,11; 4:19,20), and the Christians in the churches had a great fondness and appreciation for Paul as their founding father (4:14,15). Sometime (the interval of time is unknown, but it would appear not to be an extended period - cf. 1:6) after Paul had departed from their cities, having left designated men in charge as teacher/leaders, some other teachers arrived with a modified belief-system that inculcated adherence to the Judaic law of the old covenant. It is difficult to reconstruct the precise identity of these interlopers, but it is obvious that they were advocating the necessity of religious observances (4:10), as well as male circumcision (5:2; 6:12), and attempting to seduce these new Christians into legalistic old covenant concepts (3:2; 4:21).

Paul's reaction to this decimation of the gospel of grace by reversion to religious legalism is a passionate polemic of defense for what he considered to be of eternal consequence. Paul comes out "firing." He "pulls no punches." Here was a little guy (the name Paul means "little"), who may have earlier in his life suffered from a "banty-rooster complex" in his combativeness, but when he was incensed he could still be a forceful and ferocious freedom fighter. Those who dared to engage in dialectic forensics with Paul soon found that he could chew you up and spit you out in no time. He could have you anatomically mutilated (5:12) and spiritually damned (1:8,9) before you knew what hit you! Merrill C. Tenney notes that this epistle "crackles with indignation, though it is not the anger of personal pique but of spiritual principle."[1] Paul was not about to stand by and allow the new Christian believers in Galatia to be duped, deceived and defiled by the religious accoutrements of the Judaizing false-teachers. Without any comments of praise, commendation or thanksgiving, Paul faces the issue of the misrepresentation of the gospel with a forceful fervor that some have referred to as "explosive", "dynamite", and "warlike."

The gospel that Paul had preached to the Galatians was the "good news" of God's grace in Jesus Christ. It was a liberating message that emphasized God's action in accord with His di-

Introduction

vine character, taking the initiative to do everything necessary on man's behalf to restore mankind to God's created functional intent. All of man's attempts to reach God, appease God, and perform in a manner pleasing to God – the essence of religion throughout the history of man – were now *passé* and unnecessary. There was no need for religious conformity to traditions, or for obedience to law-based rules and regulations such as "thou shalt..." and "thou shalt not..." God has done everything that needed doing in the "finished work" (cf. Jn. 19:30), and by the provision of His presence in receptive mankind by the person of Jesus Christ and the power of the Spirit, God continues by His grace to enable and empower the Christian believer to manifest His character and minister to others. Such was the gospel of grace and liberty that Paul had preached to the Galatians, and such was the spiritual reality that formed the basis of their Christian community as a church.

So when Paul was informed that foreign infiltrators had influenced the young Galatian Christians to revert to the performance of religious legalism, he was so incensed that he was compelled to write and set things straight. In this confrontational letter he delineates the dichotomous difference between the gospel of Jesus Christ that he had introduced them to, and the religious trappings of behavioral bondage that these subversive intruders were trying to impose upon them. The epistle is necessarily theological as Paul defends the ontological essence of Christianity in Jesus Christ, but whereas the epistle to the Romans explains Christian theology in logical sequence, Galatians defends Christian theology in the polemic "heat of the battle."

An underlying sub-theme of the epistle might be entitled, "The Gospel *versus* Religion." Though Paul does not use the word "religion" in the text of the letter, it is obvious that the performance-based "works" that the new Galatian Christians are being asked to add to the pure and simple gospel of grace in Jesus Christ is indeed the essence of all religion. This comprehensive theme thus becomes the lens through which the various details of the letter must be interpreted.

The effect of this letter when it arrived in the churches of Galatia in the middle of the first century A.D. was, no doubt, explosive. Just think of the controversy it must have provoked, and the reactions of the itinerant false-teachers who were probably present when it arrived! We do not know the effectual outcome of the impact that this letter had upon the Galatian churches, but we can document some of the effects that the statements of this letter have had on others in church history. Particularly in the sixteenth century Protestant Reformation, the message of the epistle to the Galatians served as the defense of the gospel against the religionism of Roman Catholicism. Martin Luther regarded this as his favorite book of the New Testament, and once wrote, "I have betrothed myself to it; it is my wife!"[2] Frederick Godet later explained that "this epistle was Luther's pebble from the brook, with which, like another (David), he went forth to meet the papal giant and smote him in the forehead."[3] This epistle to the Galatians can rightfully be said to have inspired the Protestant Reformation, but it should serve in every age to inspire reformation and restoration that sets Christians free from religious legalism, behaviorism, moralism, traditionalism, formalism, fundamentalism, denominationalism, etc., in order that they might appreciate the freedom of God's grace in Jesus Christ. Let it be noted, though, that since this epistle inevitably challenges the status-quo of static religion, it is almost impossible to exegete and expound this portion of Scripture accurately without raising the ire of those who have a vested interest in such religion.

The abiding value of Paul's correspondence with the Galatians is that it perpetually reveals the propensity of mankind to revert to performance-based acceptance before God in religion, rather than accepting the ontological dynamic of God's grace in Jesus Christ to manifest divine character to the glory of God. Whenever Christians begin to think that the performance standards of what they "do" or "don't do" is the basis of or the quality of their Christian life or their "spirituality," then they have lapsed into "Galatian thinking." "If only I didn't smoke, drink, swear, or fall into my besetting sin. If only I prayed more, read my Bible more, witnessed more, was more regular in church attendance, got along better with my spouse, or was a better parent, etc., then I would be a better Christian and would be more blessed by God." No! That is "Galatian thinking," that evaluates Christian life by achievement, merit, and reward, rather than by constant receptive trust in the grace-working of God in Christ. Such "Galatianism" is so pervasive and prevalent in the churches today as the religious legalists have duped Christians with the didactic declarations of "how-to" Christianity in prescribed procedures, formulas, techniques and duties which allegedly determine the distinguishing marks of a true disciple. Like Paul, we must reject such as a false gospel, and clearly explain that the only distinguishing mark of a genuine Christian is the manifestation of the life and activity of Jesus Christ in his or her life by the dynamic of God's grace.

Brief Outline

I. Paul *defends* the gospel revealed to him. (Chapters 1 & 2)
II. Paul *documents* that this revealed gospel was God's intent from the beginning. (Chapters 3 and 4)
III. Paul *demonstrates* the behavioral implications of this revealed gospel. (Chapters 5 and 6)

ENDNOTES

1. Tenney, Merrill C., *Galatians: The Charter of Christian Liberty*. Grand Rapids: Wm. B. Eerdmans Pub. Co., 1971.
2. Luther, Martin, *A Commentary on St. Paul's Epistle to the Galatians*. New York: Robert Carter & Brothers. 1860.
3. Godet, Frederick, source unknown.

Grace Greeting

Galatians 1:1-5

Conforming to the customary style of correspondence, Paul utilizes a typical and proper first-century epistolary form of greeting. In only two sentences, which comprise five verses in the popularly accepted versification of the scriptures (not part of the original), Paul identifies himself as the author, the Galatians as the recipients, and extends his greetings.

Writing, as was the custom in the first-century, on the cumbersome writing surfaces of leather or papyrus, there was obvious benefit to naming the author at the beginning (cf. Acts 23:26 for example), rather than at the conclusion as is customary in contemporary letter writing. Otherwise the entire document would have to be scanned to ascertain the identity of the letter-writer. Though Paul is the author of this letter, it is likely that he utilized the services of a scribal amanuensis as he often did in his correspondence (cf. Rom. 16:22). The secretary to whom he dictated remains unnamed in this letter, but it appears that Paul took the pen and signed off in "large letters" (6:11) at the conclusion to verify his authorship.

Paul could hardly wait to get to the issues that were unsettling him, but with epistolary propriety he begins the letter with two sentences of greeting. The form is formal and functional. The tone is tense and terse. The mood is muted and matter-of-fact. The statements are succinct and staccato.

One might be tempted to think that these are just gracious words of greeting in customary courtesy, but these are

1:1

much more than just a formulaic stereotypical prescript of opening words. These two initial sentences are freighted with foundational theological import which give us a foretaste of the themes of the entire epistle as Paul defends his personal apostleship and defends the soteriological significance of the "finished work" of Christ in His crucifixion and resurrection. We do well to give due attention to the words Paul uses in his greeting.

1:1 Paul identifies himself with his Roman name, ***"Paul."*** As the "apostle to the Gentiles" he seldom utilized his Hebrew name, "Saul" (cf. Acts 7:58; 9:4; 13:9; 26:14), a probable name-sake of the great Benjaminite king of Israel (cf. Phil. 3:5), perhaps regarding such as his former name.

When reviewing Paul's Hebrew background, it would appear that if ever there was a least-likely candidate to become the "Christian apostle of grace," it might well have been Paul. All natural phenomena were stacked against him. By race and culture he was a Hebrew, a Jew, taught from birth his inherent superiority as one of "God's people," and driven to excel to prove the propriety of such pride. By religion, which was melded with his culture, he was engaged in the performance righteousness of keeping the Law of old covenant Judaism. By denomination he was identified with the meticulous perfectionism of the traditionalist separatists, the Pharisees. By vocation he was apparently trained as a lawyer-priest under Gamaliel, perhaps being groomed for the Sanhedrin, the Jewish Supreme Court. By stature Paul was likely a little man, for that is the meaning of the name, "Paul." He may have been repulsive in his physical appearance (cf. 4:14,15). Just visualize a little Jewish lawyer of the strictest Jewish sect; physically bald-headed, bug-eyed, hump-backed and bow-legged. His size may have contributed to a "banty-rooster complex" that carried over into his personality as he combatively attempted to prove himself capable, arrogantly striving to prove himself self-sufficient. If

God could transform such a man into the "apostle of grace," then God can transform any man by His grace! To think that such a man could have written this epistle of grace-emphasis to the Galatians is "amazing grace" indeed!

Immediately after his name, Paul identifies himself as *"an apostle."* In its generic meaning in the Greek language this word referred to someone who was sent or dispatched as an envoy, emissary or messenger to perform a particular task as a delegate or ambassador. The Greek Orthodox churches have traditionally referred to their missionaries as "apostles" throughout the centuries. In Christian terminology the designation of "apostle" also had a more specific or inclusive meaning stemming back to Jesus' selection of twelve disciples, also known as the twelve "apostles" (cf. Lk. 6:13). These men were regarded as having been called to a specific foundational mission-task wherein they carried with them the authoritative empowerment of Christ Himself (cf. Matt. 28:18). When one of the twelve, Judas, committed suicide after his betrayal of Jesus, a replacement was carefully selected in the person of Matthias (Acts 2:21-26), but thereafter additional persons were regarded as having such foundational authority as apostles also (cf. Acts 14:14; Rom. 16:7; Gal. 1:19; Phil. 2:25; I Thess. 2:6). In identifying himself as "an apostle," Paul is apparently including himself among those who were called by Christ Himself for such a foundational mission-task. There were others who were "apostles of the churches" (II Cor. 8:23), being sent out by the commission of local churches, as Paul himself was from Antioch (Acts 13:2-4), but Paul was keen to identify himself as having more than an ecclesiastical commission as a missionary of a local church. He considered himself as being specifically selected by Christ Himself in His risen form, thereby having divine authentication and invested with divine authority as an apostle.

The necessity of defending his apostleship seems to have been a result of such being questioned and challenged by the trouble-making agitators who had infiltrated the Galatian churches. Their argument might be reconstructed thusly: "What right does Paul have to claim to be an apostle? He is not one of the original twelve appointed by Jesus during His earthly ministry. When they selected a successor for Judas, it was Matthias who was picked, not Paul; Paul was not even in the running. This little pip-squeak was a leader in the Jewish hit-squad of murderous, terrorist persecutors of the church, killing Christians far and wide. How can he be considered an apostle? He is a 'Johnny come lately' with no valid credentials or certification. He has no official appointment of the hierarchy of the church in Jerusalem, complete with proper ordination papers. He is just a self-appointed apostolic impostor!" Religion in general is absorbed in seeking such external credentials. "What seminary did you graduate from? What degrees do you have? Have you been duly appointed, licensed or ordained after having met the scholastic qualifications of an accredited institution and creditable denomination?" It does not matter if what one has to say is true or not; only if one is a qualified speaker, having met the self-determined qualifications of agreement with the belief-system and procedures of those offering the credentials. Such ingrown accreditation was equally prevalent in Jewish religion as it is in Christian religion. What a far cry from the biblical model of a Christian indwelt by the Spirit of Christ, called to minister by the authority of Christ, accredited by the manifestation of the divine activity of the life of Jesus Christ, and authenticated by the grace-dynamic of the ontological presence and activity of Jesus Christ by His Spirit.

Countering their religious misrepresentation of his call to be an apostle, Paul defends the authenticity and authority of his apostleship by parenthetically noting that his apostolic sending was ***"not from men, or through a man."*** His commissioning as an apostle was not just an ecclesiastical commissioning from a local church, as occurred in Antioch (cf. Acts 13:2-4), nor even from the church in Jerusalem, but was more extensive.

Neither was he commissioned with a subordinated-commission from Peter or one of the original twelve apostles. His was not a mediated human commission. He was not a religious representative or agent, sent out by men under denominational directive to build their empire.

Paul maintained that his apostolic commissioning was ***"through Jesus Christ, and God the Father, who raised Him from the dead."*** As "the authority of the person commissioned is that of the person who commissioned him"[1] (cf. Jn. 13:16), Paul was asserting that his was a divine authorization, authentication and credentialization, supernaturally imparted by the risen Lord Jesus Himself. It was not human action or the action of an organizational "...ism" that authenticated Paul's apostolic ministry, but the divine action of God, by Whom he was sent, placed and empowered. This did not make him an "independent" apostle, but one who was dependent on Jesus Christ alone, as he remained receptive to the direction of the divine Spirit.

Jesus Himself was sent into the world by the Father (cf. Jn. 17:18), and is thus to be regarded as the prototypical "apostle" (cf. Heb. 3:1), who in turn sends others into the world to minister and proclaim the gospel of grace in Him. By His resurrection from the dead He was authenticated as the Messianic Savior, "declared to be the Son of God with power by the resurrection from the dead" (Rom. 1:4). In identification with the Lord Jesus Christ, having been confronted with the risen and living Lord Jesus on the road to Damascus (Acts 9:4-6; 22:1-9; 26:12-19; I Cor. 15:8-10), and called to be an apostle to the Gentiles (Acts 26:17), Paul believed such to be the divine, supernatural authentication of his apostleship. Knowing that he was who he was by the grace of God (I Cor. 15:10), Paul was confident that he did what he did as an apostle by the spiritual empowering of the ontological dynamic of the resurrected Christ, the very divine power that "raised Jesus from the dead" (Eph. 1:18-21), becoming the "power of His resurrection" (Phil. 3:10), as

Jesus who said, "I am the resurrection and the life" (Jn. 11:25) functioned within him. Paul's theology was a resurrection-theology that recognized the dynamic empowering of the risen and living Lord Jesus in himself and all other Christians as God functioned by His grace. Paul's unwavering confidence of such spiritual identity and commission may have sounded arrogant, but when one knows beyond a shadow of a doubt that he has been met by God and sent by God, then he can bank everything on that identification, even to the point of saying that "to reject me is to reject Christ in me." That was Paul's sense of authenticity and authority as an apostle.

The fact that Paul links "Jesus Christ and God the Father" twice in these first two sentences of the epistle (1:1,3), may serve to indicate that there was a deficiency in the Christological and Trinitarian understanding of the intrusive false-teachers in Galatia. As the Christian gospel is based upon the intrinsic and essential oneness of the mutual deity of God the Father and God the Son, Paul categorically affirms such in these verses. Jewish theology denies such a divine oneness in distinction, and the theology of the Judaizers may have equivocated on this unity as well. Regardless of the reason, Paul affirms the Christological oneness that Jesus Himself explained when He said, "I and the Father are one" (Jn. 10:30).

1:2   Paul does not stand alone in his position concerning the gospel of grace in Jesus Christ alone. He indicates that he ***"and all the brethren who are with me"*** are sending this concerned correspondence to the Galatians. Such a generalized and inclusive reference to "all the brethren" would surely include his co-laborers and fellow-workers, perhaps Barnabas, Timothy, Silas and Sosthenese (depending upon where he was when the letter was written) who were his colleagues and associates in the ministry. "All the brethren" could also refer to all of the Christians in the local congregation in the community where he was residing at the time of writing, or even to the entirety of the Christian brethren in the universal household of faith (Eph. 2:19), God's family. Since he indicates that they are "with him," and this probably has reference to physical location rather than to ideological solidarity, Paul is likely referring to those physically surrounding him in the location where he wrote the letter.

Where was Paul when he wrote this letter? We do not know! If this letter is the earliest of Paul's epistles as we have speculated, then it may well have been written from Antioch of Syria between the first and second missionary journeys.

The import of Paul's including his co-laborers and/or the local congregation in this greeting was probably to indicate that he was not an independent, "loose cannon," "lone-ranger" apostle, as may have been the charge of the infiltrating teachers in Galatia. Paul had the solid support of many others who endorsed what he taught and lived. Obviously, "all the brethren" did not participate in the writing of this letter, but they stood with him in the advocacy of the gospel of grace.

As Paul addressed this letter *"to the churches of Galatia,"* we confront once again the question of the identity of the recipients. As noted in the introductory chapter, there have been two primary interpretations of the identity of "the churches of Galatia": (1) the "north Galatia" interpretation which prevailed for eighteen centuries of church history, identifying the Galatians according to their ethnic settlement in the north of Anatolia, in conjunction with the early (pre 25 B.C.) and later (second and third century A.D.) borders of the Roman political province of Galatia, and (2) the "south Galatia" interpretation which has predominated in modern nineteenth and twentieth century biblical interpretation, which takes into consideration the well-documented southern extension of the Galatian political province in 25 B.C. to include the cities of Lystra, Derbe, Iconium and Antioch of Pisidia, making this the proper designation of the territory when Paul wrote this letter in the middle of the first-century A.D. The historical evidence, as well as the biblical evidence of Paul's having visited these southern cities on his first missionary journey (Acts 13,14), with no record of his having established churches in the northern part of the province, combine to present a most reasonable option of identifying the recipients as the Christians of the churches in the aforementioned southern cities.

Since the problem of the interloping false-teachers appears to have been a regional problem, and not just centered in one particular local church, Paul addresses the letter to all the churches in the region. There was probably only one copy of the letter affixed with Paul's signature of "large letters" (6:11), so the letter became a circular letter carried from city to city by the courier, or (less likely because it might have been intercepted by the infiltrators) passed on from church to church.

Paul wanted those Christians who had been "called out" in the "churches of Galatia" to recognize that their calling was to live by God's grace in Jesus Christ in order to manifest the life of Jesus (cf. II Cor. 4:10,11) in their Christian lives. They were not "called out" to fall back into Judaic performance, but to be a radically different community living individually and collectively in the dynamic of God's grace.

1:3   As Paul, the "apostle of grace," begins and ends all of his epistles with some reference to the grace of God, the Galatian epistle is no exception (1:3; 6:18). The first word of the second sentence is ***"Grace."*** The standard salutation used in Greek letters of that day was the Greek word *charein,* meaning "greeting" or "rejoice." Paul does not use the customary formulaic greeting, but chooses a similar Greek word, *charis,* which expresses the totality of the function of the gospel of Jesus Christ. From Paul's perspective the entirety of Christianity could only be explained by God's grace, the complete and all-sufficient activity of God, deriving out of His Being, and expressed in the living Lord Jesus. Paul had experienced grace in a personal way. Grace had overwhelmed him and transformed him on the road to Damascus, radically changing him from an adamant advocate of the Judaic Law to an available vessel of God's continuing grace. For Paul, grace was not an impersonal force detached from the living Lord Jesus. Grace was not merely a kindly-inclined disposition of God's unmerited favor toward sinners. Nor was grace just an initial threshold endowment sufficient for personal conversion in regenerative grace. Grace is the personal and divine action of God in the Person of Jesus Christ – the ontological dynamic of Christological activity as the risen Lord Jesus in the form of the Spirit of Christ functions to be all and do all in the Christian. Christianity is the dynamic grace of God in Jesus Christ![2]

Thus understood, one can understand that grace stands in diametric opposition to any functional performance of the Law – from all legalistic performances to please God, appease God, or seize God. The old covenant Law was a document with no dynamic, a proposition with no provision, a regulation with no resource, an explanation with no empowering, an expression with no energizing, letters with no life, a mandate with no Messiah, governance without grace. So when Paul heard that the Galatian Christians were being seduced into defection and desertion from the grace-dynamic of Jesus Christ by reverting back to legalistic performance of the Law, he was appalled that they would go backwards from the greater to the lesser, from the superior to the inferior, from the gospel to religion, from grace to law, from freedom to bondage, from faith to "works," from son to slave, from fulfillment of promise to functional performance. The severity of the situation, which amounted to the abandonment of the gospel, prompted Paul's tirade of rebuke and censure in this epistle.

How can it be that so many religious commentators down through the centuries have failed to grasp the importance and intensity of Paul's conception of grace? So often there is less comment on this verse with its foundational greeting of grace than on the verses fore and aft in this introduction. Does this not expose that many commentators are spiritually sterile and theologically constipated, with no real understanding of the grace of God in Jesus Christ? They fail to recognize that Paul's reaction to the Galatian problem is predicated on his understanding of grace, which is referred to throughout this epistle (1:3,6,15; 2:9,21; 5:4; 6:18).

Along with grace, Paul mentions *"peace,"* which, as a concomitant to grace, is derived *"from God our Father, and the Lord Jesus Christ."* Although this could be regarded as but an equivalent to the Hebrew greeting "*shalom*," this word is also best understood as being invested with the full force of Christian theological understanding. It obviously conveys far more that the classic Greek understanding of the absence of conflict or war. In Pauline theological thought peace was always a result of God's grace activity in Jesus Christ. By God's grace one can have the spiritual condition of "peace with God through our Lord Jesus Christ" (Rom. 5:1), in place of spiritual animosity and alienation. By the indwelling presence of God's grace in Jesus Christ, the Christian can have the "peace of God which surpasses all comprehension" (Phil. 4:7) ruling in his heart (Col. 3:15). As the Spirit produces the fruit of peace (Gal. 5:22) as internal character, the living Lord Jesus who is Himself "our peace" (Eph. 2:14) manifests His life in peaceful external relationships with others (I Thess. 5:13; Heb. 12:14). Such peace is always a result of God's grace.

Perhaps Paul's mention of peace is a precursor of the freedom motif that will be presented later in the epistle. The peace of God is experienced as contentment when the Christian is free to be man as God intended, manifesting the character of Christ by God's grace. On the other hand, legalistic performance of behavioral rules and regulations never brings inner peace, only the chafing and frustration of imperfect performance and inability.

Note once again, as mentioned in verse 2, the combination of "God our Father, and the Lord Jesus Christ." In Christian theology it is impossible to disconnect God the Father and God the Son. They are inextricably one! The Greek word *kurios*, translated as "Lord," is constantly employed throughout the New Testament as the translation of the Hebrew word *Yahweh*, signifying that Jesus is indeed one with Jehovah-God.

1:4 In further explanation of the grace of God, Paul continues to explain that it was the Lord Jesus Christ ***"Who gave Himself for our sins."*** What an act of divine grace! We owed a debt we could not pay; He paid the debt He did not owe. Voluntarily submitting to the sacrifice of His own life in death by crucifixion, Jesus vicariously and substitutionally paid the price of death for the sin of mankind. He took the death consequences of our sin, that we might have the grace of His life. It was this remedial action of death by crucifixion, with the subsequent restorative action of resurrection-life, that was the objective of Christ's redemptive and regenerative advent. "He came to give His life a ransom for all" (Mk. 10:45; I Tim. 2:6), and "gave Himself for us" (Gal. 2:20; Eph. 5:2,25; Titus 2:14), "obedient to the point of death, even death on the cross" (Phil. 2:8), doing everything necessary to allow man to be restored to God's intent by His grace. The crucifixion of Jesus is the crucial defining event wherein we can behold the crux of differentiation between the human performance of religion and the once-and-for-all performance of the "finished work" (Jn. 19:30) of Jesus Christ, whereby God "not sparing His own Son, freely gives us all things" (Rom. 8:32) by His grace. What more can we do? Nothing! Only receive His divine life and activity.

But this is not all! The effects of God's grace go beyond the remedial benefits of propitiation, and lead on to the liberation of mankind in the triumph of *Christus Victor*,[3] as Christ's crucifixion and resurrection allow Him ***"to deliver us out of this present evil age."*** Mankind, by their failure to understand spiritual derivation (cf. I Cor. 2:14), have misunderstood the extent to which the fallen world of men "lies in the Evil One" (I Jn.

1:4

5:19), the "god of this age" (II Cor. 4:4), the diabolic power of the devil "energizing in the sons of disobedience" (Eph. 2:2). When the risen Lord Jesus confronted Paul on the road to Damascus He commissioned him to go to the Gentiles in order to "turn them from darkness to light, from the dominion of Satan to God" (Acts 26:18). Paul understood clearly that he had been "delivered from the domain of darkness, and transferred into the kingdom of Christ" (Col. 1:13). It is in that light that Paul here explains that the grace of God in Christ has delivered and rescued us by lifting us out of, and extricating us from, the context of the enemy's controlling power. This does not mean that we are delivered out of the physical world in some form of escapist withdrawal, for we are still "in the world," but "not of the world" (Jn. 17:11,16). Nor does it mean that the fallen world-order is being transformed into the kingdom of God. Rather, "once and for all" by the death, burial, resurrection and Pentecostal outpouring of Jesus, God has delivered mankind from Satan's power. "He has disarmed the rulers and authorities, having triumphed over them through Him (Jesus)" (Col. 2:15). This ultimate victory of Christ over all diabolic forces is the theme of John's *Revelation*.[4]

Such deliverance and extrication from Satan's dominion becomes efficacious for each individual Christian when he/she is spiritually regenerated. It is not just a futuristic expectation that is progressively realized as we are delivered from the present evil age by the suppressionism or perfectionism of behavioral performance, even though there are "not yet" ramifications of deliverance. Paul's point is that we have been delivered from the devil's power at a definitive point in time (aorist tense) – objectively in the redemptive work of Jesus Christ on the cross, and subjectively in spiritual regeneration.

The Christian has been lifted up out of, and above, the diabolic dominion of the Evil One who presides over "this present evil age." We have been "saved from this perverse generation" (Acts 2:40). This is not a linear conception where two ages abut one another on a chronological time line; one ending where the other begins. Rather, the two ages, world-orders, or kingdoms overlap and exist simultaneously in the present. This allows for the cosmic dichotomy and conflict between the satanic and divine spiritual orders of operation – between the fallen, evil world-order and the kingdom of God in Christ. The Christian has been "taken up out of the present evil age" in order to live in the Lordship reign of Jesus Christ in the kingdom of God. Though he still has his feet on the ground living in the world, the Christian individual is no longer a slave to sin (Rom. 6:16-18) and self-orientation via satanic energizing (Eph. 2:2). We are no longer in "bondage to the elemental things of the world" (Gal. 4:3), the "weak and worthless elemental things" (Gal. 4:9). We do not have to be sucked into the conflict of the fallen world's ways, or succumb to the seemingly irresistible conformity of the ideologies and methodologies of the present age. Because we "have been delivered out of this present evil age," we do not have to "be conformed to this world, but can be transformed by the renewing of our minds, that we might prove what the will of God is" (Rom. 12:2).

One of the major players on the plane of the perverted and diabolic world-order is religion. Yes, religion is the devil's playground![5] The religious Judaizers who had pushed their way into Galatia are surely to be represented in the same manner that Paul describes the troublemakers who invaded Corinth: "false apostles, deceitful workers, disguising themselves as apostles of Christ. And no wonder, for even Satan disguises himself as an angel of light. Therefore it is not surprising if his servants also disguise themselves as servants of righteousness." (II Cor. 11:13-15). When Paul indicates that Christians "have been delivered from this present evil age," he is countering the intrusive servants of Satan, religious though they be, who were advocating legalistic performance of the Law in order to deliver them from the evil age. Paul regarded such as "worthless" (Gal. 4:9) and antithetical to the gospel of God's grace-dynamic in Jesus Christ within the kingdom of God.

Only by the operative of God's grace in the past and present work of Jesus Christ can we recognize ***"the will of our God and Father,"*** and realize that this as been God's plan from the beginning, to restore man by the "finished work" of Christ to function as He intended by His grace. The continuity of that divine grace (cf. Rom. 8:32), operative by the Spirit of Christ, enables and empowers Christians to live in conformity to God's will for man, which is always the expression of the divine character of Christ in our behavior. God's will is not a mystical maze to be analyzed or a problematic puzzle to be deciphered. God's will is always Jesus Christ – His life lived out in humanity to the glory of God!

1:5   Recognizing that the grace-dynamic of God in Christ is essential to the teleological objective of God in His creation, Paul concludes his introductory greeting by noting that it is God the Father ***"to whom be the glory forever."*** God can only be glorified by the grace-expression of His own all-glorious character being expressed in His creation. For mankind this necessitates the presence of God in Christ by His Spirit dwelling in the spirit of man in order to manifest His character by His grace unto His own glory. Man is "created for God's glory" (Isa. 43:7), and we are to "do all to the glory of God" (I Cor. 10:31), but this can only be accomplished as God by His grace "does exceedingly abundantly beyond all that we ask or think, according to His power that works within us, unto His glory in the church and in Christ Jesus to all generations forever and ever" (Eph. 3:20,21). The glory of God is not a result of the utilitarian productivity of religious performance, whereby men of utmost sincerity and tireless activity attempt to do great things for God. Such endeavors only carry the designation, "Ichabod" – the glory of the Lord has departed (I Sam. 4:21). God is only glorified by His own grace-activity expressing His own all-glorious character unto His own glory. Such doxological teleology is the intent of God "unto the ages of the ages," forever and ever, eternally, perpetually, without limit and without end.

"Amen." So be it. Let it be. May God confirm such as a verity by His grace.

What an introductory greeting in two sentences! As noted earlier, these are far more than customary courtesies to be read at a glance. In these opening sentences Paul has laid the foundation for his understanding of the Christian gospel and for all that he has to say in the remainder of the letter. Granted, when we continue the letter these words of greeting appear to be "the calm before the storm," but they are most important if we are to understand Paul's perspective of the severity of the situation in the Galatian churches. Only by understanding the gospel of grace in Jesus Christ which Paul preached and lived, can we begin to comprehend and appreciate the reaction he unleashes as he continues this epistle.

Be forewarned, though, that when anyone, in any age, stands with Paul in proclamation and defense of the gospel of grace in Jesus Christ alone, he/she will inevitably be charged with trafficking in the abstract, the nebulous, and the ambiguous. He/she will be labeled as advocating mysticism, subjectivism, or existentialism. He/she will be cautioned about allowing too much freedom wherein people might become lawless or licentious libertines. Natural, religious men are afraid that if Christianity is not structured, regulated, and administrated with clear-cut and concrete guidelines, then it will disintegrate in myriad perversions. Apparently there is no faith that God is competent in His omnipotence to control His people and His church by the power of His Spirit.

The self-promoting religious teachers will inevitably appear whenever and wherever the gospel of grace is introduced, and like the religious moles in the churches of Galatia, they will be advocating legislated behavior by keeping moralistic rules according to pre-set parameters, thinking that such will "deliver them from the evil age." Religion always seeks a codification of conduct in "thou shalts" and "thou shalt nots," with defined procedures and techniques for achieving such a self-defined criteria for "spirituality." Seeking "pat answers," they develop a static *ordo salutis* which is part of their "statement of faith" in an epistemological belief-system. Leadership is regulated by acceptable qualifications and credentials to develop a "chain of command" structure wherein everything is controlled and predictable. Success will be measured by quantifiable statistics in buildings, budgets and baptisms. Tangible expression of Christian commitment will be encouraged through financial giving, regular attendance, and personal involvement in church programs.

Meanwhile, the Christian peoples, like sheep willing to follow a shepherd, will probably be open and receptive to such religious direction. Grace seems so risky and unpredictable. It cannot be managed or controlled. One cannot even project the probability of its results. Yes, as Jesus Himself said, "The wind blows where it wishes and you hear the sound of it, but do not know where it comes from and where it is going" (Jn. 3:8). Religious performance, on the other hand, seems so safe and secure with its well-defined parameters of rules and regulations, complete with "how-to" books full of techniques and formulas for obedience. The leaders clearly explain their expectations, and tell you what to do, offering tangible criteria of success with visible rewards. What people cannot seem to see is that when you have such a perimeter of fences, such a regimen of enforced labor, and such strong links to hold you together, you are enslaved in the confining prison of religion, and no longer free to participate in the gospel of grace in Jesus Christ.

It appears that the majority of Christians, if given a choice of working on a chain-gang or walking across a swinging suspension bridge with no handrails, would opt for the chain-gang labor. It is tiring and monotonously predictable, but you can't fall off. It may kill you, but it's a methodical way to go! The swinging-bridge of grace is scary. It is as unpredictable as God Himself. Security is only found as we "fix our eyes on Jesus" (Heb. 12:2) and are "led of the Spirit" (Rom. 8:14; Gal. 5:18), trusting Him to keep us standing by His power (I Pet. 1:5). That requires faith! Many there are who will choose the chain-gang of religion over the swinging-bridge of grace, but Paul's epistle to the Galatians will forever be the clarion call to such peoples, encouraging them in no uncertain terms to accept nothing more and nothing less than the grace of God in Jesus Christ alone.

ENDNOTES

1. Bruce, F.F., *The Epistle to the Galatians: A Commentary on the Greek Text.* The New International Greek Testament Commentary series. Grand Rapids: William B. Eerdmans Publishing Co. 1982. pg. 72.
2. cf. Fowler, James A., *The Grace of God.* Fallbrook: C.I.Y. Publishing. 1993.
3. cf. Aulén, Gustaf, *Christus Victor: An Historical Study of the Three Main Types of the Idea of the Atonement.* London: S.P.C.K. 1931.
4. cf. Fowler, James A., *Jesus Christ: Victor Over Religion, A Commentary on John's Revelation.* Fallbrook: C.I.Y. Publishing. 1993.
5. cf. Fowler, James A., *Christianity is Not Religion.* Fallbrook: C.I.Y. Publishing. 1995.

Distorting the Gospel

Galatians 1:6-10

The initial two sentences of "grace greeting" were more than customary courtesies – certainly more than schmaltz before the assault. They were laden, as indicated, with theological import that served as the foundation for Paul's argument throughout the epistle.

Whereas most of Paul's letters commence with some words of commendation, praise or thanksgiving (cf. Rom. 1:8; I Cor. 1:4; Phil. 1:3,4; Col. 1:3-5; I Thess. 1:2,3), Paul forgoes such in the opening words of this letter. He was "champing at the bit" to unleash his impassioned remonstrative rebuke of the Galatians' reversionism, which he was only able to hold in check until the third sentence. Paul's preference would have been to engage in a face-to-face confrontation with the Galatians and their seducers (4:20), but for whatever reason he had to settle for addressing the issues in this letter. He wastes no time in getting straight to the point.

The apostle loved these young Galatian Christians. He was so concerned about their being sucked into the dead-end religion of behavioral performance that he could not remain silent, but felt compelled to confront the intolerable situation. His grieving soul was full of emotional intensity that would criticize their credulity and denounce their defection, but it was the infiltrating false-teachers that most roused his seething consternation and indignant invectives. New Christians are so fragile, vulnerable and susceptible to the introduction of distortions

1:6

and perversions. They so want to believe that religious teachers have their highest good and intent in mind, and will lead them on in their walk with God. They often lack the discernment to recognize that diabolically inspired religious peddlers (II Cor. 2:17) will inevitably misrepresent the gospel of God's grace in Jesus Christ for their own selfish benefit and ends. This is not to imply that the neophyte Galatian Christians were not to be held responsible for their backsliding, for Paul certainly holds them accountable. They should have been able to recognize that when the peripatetic outsiders began to criticize Paul and the gospel he shared, there was "a skunk in the woodpile." Apparently some of them did realize the perversion, and they were probably the ones who initiated or participated in the delegation who traveled to give a full report of the tragic situation to Paul.

1:6   Have you ever been blind-sided, or hit-up-alongside the head having never seen the approaching object that hit you? That must have been how the Christians in the Galatian congregations, and especially the religious purveyors of performance righteousness, must have felt when these forceful words of Paul were first read to them. It must have hit them like a brick!

Abruptly and explosively, like throwing a grenade into their midst or dropping a bombshell, Paul expresses his astonishment at the propensity of the Galatian Christians to abandon the gospel of Christ. ***"I am amazed that you are so quickly deserting Him who called you by the grace of Christ."*** Shaking his head in incredulous disbelief, Paul must have been questioning: "How can they do this? How can they be so blind? Why are they so easily led like sheep to the slaughter? Why are they so easily led down the primrose path of religion, like pigs back to mud, or like prisoners back to the chain-gang?" He was perplexed (4:20), stupefied, and flabbergasted, as well as displeased, irritated and grieved. The unstable fickleness of the Galatians was astonishing and alarming. It had happened "so quickly," apparently indicating a short interval of time had transpired since Paul's ministry among them, and since their conversion (or perhaps, though not likely, referring to the rapidity of their transference of allegiance since the time when the false-teachers arrived).

The charge that Paul made against them is that of desertion or defection. This was a serious charge! The Greek word was used of those who betrayed their allegiance to a community, becoming deserters, defectors, or turncoats in treasonous abandonment. Those having any Jewish background, including the Judaizing infiltrators, may have remembered God's words to Moses about the Israelites, who "having quickly turned aside from the way which I commanded them, made for themselves a molten calf and worshipped it," for which God's "anger burned against them" (Exod. 32:8; Deut. 9:16). In more recent history they may have recalled those who were turncoats and defectors during the Maccabean revolt (II Macc. 4:46; 7:24; 11:24). They would have been appalled to have their actions identified with such desertions.

Paul makes it clear that the actions of the Galatians was the result of personal choice. Though they may have been duped and deceived, seduced and snookered, they were not passive dupes and were to be held personally responsible for their choices. Only the tense of the verb that Paul used mitigated the situation, for he did not employ a past tense that indicated they were fixed in their defection or that their apostasy was complete, but he used a present tense that implied they were only in the process of deserting which meant they could still change their minds and stop their wrong course of action.

When Paul wrote of their "deserting Him who called you," he was not alluding to their having forsaken their allegiance to him, Paul, who had preached to them. The obvious reference is to their falling away from and turning against God. The Christian gospel is a personal gospel of a personal God who sends His Son as a personal Savior to personally reconcile mankind to Himself. In a personal calling of His Spirit to the hearts of men (cf. 5:8), receptive individuals can enter into a personal faith-love relationship with Jesus Christ as He personally indwells their spirit in the form of His Spirit (cf. Rom. 8:9,16). The problem was not that the Galatians were abandoning one theological ideology for another, exchanging an orthodox belief-system for one of heretical error and falsity (as these verses have often been misinterpreted and misapplied), rather, they were deserting their personal and ontological relationship with God who had "called" them, not just in the past objective "calling" of all men in the work of Jesus Christ (cf. Rom. 8:28-30), or in a solicitous summons to a decision about doctrine and church membership, but in the gracious beckoning of "calling" them into His own Being in spiritual oneness and unity.

This divine "calling" into His own Being is "by the grace of Christ." This does not mean that grace is the instrumental means of God's calling, nor the locative position into which God calls men, but that grace is the essential action of God's calling in Christ. All that God does, including His "calling," is by the expressive dynamic of His grace-activity in His Son, Jesus Christ, as He calls mankind into an ontological relationship with Himself. What amazes Paul is that the Galatians would turn their backs on such a dynamic Christ-energized grace-calling of an ontological relationship with the living Lord Jesus, to settle ***"for a different gospel."***

Apparently the Jewish-Christian didactors who had descended upon the Galatian churches referred to their moralistic and epistemological teaching as "gospel," but with a few "different" tenets of belief. Their concept of "gospel" included traditions that attached the Jewish heritage of observance of the old covenant Law with the acceptance of Jesus as the Messiah. This was, indeed, an heterodoxically "different" concept of "gospel," for the Christian gospel is not an epistemological belief-system, nor a moralistic modification of behavior, despite the fact that the preponderance of Christian religious instruction has failed to understand this any more than the Judaizing instructors. The biblical and Christian concept of "gospel" is the good news of the vital indwelling dynamic of the risen Lord Jesus living out His life in a Christian's behavior by the power of His Spirit, thus allowing for the restoration of functional humanity as God intended. The gospel is the ontological essence and dynamic of the life of Jesus Christ. Another gospel of a different kind would, therefore, have to be something other than the grace of God in Jesus Christ; a completely different entity of authority structures, epistemological formulations, or ethical strictures, far removed from the essential Being of Christ's life. So it was that the religious rabble-rousers in Galatia were propagating a performance-package completely antithetical to God's grace in Christ, advocating meritorious Law-keeping that would allegedly earn favor with God and "deliver one from the present evil age" (1:4). Paul was fully aware that this was a total denial of the all-sufficient "finished work" (cf. Jn. 19:30) of Jesus Christ, and the ongoing dynamic of the life of Jesus as the total essence of the gospel. This is why he was so distressed and dismayed at their departure from the gospel by detaching the very concept of "gospel" from the dynamic of Christ.

1:7 A different concept of "gospel" is *"not really another gospel"* of the same kind or category with slight variations or accretions, concerning which Christians might agree to disagree. The intruding instructors in Galatia may have been intimating that their presentation of the gospel was not essentially different from that proclaimed by Paul, but they were just explaining additional implications of the gospel which could take Christians to a higher level of spirituality. Paul would have none of that amalgam and admixture. The gospel of grace in Jesus Christ allows for no adjuncts, and will never serve as an adjunct to anything else. It stands alone as nothing more and nothing less than Jesus Christ. There is no other gospel! There can be no plurality of gospels. There is only one gospel – the "good news" of what God has done and continues to do by His grace in His Son Jesus Christ. Anything else is so essentially different that it cannot be legitimately called "gospel." It will not be "good news," but will necessarily be the "bad news" of religious bondage.

What is happening, Paul went on to explain, is that *"there are some who are disturbing you."* He does not identify these trouble-making "disturbers of the peace" by name or theological label, but the plural pronoun "some" indicates a multiple number in the band of propagandists. Luke's account of the intrusive teachers in Antioch bears many similarities: "*Some* men came down from Judea and began teaching, 'unless you are circumcised according to the custom of Moses, you cannot be saved'." (Acts 15:1). After the Jerusalem council rejected such teaching, a letter of apology and explanation was written to the Christians in Antioch, noting, "We have heard that some of our number have *disturbed* you with their words, unsettling your souls" (Acts 15:24), which was carried back to Antioch by Paul, Barnabas and Silas. So Paul was quite familiar with this type of Judaizing agitators, and must have suspected from whence they had come.

Apparently there were a few of the new Christians in Galatia who were disturbed enough about the aberrant teaching they had heard from the mouths of these false teachers that they determined to send a report to Paul to inform him of the situation. Writing in response to such, Paul does not appear to have much tolerance for those who would engage in such seditious activity of harassing, intimidating, threatening and troubling (5:12) the new converts. Later in the epistle he warns that "the one who is *disturbing* you shall bear His judgment" (5:10).

Though the pernicious propagandists probably explained that they were merely attempting to improve on Paul's presentation of the gospel, Paul adamantly charges that they are deliberately *"wanting to distort the gospel of Christ."* It wasn't just Paul's version of the gospel to which the pesky proponents of legalism were attempting to make permutations. The gospel is Christ! Christ is the gospel! It is not the gospel about or concerning Christ, nor simply the gospel introduced and preached by Christ, but it is the gospel of which Christ is the ontological essence. Any attempt to change or alter, to twist, turn or tamper with the personified Truth (cf. Jn. 14:6) of the gospel in Jesus Christ Himself, will of necessity transform the essential nature of the presentation into that which is no longer gospel. To distort the gospel is to destroy the gospel. To annotate the gospel is to annihilate the gospel. To modify the gospel is to mutilate the gospel. To emend the gospel is to eliminate the gospel. To revise the gospel is to reject the gospel. To negotiate the gospel is to negate the gospel. To attempt to improve the gospel is to invalidate the gospel. To supplement the gospel is to supplant the gospel. To reduce the gospel is to repudiate the gospel. To diminish the gospel is to decimate the gospel. The gospel is what it is (Who He is) only in the ontological dynamic of the Person and work of Jesus Christ.

The distortion of the gospel that Paul is referring to here is not a slight deformation of doctrinal data. The Greek word denotes turning something into its opposite, as in "sun turned into darkness" (Acts 2:20), or "laughter turned into mourning" (James 4:9). When any attempt is made to change the gospel into anything other than the life of Jesus Christ alone, then the essential nature of that being discussed has been turned 180 degrees from gospel to religion, from grace to law, from faith to works, from God to Satan. Such transformation Paul finds intolerable.

1:8 That explains why Paul proceeded to declare that *"even though we, or an angel from heaven, should preach to you a gospel contrary to that which we have preached to you, let him be accursed."* The exclusivity of the gospel in the reality of the Being of Jesus Christ is to be maintained regardless

1:8

of the messenger. Paul is not attempting to defend himself as the messenger, nor is he attempting to defend an ideological message that he presented. Rather, he defends with unshakable certainty the unchangeable and immutable gospel of "the one mediator between God and man, the man Christ Jesus" (I Tim. 2:5). In his German translation of the Bible, Martin Luther wrote, "That which does not teach Christ is not apostolic, even if Peter and Paul be the teachers. On the other hand, that which does teach Christ is apostolic, even if Judas, Annas, Pilate or Herod should propound it." Paul would have agreed with Luther, for he includes himself and all of his co-laborers in ministry as unqualified to alter the gospel of Christ only. Then, in a stretch of hyperbolic extension, Paul includes even Michael, Gabriel and the angels of heaven as incapable of changing the gospel without the most severe consequence. Paul knew full well that Jesus was higher than the angels (cf. Heb. 1:3-14), so he did not hesitate to state that even the angels cannot make variances to the Christocentric gospel. This comment may have been prompted by the itinerant tutors' claims to have been led by, or to have received revelations from, angels for the revision and amplification of the gospel, as such claims of angelic intervention have been employed by religious innovators through the centuries.

Paul was so convinced that the gospel of grace in Jesus Christ alone, that he received and was commissioned to share on the road to Damascus, was the exclusive good news of the singular divine reality for the restoration of mankind, that no matter who advocated anything else, be they men or angels, they were dead-wrong and damnably in jeopardy. That, of course, included, and was specifically aimed at, the Judaizers who were seeking to add legalistic observances as necessary accretions to Christianity. Any addition to Christ necessarily implies the insufficiency of the all-sufficiency of Christ, and is therefore at variance with and antithetical to the gospel.

The consequence for those who would thus cut the heart out of the gospel by reducing Jesus Christ to an adjunct redundancy is that they should receive the anathema curse of God's condemnation to final doom and destruction. This is not Paul's personal passion or pique that pronounces a curse upon others, saying, "To hell with them!" Only God can pronounce the divine ban of His wrath on those who will be damned to final destruction by His retributive judgment. Paul's reasoning is based on the fact that God's anathema curse is the opposite of His blessing, and if "God has blessed us with every spiritual blessing in heavenly places in Christ Jesus" (Eph. 1:3), then the only alternative to accepting the blessings of the "finished work" of Jesus Christ is to experience God's anathema for thinking that we can finish off God's work and be blessed thereby.

What an indictment on so much of Christian religion that sells the gospel short by demanding ethical duties in addition to the grace of God in Christ. These moralistic inculcations are not innocuous diversions and contingencies, but are diabolic misrepresentations worthy of the indictment of God's anathema for the damnableness of religion. Who could better issue the pronouncement of "Religion be damned!" than the former Pharisee who knew the bankruptcy (cf. Phil. 3:2-9) of Judaic religion, and would under no circumstances allow its encroachment upon the Christian gospel?

1:9 The avalanche of justifiable reaction to the decimation of the gospel continues as Paul writes, *"As we have said before, so I say again now, if any man is preaching to you a gospel contrary to that which you received, let him be accursed."* Based on the wording in the original Greek language, it is doubtful that Paul is merely reiterating what he said in the previous sentence. Instead, he is explaining that he had forewarned them during his previous visit to the churches of Galatia, and is "now" (as opposed to "then") repeating his warning of the consequences of attempting to make the gospel something other than the dynamic reality of Jesus Christ. Regardless of his scholarship, charisma, ecclesiastical position, or any other criteria, if "any man," without exception, should attempt to advocate supplemental requirements to the simple reception of the singular reality of Christ's life, he stands culpable for the dire consequences of God's anathema.

Paul is appealing to the Galatian Christians to recall their own experience of having "received" the essential gospel of the living dynamic of Jesus Christ. It was not that they had assented to a new belief-system, or agreed to participate in a different religious tradition, but they had "received" Christ Jesus (cf. Jn. 1:12; Col. 2:6), His very Spirit (cf. Gal. 3:2) by faith at the time of their initial conversion and regeneration. Such faith is the receptivity of His divine activity, the very life of Jesus, wherein are all the blessings of God, and apart from which are God's consequential curses upon sin. Having received the reality of the living presence of God in Christ, the Galatians should have been able to recognize that the rival teachers advocating reversion to religious rules and regulations (even though they probably claimed it was an advancement in spirituality) were promoting a fallacious gospel contrary to the ontological dynamic of Jesus Christ and the blessings of God in Christ.

1:10 This verse serves as a transitional connection between the denunciatory rebuke of verses 6-9 and the defense of his divine calling to share the gospel as an apostle (1:1) in the following paragraphs of 1:11–2:21. Paul was so convinced that the only explanation of his life and ministry activity was the dynamic of Christ in him, that his defense of the gospel and the defense of his life in sharing the gospel are intertwined. To the Corinthians, he wrote, "By the grace of God I am what I am" (I Cor. 15:10), and to the Romans he testified, "I will not presume to speak of anything except what Christ has accomplished through me" (Rom. 15:18). Paul found his identity and reason for being in the fact that Christ was his life (cf. Gal. 2:20; Col. 3:4).

Apparently Paul's detractors in Galatia had sought to discredit him by casting aspersions on his *modus operandi* and his motivational ambition. It appears that his procedures and tactics of preaching may have been questioned by suggesting that he engaged in the subterfuge of cheapening the gospel into a watered-down version of "cheap grace" that did not cost anything or require anything. Perhaps he was charged with attempting to placate the people with a persuasive propaganda that cut corners by explaining only half of the gospel. Their argument could have been: "He didn't tell you the rest of the story, as we are doing, about how you need to observe the commandments of the Law, and submit to male circumcision. Paul was luring you in with a lax, less arduous, Law-free gospel message of 'easy believism,' that sought to conciliate you into making a decision without counting the cost." Religion through the centuries has attempted to discount the grace of God as being too soft, too easy, too cheap, too free, because they want to impose their oppressive dictates of doctrine and duty upon people.

Having just lambasted those who would distort the gospel the gospel into something other than the grace of God in Jesus Christ, and suggested their liability to damnation, Paul asks, **"Am I now seeking the favor of men, or of God?"** "Does what I have just written sound like conciliatory "playing to the crowd" that seeks to seduce you and sell the gospel short? If I were courting and currying to the favor of my audience, would I be expressing myself in such straightforward polarizing terms that depict the alternatives in such either/or categories of blessing or cursing, gospel or religion, grace or law, faith or works, God or Satan? No! Opportunistic flatterers don't call for the anathema of God, as I have just done. I am not inconsistent. I did not "then," when I was previously sharing the gospel with you, nor do I "now" in this letter, mince my words in rhetoric that seeks to gain your confidence by the art of persuasion. I am not a confidence-man who is trying to put something across on you or God. My only concern is that the gospel of God's grace in Jesus Christ is clearly proclaimed and maintained."

In a slight variation on the preceding question that proceeds to address his motivation and ambition rather than persuasive procedures, Paul continues by asking, *"Am I striving to please men?"* Once again the challengers in Galatia had apparently suggested that Paul was seeking the accolades of prestige and popularity by engaging in his mission work. Their argument might have gone something like this: "The reason Paul omitted telling you about the need for circumcision and the observance of the Law, you know, was because he knew that by lowering the standards he could achieve greater statistical success and build a more impressive personal empire of supportive churches. That man is driven to do what he does by the desire for self-seeking significance and superiority." Paul's response to such accusations is basically that, "Men-pleasers usually 'pull their punches' and do not 'shoot as straight' as I have just done in explaining the absolute intolerance for any distortion of the gospel of Jesus Christ. If I were seeking the self-enhancement of personal popularity, then my 'all or nothing' approach to the gospel that I have just presented is certainly not the way to 'win friends and influence people.'" Though Paul knew that there were some who "proclaimed Christ out of selfish ambition, rather than from pure motives" (Phil. 1:17), he explained to the Thessalonian Christians that he and his fellow ministers "had been approved by God to be entrusted with the gospel, so they spoke, not as pleasing men but God, who examined their hearts" (I Thess. 2:4).

In further explanation of the logic of his argument, Paul states, *"If I were still trying to please men, I would not be a bond-servant of Christ."* The "if" is an unfulfilled condition that is contrary to fact, and not true, either when he visited Galatia or at the time of the present correspondence. But apparently there was a time in Paul's life when he was a religious man-pleaser, for he sets up the hypothesis about "*still* trying to please men." As a Jewish Pharisee he was undoubtedly given to ostentatious display in his personal ambition to climb the ladder in the religious and political hierarchy of Judaism in Jerusalem. He would go to any length to please his superiors, even pursuing Christians as far away as Damascus of Syria. Paul knew well the defense of belief-system, the meticulous observance of moral Law, the propagandizing proselytizing of those driven to force all others into conformity with themselves, and the pride of "confidence in the flesh" (Phil. 3:4-7). He wanted nothing to do with such religion anymore. If he were to continue to engage in such religious activities, as the Jewish-Christian proponents in Galatia were now advocating, then he would not and could not "be a bond-servant of Christ," for they are mutually antithetical.

Paul recognized, as few religious men ever do, the total incongruity between being a self-oriented religious man-pleaser and attempting to be pleasing to God as a selfless servant of Jesus Christ. The Roman slave was regarded as but a vessel or instrument who existed in order to serve at the disposal of his master's use or pleasure. In like manner, Paul saw himself as totally available to serve and please his Master, the Lord Jesus Christ, by abandoning himself to the control of Christ's Lordship in the dependency and receptivity of faith. Christian servanthood is not indentured coercion to the capricious dictates of the divine Lord, but is the self-chosen willingness to be bonded to the very Being of God in Christ, and the faithful availability to serve as the ontological expression of Christ in active ministry. The incongruity that Paul is emphasizing obviates that one cannot be a slave of Jesus Christ, and at the same time a slave to men's opinions. "No man can serve two masters" (Matt. 6:24).

These bombastic words of Paul, coming as they do, immediately after the letter's brief greeting, reveal how severe Paul regarded the situation in the churches of Galatia. This was no minor matter that could be delayed and resolved in future negotiations. The essential nature of the gospel was at stake, and had to be addressed immediately.

Paul's understanding of the gospel was nothing other than the vital dynamic of the life of the risen Lord Jesus, "the gospel of the grace of God" (Acts 20:24) in Christ. There is no *different* gospel. There is no *other* gospel. Christianity is Christ. The entirety of the gospel is in the ontological dynamic of the life of Jesus Christ, or there is no "good news." The life and activity of Jesus Christ is all of the gospel, or there is nothing that deserves the name "gospel." Everything that God has for man is in the "finished work" of Jesus Christ, or there is no hope.

Those who would attempt to add to or subtract from the gospel have already misunderstood the essence of the gospel, and turned it into something that can be supplemented or annotated. They have already detached the gospel from the dynamic grace of God in the "finished work" of Jesus Christ. Any attempt to alter, adapt or annotate the gospel does not create a different gospel, but is a total denial of the gospel. It is not a diminishment of the gospel, but a total destruction of the gospel. It is not a distortion of the gospel, but the total dissolution of the gospel.

How tragic, then, that religious interpretation of these verses down through the centuries, has for the most part failed to grasp Paul's understanding of the gospel and thus misused this text. The religious commentators have usually thought that Paul was arguing about the *ordo salutis* of an orthodox soteriological belief-system. They have therefore surmised that the "distortion of the gospel" in a "different gospel" is to be discovered in divergent doctrines or unacceptable behavioral practices, thus using these verses to justify hurling charges of "heresy" at those with differing opinions or interpretations.

What they do not recognize is that their religious misinterpretations fall under the same indictment of "distorting the gospel" as did the aberrations of the Judaizers in Galatia, with the same consequent pronouncement of anathema upon their religious perversions.

On the other hand, the more liberal religionists might fault Paul for having an unduly exclusionist concept of the gospel, and for being narrow-minded, intolerant and discriminatory towards those advocating alternative opinions and approaches. "Progressive sensitivities call for open-minded, non-judgmental acceptance and accommodation of pluralistic thought. All antitheses must be merged in syntheses. Criticism, confrontation and condemnation have no place in the undiscriminating amalgam of modern thought," argue the progressive modernists.

Paul may well be out of step with the modern world of "political correctness" and its epidemic of tolerance, but he had the spiritual appraisal (I Cor. 2:14,15) and discernment of God's Spirit, the Spirit of Christ, to "test the spirits" (I Jn. 4:1) and ascertain that which was contrary to the singular essence of the gospel in Jesus Christ. He had the boldness of Christ to "make a defense" (I Pet. 3:15) and "contend for the faith" (Jude 1:3), so that people would not be "taken captive through empty deception, according to the traditions of men" (Col. 2:8). Would that more Christians today would have such a clear concept of the gospel which is Christ, and take their stand against all religious distortion and perversion.

＃ Defending the Christocentric Gospel

Galatians 1:11 – 2:10

Having just wiped out all pretense of a different gospel other than the dynamic reality of Jesus Christ alone, there is no doubt that the congregations in Galatia were waiting with bated breath for what the reader would say as he continued to read Paul's letter. Their attention would now be keenly drawn to the defense of the Christocentric gospel, as Paul continued in his letter to the Galatians to defend his life and ministry and gospel as revealed in Jesus Christ.

Although this is the longest autobiographical passage in Paul's writings (cf. I Cor. 11:22-33; Phil. 3:4-6), Paul is not just sharing his testimony, but has selected events in his life which document how Christ has worked in his life to reveal Himself as the gospel. Paul is not just egotistically defending his personal reputation against the derogation of the detractors who had entrenched themselves in the Galatian churches, but his desire was to explain how the real dynamic of the gospel of the life of Jesus Christ had impacted his life and become his life. The ontological reality of the gospel had been ontologically experienced by Paul to the extent that the man and his message were inseparably linked. The living Lord Jesus was the only gospel Paul knew. The living Lord Jesus had so integrally become Paul's life that he could say, "for me to live is Christ" (Phil. 1:21), "Christ lives in me" (Gal. 2:20), "Christ is our life" (Col. 3:4). The gospel reality of Jesus Christ indwelt Paul and was embodied in him as the basis of all that he was and did, leading Paul to declare "I am who I am by the grace of God" in the risen Lord Jesus (I Cor. 15:10). Paul could not defend himself without defending Christ who had made him a "Christ-one," a Christian. Since Paul regarded Jesus Christ to be the essence of the gospel and the essence of his own life, self-defense and gospel-defense were both Christ-defense.

There is still a polemic turbulence in these words as Paul is countering and refuting the so-called "gospel" proffered by the pseudo-preachers of performance-piety. If, as in Acts 15:1, these Judaizing church-crashers had come from Judea, from the church in Jerusalem, they may have regarded such as the "mother-church" headquarters of genuine Christianity. Paul takes pains to distance himself from any derived gospel emanating from Jerusalem or from any apostolic leadership of the Judean church. He is intent on showing that the divine revelation of God's grace in Jesus Christ is the essence of his life and ministry (1:11-24), as well as the essence of the gospel and the unity of the church (2:1-10).

1:11   Transitioning from the denial of any gospel other than the living dynamic of God's grace in Jesus Christ(vss. 6,7), and the consequences of divine anathema upon any attempt to develop such (vss. 8,9), Paul explained, ***"I would have you know, brethren, "that the gospel which was preached by me is not according to man."*** "Let me make this clear, my dear spiritual brothers in Christ, that the gospel which I preached to you in Galatia – the very gospel which you heard and received (1:9) – is not a gospel of human origin." Still regarding the Galatian Christians as "brothers," as distinct from the "false brothers" he will refer to later (2:4), Paul is concerned that his spiritual family members should clearly recognize that the gospel is the divine reality of the risen and living Lord Jesus. The gospel is not some systematized construct of human thought, for man's natural reasoning would never have devised a triune God and a dying Savior. The gospel is not a continued development of

Jewish religious tradition authorized by the original apostles in Jerusalem. The gospel is not something that Paul invented as his own personal interpretation and opinion. The gospel is not "according to man," but "according to God," as the divine dynamic of His own Being and life. There are many forms of "self-made religion" (cf. Col. 2:23) that are "according to man," but they are not God's gospel in Jesus Christ.

1:12 In contrast to the misleading missionaries in your midst, ***"I neither received the gospel from man, nor was I taught it by man."*** "The conveyance of the gospel to me was straight from God's supernatural activity of grace in Jesus Christ, both on the road to Damascus and in all subsequent outpourings." The recent religious rough-riders in Galatia may have claimed that they learned the gospel from the original apostles down in Jerusalem, and that Paul must have been taught through some subordinated instructors as well, but their version was obviously closer to the original tradition and more complete than what Paul had preached. Paul, on the other hand, was adamant that the gospel he shared did not come through human channels, for he was never "discipled" by any man, nor served as any man's apprentice. He did not accumulate the gospel through didactic transmission of data, doctrine, or tradition. He did not attend catechism or seminary to be instructed in the necessary epistemological tenets of a Christian belief-system. To know facts *about* Jesus Christ is not to know Jesus Christ, who is the gospel.

"I received the gospel through a revelation of Jesus Christ," Paul declared. "The gospel I share is of divine origin for I received Him in faithful receptivity of His activity when He personally and unilaterally revealed Himself to me on the road to Damascus. The gospel I share is 'according to God,' because God opened heaven to reveal Jesus to me in a personal revelation." Jesus is both the subject and the object of the revelation of God; both the source and the content of the revelation.

1:13,14

It is not just the revelation *about* Jesus Christ, nor merely the revelation conveyed *by* Jesus Christ, but the revelation which *is* Jesus Christ as its very essence. Jesus is the ontological essence of God's revelation. This is the basis for Karl Barth's statement that "revelation is the abolition of religion,"[1] which is the very point that Paul is attempting to make to the Galatians.

1:13 "Now this was a radical transformation in my life when I received God's revelation in Jesus Christ, ***"for you have heard of my former conduct of life in Judaism."*** Paul had quite a "reputation" among the Christian communities concerning his pre-conversion activities. The intrusive instructors had surely brought this to the Galatians' attention by way of derogation and suspicion. ***"I used to persecute the church of God beyond measure, and tried to destroy it."*** Luke noted that "Saul was ravaging the church, entering house after house; and dragging off men and women, to put them in prison" (Acts 8:3), "breathing threats and murder against the disciples of the Lord" (Acts 9:1). The risen Lord Jesus asked Saul on the road to Damascus, "Saul, Saul, why are you persecuting Me?" (Acts 9:4). With utmost regret and remorse, Paul admits that he "persecuted the church of God" (I Cor. 15:9; Phil. 3:6). To persecute the "church of God," the "people of God," is to persecute Jesus Himself, for He is the ontological essence of the Church, which is His Body. But Paul had no concept of the spiritual fulfillment of the old covenant concepts of God's people, Israel, Jews, Jerusalem, and the temple, when he so vigorously, vehemently and violently attempted to annihilate and eradicate Christianity from the face of the earth. Paul seemed to approach everything from an excessive "all or nothing" perspective, and he had gone on a murderous rampage of "religious cleansing" to wipe out Christians.

1:14 Paul was motivated by the personal ambition of "trying to please men" (1:10), and in his fierce, fanatical zeal to compete against all others and earn more performance points by cutting down all opposition, he admits, *"I was advancing in Judaism beyond many of my contemporaries among my countrymen."* Paul knew how to climb the ladder in the game of ecclesiastical politics! He had impeccable credentials in Jewish religion, *"being more extremely zealous for my ancestral traditions."* Highly motivated and task-oriented, Paul was never one to approach anything "half-heartedly." Since religion is fueled by "zeal without knowledge" (Rom. 10:2), Paul was obsessed in his violent defense of religion. Religion too often embodies violent conflict against those who disagree and will not conform to their traditions, causing religious fundamentalists to become terrorists, willing to go to any end, even death, for their cause. Paul was a good Pharisaic student who knew the minutia of Jewish traditions well, with all their "fence laws" of religious performance and conformity. Under the surface Paul may have been indicating to the Galatians, "If you want addendums of Law-performance, I know about those better than anyone, for 'concerning righteousness in the Law, I was found blameless'" (Phil. 3:6). But Paul knew that such performance had nothing to do with the gospel of grace in Jesus Christ. If ever there was a person whose personal and religious background dictated against any predisposition to become the "apostle of grace," it was Paul! It took a radical action of divine intervention to transform him and totally restructure his thinking.

1:15 The first-person pronouns of the previous two verses are now exchanged for the second-person pronouns of Deity as Paul expresses the initiative of God's grace in his life. As an exemplary Pharisee, Paul knew about religious separationism, but now he refers to the divine action of God, *"Who set me apart, even from my mother's womb."* It was no accident, no incident of fortuitous luck, that transformed Paul into a grace-Christian. Paul attributed what happened in his life to God's pre-ordained plan to sovereignly act in his life, even before he was born. This was no fatalistic, arbitrary predeterminism or predestinarianism that disallowed Paul's responsibility to be receptive to God's activity, but Paul recognized God's foreordination and foreknowledge to "set him apart unto the gospel of God" (Rom. 1:1), the spiritual union with Jesus Christ. Like Isaiah (Isa. 49:1,6) and Jeremiah (Jere. 1:5) before him, Paul believed that God could select and call an individual "even from his mother's womb" for His divine purposes. Paul certainly was not looking for Jesus on the road to Damascus. It was not his idea; it was the last thing he could have conceived of. But God **"called me through His grace, and was pleased to reveal His Son in me."** The grace-activity of God revealed Jesus Christ *to* Paul objectively, and *in* Paul subjectively in regeneration and the on-going dynamic of His life. God did not just reveal factual data, informational propositions of a beliefsystem of doctrine or theology, but He "revealed His Son," the "revelation of Jesus Christ" (1:12), the personal revelation of the ontological reality of the Son of God indwelling Paul's spirit and living in Paul as his life (cf. Gal. 2:20; II Cor. 13:5).

1:16 The purpose of this revelation of Jesus Christ in Paul was "*that I might preach Him among the Gentiles.*" Paul's conversion and commissioning both occurred on the road to Damascus (cf. Acts 9:3-22; 22:6-21; 26:12-18). Notice that he was commissioned to "preach *Him*," Jesus Christ, not some denominational party-line or some systematized package of doctrine. Jesus is the subject and the object, the dynamic and the content of genuine Christian preaching. That Paul should become the "apostle to the Gentiles" (Rom. 11:13; I Tim. 2:7) was a revolutionary reversal for such a Jewish, Pharisaic exclusionist, who would have regarded all ethnic diversity other than Jews to be unclean *goyim* who were "strangers to the covenant" (Eph. 2:12). But again, like Isaiah, he knew he was called to be "a light to the nations" (Isa. 49:6; Acts 13:47), proclaiming a universal gospel in Christ, and "not presuming to speak of anything except what Christ had accomplished through him, resulting in the obedience of the Gentiles" (Rom. 15:18).

Since Paul was convinced of God's calling and commissioning, he *"did not immediately consult with flesh and blood."* He did not consider it a priority to consult with any human leadership delegation for legal or spiritual authoritative counsel. Knowing that the gospel was the vital dynamic of the living Lord Jesus, and not an informational system compiled by human conference and requiring consensual ratification, Paul didn't consider it necessary to consult with any "district superintendents" or other human mediators. He knew that there was only "one mediator between God and man, the man Christ Jesus" (I Tim. 2:5).

1:17 *"Nor did I go up to Jerusalem to those who were apostles before me,"* Paul continues to explain. He did not seek authentication of the gospel reality of Jesus Christ in his life from the original apostles who had been disciples of Jesus, and who were apparently still localized, for the most part, in the "First Church of Jerusalem." Regarding their apostleship to have precedence in time, but not precedence in authority, Paul did not consider his apostolic commission to be in any way inferior or secondary to the original apostles. His was an independent divine commissioning, and not a subordinated ecclesiastical commissioning requiring validation from the Jerusalem jurisdiction. (Whether the traveling traditionalists who had come to Galatia thought that it was, or that it should be, is not clear.)

Instead, Paul reports, *"I went away to Arabia, and returned once more to Damascus."* As there is much ambiguity about the geographical location of Arabia, and no other details about this period in Paul's life, we can only speculate that Paul probably went into the area known as the "kingdom of the Nabateans" which was to the south and east of Syria. In his

1:18,19

letter to the Corinthians, Paul indicates that the ethnarch of Damascus, who took his orders from Aretas, king of the Nabateans, sought to seize him in Damascus for some reason (cf. II Cor. 11:32). The purpose of this diversion in Arabia was probably to be taught of the Spirit of Christ, and to listen to God in obedience (*hupakouo*). Others, like Moses, David and Jesus, had been taught of God in the wilderness, and Paul needed time to meditate and reflect in order to reorient his thinking to accommodate the fact that all Jewish expectation was fulfilled in Jesus Christ. His return to Damascus was probably brief, and likely the occasion of his being lowered in a basket over the city wall at night (II Cor. 11:33).

1:18 Thoroughly taught by Christ Himself in Arabia concerning his ministry to the Gentiles, Paul *"then, three years later, went up to Jerusalem to become acquainted with Cephas, and stayed with him fifteen days."* Some have noted that Paul's three years of personal instruction from the risen Lord Jesus in Arabia seems to correspond to the approximately three years that the original disciples were taught by the physical Jesus in Palestine, indicating that the "historical Jesus" is not to be separated from the "spiritually indwelling Jesus" as of any more or less consequence, and Paul's apostleship is not to be regarded as inferior to that of the others who were with Jesus in the flesh. The point that Paul seems to be making is that though he did eventually go to Jerusalem (cf. Acts 9:26) for a brief visit of fifteen days, that was certainly not sufficient time for Peter to have discipled him in all there was to know about the gospel, verifying again that he did not receive his gospel understanding from men, but from God.

1:19 Then, to further illustrate that his was not a humanly derived and subordinated apostleship commissioning, Paul explains that he *"did not see any other of the apostles except James, the Lord's brother,"* while in Jerusalem. Though not alienated from the other apostles, Paul wanted to make it clear that he was not dependent upon them as a protégé or pupil. Some, especially those in the Roman church who wish to preserve the perpetual virginity of Mary, attempt to explain that James was a cousin of Jesus, or a step-brother who was the son of Joseph from a previous marriage. The most logical explanation, however, is that James was the son of Joseph and Mary, the first male child born of Mary after Jesus (note order in Matt. 13:55), who later became a Christian and an apostolic leader in the Jerusalem church (cf. Acts 12:17; 21:18).

1:20 Parenthetically, Paul explains, *"(Now in what I am writing to you, I assure you before God that I am not lying.)"* "As incredible as it may sound," Paul seems to be saying, "I assure you it is true." Employing what sounds like a legal oath, Paul insists, "I am telling the whole truth, and nothing but the truth, so help me God!" "I am willing to explain every place I went and everyone with whom I spoke." This may have been in response to an accusatory charge by the Galatian intruders that Paul was not telling the whole truth about his background and motives. Perhaps they were insinuating that Paul must have learned the gospel from such apostles as Peter or James, or at least had his understanding validated and affirmed by such authoritative apostles, and then subsequently deviated from such acceptable doctrine by becoming a radical renegade who set off on his own independent mission to the Gentiles. He may have been faulted for being too independent in going his own way and teaching his own personal interpretation, as well as for being too liberal in not conserving the continuity with Judaic heritage in the performance of the Law – a "Torah-traitor." Paul denies such.

1:21 Continuing his recital of the sequence of events that were pertinent to his explanation of his divine calling and commissioning in Christ, Paul notes that *"Then* (after some confrontations with the Jewish hierarchy in Jerusalem - cf. Acts 9:26-30; 22:17-31) *I went into the regions of Syria and Cilicia."* The order of these provinces, which were combined by the Romans between 25 B.C. and 72 A.D., may indicate the route he traveled from Jerusalem, going first through Antioch in Syria, and then to Tarsus, the capital of Cilicia, where Paul had been reared (Acts 9:11; 21:39). There is no better place to learn how to live out the practical implications of the Christian gospel than in your old home town! Exiled from the center of Christian activity in Jerusalem, Paul settled in Tarsus to continue to learn the implications of the gospel of Christ in him.

1:22 Still distancing himself from any implications of his being a deviant product of Judaic Christianity, Paul reports that he *"was still unknown by sight to the churches of Judea which were in Christ."* He was "out of touch" with the mainstream Christianity of his day, having been independently called and taught by Jesus Christ, the essence of the gospel. He was never a celebrity speaker, put on display as a trophy among the Judean churches around Jerusalem. The only "sight" the Christians in the churches of Judea may have had of him was when he was still a Jew engaged in his efforts to eradicate Christians. It is interesting that he refers to these local churches as being "in Christ," rather than "in Judaism," exposing once again the ontological dynamic of the risen Lord Jesus in the gospel and in the Church.

1:23 The Christians in the churches of Judea *"kept hearing, 'He who once persecuted us is now preaching the faith which he once tried to destroy.'"* The reports were relayed despite the absence of any "Judean press," that the notorious Paul had been radically changed from a persecutor to a preacher. Skepticism surely abounded at first that one so thoroughly entrenched in Judaic exclusivism that he sought to exterminate Christians, could possibly be converted and transformed as a Christian.

That he was now preaching "the faith," an identification tag used for Christians who were allowing for the receptivity of the activity of Jesus Christ in them by faith, was a remarkable phenomenon.

1:24 *"They were glorifying God because of me,"* Paul adds. The Jewish Christians in Judea were praising God for Paul. "To God be the glory, great things He as done!" Why, then, Paul must have been questioning in his own mind, and hoping that the Galatian Christians would ask themselves also, were these Jewish Christian agitators (probably from Judea) dogging his heels and attempting to undermine and counter the gospel of grace in Jesus Christ that he preached?

2:1 Paul's training as a lawyer may have prepared him for the forensic defense that he makes by reporting a careful chronological sequence of the selected events that establish both his independence from the other apostles (1:11-24), as well as his solidarity with the other disciples (2:1-10). ***"Then after an interval of fourteen years I went up again to Jerusalem with Barnabas, taking Titus along also."*** Likely calculating from the same point of chronological reference as the previous "three years" (1:18), Paul indicates that fourteen years after his conversion on the road to Damascus, he traveled once again to Jerusalem, probably from Antioch, having been sought out by Barnabas to assist in the ministry to Gentiles in Antioch (Acts 11:25,26). Since Paul is being so careful with his chronology here, to counter the charges of his detractors in Galatia, it is most likely that this visit to Jerusalem was the famine-relief journey that Paul took with Barnabas, as recorded in Acts 11:29,30, being prior to the first missionary journey when Paul first preached in the southern cities of Galatia. Though many commentators have identified the visit Paul refers to in this verse with the trip to participate in the Jerusalem Conference (Acts 15:2-29), since the same issue of circumcision was discussed, the precision of Paul's chronology and the difference between the private (2:2) and public (Acts 15:12) contexts of the discussions would seem to dictate against such. Taking two witnesses to conform with Jewish practice, Paul traveled to Jerusalem with Barnabas, a Jewish Christian whose name meant "Son of Encouragement" (Acts 4:36), and Titus, a Gentile Christian convert who had not been circumcised in accordance with Jewish Law.

2:2 The occasion for this visit to Jerusalem was not a result of a summons from the church leaders in Jerusalem wherein Paul was "called on the carpet" to defend his actions, but ***"it was because of a revelation that I went up"*** to Jerusalem, Paul explains. Neither did Paul initiate the visit in order to force the issue of Law-observance and circumcision, but it was God's initiative to disclose to Paul in personal revelation, however perceived, that he should make the trip. Being thus "led by the Spirit" of Christ (cf. Rom. 8:14; Gal. 5:18), Paul and Barnabas and Titus went "up" (since Jerusalem is on Mt. Zion) to Jerusalem, and the occasion of their going served as a convenient conveyance of the famine-relief contributions.

When they arrived in Jerusalem, Paul explains, ***"I submitted to them the gospel which I preach among the Gentiles, but I did so in private to those who were of reputation, for fear that I might be running, or had run, in vain."*** Though Paul defended his independent commissioning as an apostle, he obviously did not advocate independent separationism and isolationism (an attitude he knew well from Pharisaism), but sought a consensus of solidarity with the leaders in the Jerusalem church. He was not a "lone-ranger Christian," but was keenly aware of the need for unity in the Body of Christ, the Church. It was not that Paul had to submit his gospel of grace and liberty in Jesus Christ for the approval of the Jerusalem leaders, but he laid it out in explanatory declaration. He did so in private consultation with those recognized and reputed to be leaders, rather than in a public council. There is probably some questioning of the elevated "reputation" of these leaders among the Jewish Christians of Judea, both those in Jerusalem at the time of this visit, and those who were now attempting to legalize the gospel in Galatia which prompted this letter. Paul's "fear of running in vain" is not an admission of lingering doubts about the gospel of grace, thus needing the authentication and validation of the Jewish-Christian leaders, but is an athletic metaphor that indicates that he wanted to avoid the competition of separate rival factions of Jewish Christianity and Gentile Christianity in order to facilitate the unity of running together in the same race on the same team. Paul did not want division among God's people, but wanted them to be "one" (Jn. 17:21) in the unity of "one Body" (Eph. 4:4) with a universal gospel for all peoples.

2:3   Reporting on the private consultation, Paul notes that ***"not even Titus who was with me, though he was a Greek, was compelled to be circumcised."*** The inclusion of Titus in the delegation to Jerusalem was not necessarily an act of provocation, but he did serve as a tangible test-case to establish the unlegislated freedom of Gentile Christians to enjoy the grace of God apart from Judaic Law-observances. This is the first reference to "circumcision" within this Galatian epistle, though there will be several others (2:7-9,12, 5:1-11; 6:12-15), for this was one of the issues that Paul had with the subversive "circumcision party" (Gal. 2:12; Phil. 3:2; Titus 1:10) that had apparently invaded the Galatian churches. Paul knew full well (Phil. 3:5) the importance placed on circumcision as the primary physical sign and seal of male Jewish identity in belonging to the old covenant people of God, but he also knew that this physical pictorial prefiguring was superseded by the spiritual reality of the "cutting off" of sin from the hearts of men by the grace-activity of Jesus Christ in the new covenant. Under no circumstances would he stand by and allow Jewish Christians to add physical circumcision of male converts as a necessary and essential condition to the completed sufficiency of Christ's work. He knew that any supplementation of legal-performance was a sacrifice of the gospel of grace, making "grace no longer grace" (Rom. 11:6). Apparently Paul was able to convey this to the Jewish-Christian leaders in Jerusalem, for Titus "was not compelled to be circumcised." Some have conjectured that though Titus was not "compelled" to be circumcised, he voluntarily submitted to such as a conciliatory gesture, similar to the expedience of Timothy's circumcision (Acts 16:3). Very unlikely, since such a precedent would have undermined Paul's position of the singularity of grace.

2:4 As Paul writes to the Galatian Christians, his recollection of what happened while he was in Jerusalem so disturbs him still that he inserts this dangling, incomplete sentence, explaining the intense pressure that was brought to bear by some hard-line saboteurs advocating the necessity of circumcision. The pressure to capitulate and sell out the gospel by adding the ritual performance of circumcision to the grace of God, ***"was because of false brethren who had sneaked in to spy out our liberty which we have in Christ Jesus, in order to bring us into bondage."*** Paul's indignation has been brought to the surface again, for he realizes that these "false brethren" who infiltrated the meeting in Jerusalem would probably be in total sympathy with the false-teachers who were infiltrating the churches of Galatia. They could have been the same people; maybe even the same legalistic, Judaizing agitators who were beginning to appear in Antioch (from whence Paul may have been writing), declaring, "Unless you are circumcised according to the custom of Moses, you cannot be saved" (Acts 15:1). Paul regarded them as "false brethren," pseudo-Christians who did not understand or appreciate the gospel of grace and liberty in Jesus Christ, for they were willing to cut the heart out of the gospel, destroying the "finished work" of Jesus Christ, "making Christ of no value" (5:2), by advocating their agenda of adding

Jewish Law-observances, particularly circumcision, to the simple gospel of Christ. Regardless of the issue at hand, any who would advocate the supplementation of moralistic behavioral performance to the singular essence of the gospel of God's grace in Christ are to considered "false brethren" and diabolic enemies who "disguise themselves as servants of righteousness" (II Cor. 11:15). Their fallacious theology is evidenced in their furtive methodology. Paul regarded the "false brethren" in Jerusalem and the false-teachers in Galatia as sinister snakes who would "sneak in" subversively and surreptitiously to conduct clandestine espionage upon the saints of God in Christ. The gate-crashers in Jerusalem and the church-crashers in Galatia were one and the same, deliberately and deceitfully attempting to sabotage the gospel by requiring religious performance. To this day their ilk continue to "spy out the liberty" of grace that Christians have in Christ, in order to bring them into the bondage of religious rules, regulations and rituals. Religion is bondage! The Latin word *religare* from which we derive the English word "religion" means "to bind up" or "to tie back." Paul would never tolerate or allow Christianity to degenerate into the bondage of religion, but in the liberty of grace in Jesus Christ he wanted all Christians to experience the restorative salvation that allows the dynamic of Christ's life to function so that Christians are free to be all that God intends them to be. "It was for freedom that Christ set us free" (5:1).

2:5   Perhaps taking a breath to collect his emotional agitation, Paul proceeds to indicate that ***"we did not yield in subjection to them for even an hour, so that the truth of the gospel might remain with you."*** The plural "we" could refer to Paul, Barnabas and Titus standing their ground against the Jerusalem leaders, which would connect with the following verse. But the flow of thought from the previous verse might better allow the plural pronoun "we" to be inclusive of Paul, Barnabas and Titus in conjunction with the leaders of the Jerusalem church, standing firm and refusing to capitulate to the agenda of the hard-line "false brethren," for such action would have been a betrayal of the essence of the gospel. Paul was adamantly desirous that the "truth of the gospel," the ontological reality of the Personified Truth in Jesus Christ (Jn. 14:6) should be allowed to "make men free" (Jn. 8:32,36), apart from any performance supplementation. Paul did not consider the "truth of the gospel" to be contained in propositional truth-tenets of a theological belief-system, but the dynamic expression of the true reality of the Person of Christ. He was willing to take his stand and not back down an inch, so that the Gentile Christians in Galatia, and all Christians everywhere, might experience the blessing of Christian liberty in Christ, and not be imprisoned as slaves in the legalistic bondage of religion.

2:6 Returning now to his theme of personal independence from the Jewish-Christian establishment, Paul states, ***"Those who were of high reputation (what they were makes no difference to me; God shows no partiality) – well, those who were of reputation contributed nothing to me."*** Though it may appear that Paul is sarcastically referring to the acknowledged leaders of the Jerusalem church with an attitude of deprecation, derogation or disparagement, it is probably more correct to recognize that Paul is reacting to the excessive and exaggerated reverence of these leaders that verged on an idolatrous veneration of their status. The false-teachers in Galatia were apparently lifting up the leaders of the church in Jerusalem as ecclesiastical authorities whose teaching and practice should be considered as an infallible norm. Paul knew that all authority was invested in Christ (Matt. 28:18), and that all Christian leaders are mere men who should not be afforded undue exaltation or privilege, for the impartiality of God (Acts 10:34) requires all men to stand before Him only by His grace in Jesus Christ. Religion often stands in awe of human power and reputation, but every Christian should be as impartial to men's positions as God is, and as indifferent as Paul was.

After the parenthesis, Paul completes his thought by indicating that the Jerusalem leaders added nothing to his standing as an apostle, nor did they add any supplements, improvements, or modifications to the gospel which is Christ only. That they "contributed nothing to him" does not mean that they failed to give Paul any monetary funding.

2:7 The positive side of the story, Paul continues to report, is that the Jerusalem leaders, *"seeing that I had been entrusted with the gospel to the uncircumcised, just as Peter with the gospel to the circumcised,"* recognized that there was only one essential gospel in the ontological dynamic of the grace of God in Jesus Christ, though different people could be called of God to different ministries in different locations among different people-groups. There is no "different gospel" with appended performance responsibilities, but there are diversified personnel and mission strategies for the sharing of the gospel of Christ.

2:8 Paul inserts a parenthesis of explanation: *"(for He who effectually worked for Peter in his apostleship to the circumcised effectually worked for me also to the Gentiles)."* The same God energizing in the same gospel of the dynamic of His grace in His Son, Jesus, can designate different spheres of ministry for different apostles. There can be unity in the diversity of ministries within the one Body of Christ. Both Peter and Paul, as apostolic colleagues, were equally entrusted to minister in their respective fields of labor.

2:9 The lengthy, drawn-out sentence that runs from verse 6 through 9 is concluded as Paul reports that *"James and Cephas and John, who were reputed to be pillars, recognizing the grace that had been given to me, gave to me and Barnabas the right hand of fellowship, that we might go to the Gentiles,* *and they to the circumcised."* Three of the particular leaders of the church in Jerusalem are identified by name. That they are "reputed to be pillars" may be a renewed questioning of the reverence afforded to them by the Jewish-Christians in Jerusalem, by the "false brethren," and by the infiltrating false teachers in Galatia, but then again it could be an accepted designation of these apostolic leaders who were the foundational and supportive strength of the early Church. The important fact is that Peter, James and John accepted and acknowledged the grace-activity of God in Jesus Christ that had been given to Paul. This grace was not given to Paul as a possession, or as a supplemental power, but was the dynamic life of Jesus given to him as the complete basis of his being and activity. On that basis the Jerusalem leaders extended to Paul and Barnabas "the right hand of fellowship," recognizing their commonality and solidarity in Christ, and endorsing a favorable partnership and cooperation in their respective God-given ministries. This was probably acted out in a handshake that represented a formal agreement. How tragic it is that the petty squabbles of religion today, fought over the slightest of doctrinal differences, often result in "the left foot of disfellowship" as nonconformists are charged with "heresy" and given "the boot" of ostracism or excommunication.

2:10   As a final excursus to this autobiographical defense of the gospel which served as the basis of his life and ministry, Paul notes that the leaders of the church in Jerusalem *"only asked us to remember the poor – the very thing I also was eager to do."* This was not a contractual addendum that constituted an obligatory stipulation, as it might be interpreted to be if this were a synopsis of the written document drawn up after the Jerusalem Conference (Acts 15:23-29). The Jewish-Christian leaders were simply suggesting and urging the leaders of the Gentile mission to continue to remember the Christians in Judea who had been forced into economic deprivation either by

Jewish ostracism or by agricultural famine. Such a monetary collection had been given to the church in Jerusalem for distribution to deserving peoples during this visit of Paul, Barnabas and Titus, but the Jewish-Christian leaders were desirous that the Gentile Christians should not become detached from their concern for their poor Jewish-Christian brethren. Paul indicates that he was eager to continue the collections from the Gentile churches for the poor saints in Judea, for this served as a consistent expression of the love, compassion and givingness of the character of Christ in Christians. The operative grace of God will inevitably be expressed as Christ in us for others.

The question might legitimately be asked, "*What if* the Jewish-Christian leaders in Jerusalem had not agreed that the essentiality of the gospel was to be found in the grace of Jesus Christ alone? W*hat if* they had refused to accept Paul's gospel of grace and liberty to the Gentiles? *What if* they had demanded modifications of supplemental Judaic law-observance in addition to the faithful receptivity of Christ's activity? We can rest assured that Paul's declaration that "if *any man* should preach a gospel contrary, let him be accursed" (1:8,9), would have remained in place and applied to the original Jewish-Christian apostles in Jerusalem. Under no circumstances would Paul have sacrificed the gospel of grace, which had become the essence of his life and ministry, for a legalistic amalgam of performance righteousness. He would have been constrained by the divine grace of Christ's activity in him to continue to share Christ with the Gentiles as God had directed him to do. The universality of the gospel and the external unity of the Body would have been compromised and relinquished, as the Church would have been divided into two distinct groups – the Jewish Church (which could have become a Petrine or Jacobian sect of Judaism), and the Gentile Church (possibly identified as Pauline Christianity). As it is, the major splits in the Church came centuries later in the break between the Western Roman Church

2:10

and the Eastern Orthodox Church, and the division of the Western Church into Roman Catholicism and Protestantism in the sixteenth century. The question we have posed is hypothetical, for much to the credit of the Jerusalem leaders and Paul, they listened to the Spirit of God within them and preserved the unity of the Church in the essential gospel of grace and liberty in Jesus Christ.

Some have questioned whether the autobiographical chronologue of selected events that Paul wrote in this passage is of any real value to subsequent generations of Christians, other than as an historical footnote. Let us first note that history is important to Christianity! Without the documentable historical foundation of the earthly life and ministry of Jesus, Christianity would be relegated to nothing more than a subjective belief-system of mystical speculation, moralistic behavioral modification and conformity, and philosophical or theological reasonings. The gospel has definite historical moorings, as Paul so adequately pointed out to the Corinthians (I Cor. 15:3-10), which include the historical details of the impact of the gospel on Paul's life. The historical foundations alongside of the revealed theological formulations allow for the personal and spiritual formation (4:19) of Christ in the individual and the Church. Paul has shared in these verses how such a formation occurred in his own life in the most radical transformation from persecutor to preacher, evidencing the vital dynamic of God's grace in Christ. He obviously desired and hoped that it would happen in every person's life.

The second value of this recitation of events in Paul's life is that his defense of the Christocentric gospel functioning by the grace of God, serves as a model for the persistent and perennial need for Christians in every age to defend the gospel against the intrusion of religious attempts to modify the gospel with behavioristic performance requirements. Christians will always be called upon to "make a defense of the hope that is in them" (I Pet. 3:15), and would that they were as firmly convinced as

Paul was that the living Lord Jesus is the sole basis of the gospel and of their personal identity (who they are) and their personal purpose (what they do). They could and would then stand before any so-called church authority (whoever they might be), take the flak from any detractors, and bear the ostracism of any religious "false brethren," in order to declare the life-message and life-purpose that God had called them to in Christ. The reality of Jesus Christ would so be the basis of their lives that they would not be defending themselves or their reputation, but declaring the gospel of the life that is theirs in Christ Jesus. Sadly, religious understanding has so permeated Christian thinking that few understand, appreciate or experience the essential ontological dynamic of the gospel of the living Lord Jesus in them, much less attempt to defend that Christo-centric gospel.

ENDNOTE

1   Barth, Karl, *Church Dogmatics*. Vol. I, Pt. 2. Edinburgh: T&T Clark. 1956. pg. 280.

Straightforward About the Gospel

Galatians 2:11-21

In defense of the Christocentric gospel Paul would defer to no one. He had already inclusively indicated that if "any man" (1:9), even him, his associates, or an angel from heaven (1:8), should offer a gospel other than that of God's grace in Jesus Christ, he would be subject to God's anathema. Furthermore, he explained that those who were of ecclesiastical reputation (2:2,6), even "pillars" of the Church (2:9), made no difference to him (2:6) in his divinely commissioned resolve to share the gospel of grace and liberty, for he was convinced that "God shows no partiality" (2:6) concerning the messenger and his alleged position. The issue for Paul, which he would defend at all costs, was the essence of the gospel in Jesus Christ alone (*sola Christus*), expressed by God's grace alone (*sola gratia*), and received by faith alone (*sola fide*).

Immediately after the recitation of selected events from his life which evidenced his independency from the original apostolic leadership in Jerusalem, since he had not learned the gospel from them, nor been commissioned by their authority (1:11–2:10), Paul cites a particular incident that places the centrality of the gospel of grace into focus. Under no circumstances, regardless of the personages involved, would Paul allow moralistic performance accretions to supplement the gospel, either directly or indirectly. That the gospel was solely the dynamic activity of Jesus Christ by the grace of God, allowing the freedom of the Christian to function by the leading of the

2:11-21

Spirit of Christ without any legalistic requirements of ritualistic rites or behavioral regulation, was the reality that Paul would not back away from.

This letter was written at a crucial time for defense of the singular essence of the gospel in Christ. The extension of the gospel to the Gentiles, precipitated by Peter's visit to Cornelius (Acts 10:24-48), the receptivity of the Gentiles in Antioch prompting the sending of Barnabas and his subsequent alliance with Paul (Acts 11:19-26), and the commissioning of Paul as "apostle to the Gentiles" (Rom. 11:13) to which he was obedient on the first missionary journey accompanied by Barnabas (Acts 13:1–14:26), all contributed to a crisis of identity in the early Church. The Jewish religion was known for its ingrown enculturated traditions based on racial superiority, religious exclusivism, and nationalistic rights which segregated them from all others. The early Jewish-Christians were having a difficult time accepting and allowing for integration with Gentile-Christians who did not feel obliged to conform to basic traditions of the Law in which those of Jewish heritage had found their unique identification. In particular, some Jewish-Christians were keen to preserve the rite of male circumcision as the external mark of specific identity, and their extensive food laws wherein they demarcated their purity.

The differences of opinions on these issues varied among the Christians of Jewish heritage. At one end of the spectrum was Paul, who, on behalf of the Gentiles, was willing to abandon all Jewish traditions for complete freedom in Christ. Other Jewish-Christians were struggling with such broad abandonment of their heritage. The leaders of the Jerusalem church were engaged in the learning process of progressive revelation concerning the implications of the gospel. Peter had a special revelation of the inclusion of the Gentiles and the irrelevancy of Jewish food laws while on the rooftop in Joppa (Acts 10:9-23), but was still reluctantly accepting the dismissal of Jewish essentials one issue at a time. James may have been more

2:11-21

reticent to rescind the Jewish traditions. At the far right end of the spectrum were some Jewish-Christians whose attitudes were not far removed from those of the Jewish religion. They accepted Jesus as the Messiah, but thought of Christianity as a form of completed Judaism which should retain all traditions. Among this group there was a contingent of hard-line advocates who have been called "Judaizers" (though the term is not a biblical designation), who felt obliged to defend the mandatory matters of Mosaic Law with all the traditions of Judaism, with special emphasis on male circumcision which earned them the designation of "the circumcision party" (2:12; Titus 1:10). It was their tactics of activistic "politics of legalism"[1] which led to the confrontation which Paul recounts in Jerusalem (2:4,5), and in Antioch (2:12-21), and was the occasion for Paul's writing of this letter to the Galatians. They took it upon themselves as a personal mission to "spy out the liberty " (2:4) of Christians, whether of Jewish or Gentile ethnicity, in order to impose or compel rigid conformity to the behavioral specifics of the "works of the Law" (2:16,21), which Paul regarded as the "bondage" (2:4) of religion. They would travel far and wide from Judea (Acts 15:1) to infiltrate, agitate and intimidate Christian groups, employing pressure tactics to force and compel (2:3,14) conformity, and labeling all non-conformists as "sinners" (2:15,17) to be separated from (2:12). Claiming ecclesiastical authority by name-dropping the names of Peter and James (2:12), they regarded the Jewish traditions as essential to the gospel for Christian living, which Paul regarded as a distortion (1:7) and denial (1:6,7) of the "truth of the gospel" (2:5,14) of grace in Jesus Christ, thus calling them "false brethren" (2:4).

The conflict between Paul and this radical, hard-line "circumcision party" within the Jewish-Christian community in Judea was taking place on many fronts at the same time. When Paul went to Jerusalem with Barnabas and Titus for a private meeting with the Jerusalem leaders (2:1-10), which we have taken to be the famine-relief visit of Acts 11:30; 12:25, he was accosted by the "false brethren" (2:4,5) in Jerusalem. After his first missionary journey with Barnabas (Acts 13:1–14:26), during which time he preached in the southern cities of the Roman province of Galatia and established the predominantly Gentile "churches of Galatia" (1:2), Paul returned to Antioch of Syria and spent a "long time" (Acts 14:28) with the Christian disciples there. It was probably during this indefinite "long time" that the incident with Peter (2:11-21) took place, perhaps correlating with the delegation from Judea who were teaching that, "unless you are circumcised according to the custom of Moses, you cannot be saved" (Acts 15:1). It is the author's personal opinion that this letter of Paul to the Galatians was also written from Antioch during this same relative "long time" (Acts 14:28). If so, the heat of confrontation was intense as Paul was defending the gospel against the Judaizers on many fronts, and this may have been the reason why he could not revisit the Galatian churches at the time, but wrote this letter to address the issue of Judaizers in Galatia before he headed off to the Jerusalem Council (Acts 15:2-29), where some of these issues would be clarified more carefully.

Perhaps part of Paul's purpose in relating this incident of confrontation with Peter was to continue to validate his independence from Peter and the original apostles. Since Peter was apparently held in high regard by the intrusive Judaizing traditionalists, and they may have been using his name as their prime source of authority for their propaganda of supplementation, Paul may have intended to expose the fact that he had to set Peter straight on the essence of the gospel, and Peter should not be granted undue veneration as one of the original apostles, as the hard-line legalist party was prone to do. How interesting that in later Church history the Roman Catholic Church which regarded Peter as their first pope, attempted to preserve Peter's reputation and veneration by arguing that Peter was just role-playing with Paul in this account, in order to drive home the truth of the gospel. Not likely!

2:11   Immediately following the report of their private consultation with James and Cephas and John (2:1-10), Paul recounts the incident *"when Cephas came to Antioch,"* even though the first missionary journey may have intervened between the two occasions, and this latter incident may have been quite recent prior to the writing of this epistle. The connecting link is probably Paul's intent to show that Peter did not honor the consensus they had reached in Jerusalem, both by failing to stand pat in the resolve not to allow any ritualistic or moralistic additions to the gospel, and possibly by intervening in a situation outside of Judea that was largely part of the Gentile mission which Paul had been entrusted with (2:7), even though there was a sizable contingent of Jewish-Christians in Antioch also. Some have attempted to attribute the confrontation to a misunderstanding whereby Paul interpreted the Jerusalem agreement as a broad negation of all Judaic Law-observances, while Peter (and perhaps James more so) thought it related only to circumcision, with Jewish food laws still a negotiable issue. This seems somewhat untenable since Peter knew full well that food laws were abolished in the new covenant after his revelation in Joppa (Acts 10:9-23). Given Peter's personality propensity to be fickle and fallible, evidenced by previous fearful vacillation and wavering leading to a denial of what he really believed (cf. Matt. 26:69-75), it is more likely that Peter just caved in and capitulated to the pressure of the legalistic hard-liners from Judea.

The purpose of Peter's visit to Antioch is unknown, and there is no apparent reference to such in the book of *Acts*. Antioch was one of the largest cities in the Roman empire, and the capital of the province of Syria. It was the first major site of Christian development outside of Jerusalem, as Christians scattered by persecution (Acts 8:4; 11:19) first shared the gospel with Jews, and then later with Gentiles (Acts 11:19,20). After news of this mixed church reached Jerusalem, they sent Barnabas as a liaison (Acts 11:22). Barnabas, in turn, recruited Saul from Tarsus to assist him (Acts 11:25,26). The believers in Jesus were first called "Christians," that is "Christ-ones" or "those of Christ," in Antioch (Acts 11:26), possibly first as a designation of derogation, but later accepted as a most appropriate explanation of the reality of Christianity.

In response to Peter's defection under pressure (which will be explained in the next verse), Paul says, ***"I opposed him to his face, because he stood condemned."*** True to his word, Paul was indifferent to a person's position (2:6), and no longer a man-pleaser (1:10). Paul stood up against and resisted Peter in the same manner that Peter (I Pet. 1:9) and James (James 4:7) both would later indicate that a Christian should resist the devil. It was a head-to-head, face-to-face, eyeball-to-eyeball face-off, with Paul in effect saying to Peter, "I don't care who you are; you're wrong!" This was not just a personality clash or a political power-play between apostles, but this was a rebuke of Peter's behavior that sacrificed the truth of the gospel and the unity of the Church. Peter knew better, but once again his moral cowardice caused him to act contradictory to his convictions. He was guilty of pretense and inconsistency in violating his own established attitudes. What he did was condemnable because it was a betrayal of the singular essence of the gospel in the grace of God through Jesus Christ alone. This was not the condemnation of divine anathema (1:8,9), but the condemnation of misrepresentation, which every Christian is guilty of at times.

2:12   The explanation of Peter's action is subsequently made. ***"For prior to the coming of certain men from James, he used to eat with the Gentiles."*** The issue in the integration of Jewish and Gentile Christians was more than just circumcision, for the purification food-laws about types of food, killing of animals, food preparation and proper cleansing were regarded as essential by some Jewish Christians. The Judaic concept of table-fellowship regarded eating together as a sign of oneness, equality, acceptance, commonality, and intimacy within the Jewish covenant community. Some Jewish-Christians were having a difficult time giving up their traditional conceptions.

Peter had been given a graphic lesson in the unimportance of Jewish food-laws on the rooftop in Joppa (Acts 10:9-23), so when he came to Antioch he ate regularly with the Gentile-Christians, apparently disregarding the preparatory regulations about kosher foods. Perhaps he could recall that Jesus had been criticized for eating contrary to Jewish religious scruples also (cf. Mk. 7:1-8; Lk. 15:2). So Peter, consistent with the accord reached in Jerusalem (2:1-10), and recognizing that the kingdom of God is not regulated by eating and drinking rules (cf. Rom. 14:17), exercised the freedom to eat with Gentiles (probably including the Lord's Supper observance), regarding them as equals in Christ.

Peter was not a Judaizing "false-brother" (2:4) of the "circumcision party", but stood with Paul in countering such an attitude in Jerusalem (2:5-10), even if more moderate in his stance. But when the right-wing propagandists from Jerusalem came to Antioch, claiming to be connected with and authorized by James, the leader of the Jerusalem church, Peter began to backpedal. That they really represented the opinion of James is questionable since after the Jerusalem Council James and the elders drafted a letter to the Gentile churches indicating that "some of our number to whom we gave no instruction have disturbed you" (Acts 15:24).

When the Law-observance advocates came to Antioch, with the opinion that social interaction with Gentile-Christians who did not observe their traditions was unacceptable, Peter *"began to withdraw and hold himself aloof, fearing the party of the circumcision."* Such a group of religious fundamentalists can be very intimidating as they employ pressure tactics both

2:13

directly and indirectly, threatening ostracism or excommunication (even if they don't have authority to do so), and castigating those who do not conform as "sinners" or "heretics." Peter was known for his tendency to capitulate under pressure (cf. Matt. 26:69-75), and true to form he began to retreat and back-off from fellowship with the Gentile-Christians. The word used for his "shrinking violet" withdrawal is the same word used of "shrinking back to destruction" in the epistle to the Hebrews (Heb. 10:38,39). In so segregating and separating himself "aloof" from the Gentile-Christians, Peter was acting like the Pharisaical separatists (cf. Acts 15:5) of the "circumcision party." He was afraid of their right-wing political power in the Jerusalem church, and was still trying to please men (cf. 1:10).

2:13   Particularly bothersome to Paul was the fact that *"the rest of the Jewish-Christians joined him in hypocrisy"* by segregating from the Gentile-Christians also. Paul was left standing alone with the Gentile-Christians, which he was quite willing to do in order to preserve the integral essence of the gospel in Jesus Christ alone. Like sheep being led to the slaughter, the Jewish-Christians followed the lead of Peter, joining in the deceptive pretense that such Law-observance was essential to Christian living. Distinguishing oneself under a false cover is the essence of hypocrisy!

Most disappointing to Paul was that *"even Barnabas was carried away by their hypocrisy,"* joining the Jewish-Christian contingent in segregation from the Gentile-Christians he had ministered to in Antioch. Barnabas was no narrow-minded person. He was usually reaching out to others as "the Son of Encouragement" (Acts 4:36). He stood by Paul against all odds (Acts 9:27), enlisted him for the work in Antioch (Acts 11:25,26), and accompanied Paul on the first missionary journey to the Gentiles (Acts 13:2–14:26), which included the Gentile-Christian recipients of this letter in Galatia. With deep sadness Paul reports that *"even* Barnabas" was influenced and "carried away." How interesting that Peter later used the same word in warning about being *"carried away* by the error of unprincipled men" (II Pet. 3:17). The subtlety of hypocrisy is that it gives a false impression of reality. It is a "pose" of play-acting a charade that is contrary to one's genuine persona. Peter and those Jewish-Christians that he influenced were playing the farce of religion, and they knew better because they knew the reality of the gospel in Jesus Christ and the falsity of their hypocritical segregation.

2:14 When Paul ***"saw that they were not straightforward about the truth of the gospel,"*** he initiated a confrontation with the one who had led them all down the primrose path of hypocrisy. Unlike Peter, Paul had courage of conviction and was a real watch-dog for preserving the singular essence of the gospel in Jesus Christ. He could see that the segregationists were not "straight-footing" on a straight-line that led to Jesus Christ, by "walking in the Spirit" (5:25). Instead, they were "pussy-footing" and "waltzing around the problem," creating a crooked-line that would lead others astray.

Paul was willing to defend with his life "the truth of the gospel." This was not a subsidiary issue of social table graces, nor a peripheral issue of differing opinions (cf. I Cor. 9:19-23), but the issue was the real truth of the gospel in Jesus Christ. Jesus is the truth (Jn. 14:6), the reality of the gospel that sets men free (Jn. 8:32,36) to function as God intends. The "truth of the gospel" is the vital indwelling Person of Jesus Christ; not propositions, procedures and practices of religion. What these Jewish-Christians in Antioch were doing was indicating by their example that the "truth of the gospel" was in the religious and legalistic performance of what one does or does not do. Paul could not tolerate such misrepresentation of the gospel of grace in Jesus Christ, knowing that it would destroy Christian freedom and Christian unity.

2:14

Taking the bull by the horns in the strength of God's grace, Paul *"said to Cephas in the presence of all, 'If you, being a Jew, live like the Gentiles and not like the Jews, how is it that you compel the Gentiles to live like Jews?'"* This is not a personal attack, but the addressing of a theological issue. Whether Paul had broached the subject with Peter personally (cf. Matt. 18:15-20) prior to the public rebuke, we do not know, but the public nature of the wrongdoing called for public exposure and remonstrance (cf. I Tim. 5:20). How unfortunate that contemporary ministerial ethics often discourage the washing of dirty theological linen in public, desiring to keep disputes under wraps where they fester as cover-ups.

Paul's question to Peter challenges his inconsistency. Peter, a Jew by race and religion, had been a disciple of the historical Jesus and had received the indwelling Spirit of Jesus as a Christian. He exercised the freedom that was his "in Christ" to live in grace rather than by every regulation of the Jewish old covenant Law. In so doing, he "lived like the Gentiles," not observing all of the social customs and religious traditions of Judaism (although he may not have abandoned all of them), but feeling free to cross over to different cultural, racial and religious practices. When he came to Antioch he was practicing such freedom. "Why, then," Paul asks, "when you had the freedom to live like the Gentiles in the liberty of God's grace, do you now force the Gentile-Christians to conform to the performances of the Jewish Law, when you did not previously feel obliged to do so?" Such flip-flopping inconsistency is hypocrisy! It is a double-standard! You can't have it both ways! "By your example, Peter, you compel the Gentile-Christians to conform to Jewish customs, thereby, at least indirectly, indicating that such external practices are necessary and essential to genuine Christian life as tests of faith. In so doing you diminish the reality of God's grace in Jesus Christ by supplementation. You, Peter, need to decide what the truth of the gospel really is, and stick with it!"

2:15   There is a question whether vss. 15-21 are a continuation of Paul's remarks to Peter or whether they are theological summarization and application addressed to the Christians in Galatia. Without a doubt there is a transition from historical narrative to theological explanation, and it is almost imperceptible where one ends and the other starts. Since Paul's personal life and the gospel message were both defined by Jesus Christ, he could move effortlessly from personal autobiography to essential theology. The gospel dynamic of Christ was the living dynamic of his life. But in order to understand what is written here, we must attempt to discover Paul's intent, for such will determine the interpretation of his words. Some English translations punctuate with quotation marks from vs. 14 through vs. 21, considering the entire passage to be an extended quotation or synopsis of Paul's remarks to Peter (ex. NASB and NIV), while others conclude Paul's quotation at vs. 14, considering the remaining verses to be general explanation of theological summation (ex. NRSV and NAB). The lack of a clear-cut break between vss. 14 and 15, alongside of the obvious connection of the following verses to the incident with Peter (as we shall note), lend credence to the view that these thoughts were first directed to Peter. The indirect intention of Paul may have been that the Galatian Christians should understand the theological argument made to Peter, and take note, because they were also being influenced by similar performance piety proponents, and were in danger of the same forms of inconsistency that sacrificed the Christocentric gospel.

   The statement, ***"We are Jews by nature, and not sinners from among the Gentiles,"*** appears to be a recapitulation of the polemic language employed by the Judaizing traditionalists, as they retained and maintained their Jewish prejudices of racial distinction. Paul restates their boastful pride of heritage in order to project such as a typical and traditional Jewish conception lodged in the minds of those of Jewish heritage, and held over even by many of those who had become Jewish-Christians. He sets it up in order to refute the notion in the next verse. The Jews took great pride in their birthright as the "people of God," considering such natural, physical privilege to benefit them spiritually as favored and chosen before God. Paul had reveled in such pride of superiority himself (Phil. 3:4-6), but God had revealed the fallacy and bankruptcy of such physical priority and legal performance (Phil. 3:7-10). The Jews may have had precedence in the timing of the revelation of God unto them (Rom. 3:1,2), but they had no precedence of place before God. On the other hand, the Jews regarded all other ethnic groups as Gentile "sinners" because they were "strangers to the covenant" (Eph. 2:12) who were not given the Jewish Law (Rom. 2:12,14) in order to be righteous, and were thus vulgar violators of the Law of God. The Judaizing separatists may have been using a variation of the theme by regarding even the Jewish-Christians who did not retain their purity in performance rites, and instead "lived like Gentiles" (2:14), to be "sinners among the Gentiles," using such as a derisive label to hurl at nonconformists. Paul will combat such, for he knew that "both Jews and Gentiles are all under sin" (Rom. 3:9), "by nature, children of wrath" (Eph. 2:3); that "Christ Jesus came into the world to save sinners" (I Tim. 1:15), so that all men, "Jew or Gentile," might be one in Christ Jesus (Gal. 3:28) as redeemed and restored humanity.

2:16 Granted, this traditional Jewish attitude of prejudice was retained by many Jewish-Christians, and narrowed even more by the separatistic Judaizers to impinge on the less strict nonconformists, but this is not a Christian perspective. Paul contradicted this prejudiced view of racial and religious privilege, as well as the hard-liners' deprecation of nonconformist "sinners," stating, ***"nevertheless we know that a man is not justified by the works of the Law but through faith in Christ Jesus."*** The general message of the Christian gospel which every genuine Christian should know is that no man is made right or declared right with God on the basis of performance conformity to the legally prescribed behaviors of the Law, but only on the basis of the receptivity of the performance activity of Jesus Christ by faith. This is basic Christian knowledge that differentiates Judaic religion from Christianity. Neither the generalized performance of the Mosaic mandates, including the Ten Commandments, nor the specific "works of the Law" in circumcision and food-laws being compelled by the Judaizing exclusivists, are essential to rightness with God and the expression of His righteous character.

Long and intense have been the theological debates over "justification by faith," especially since the Protestant Reformation when this issue became the banner of protest against the performance-righteousness allegedly advocated and practiced by Roman Catholicism. Reacting against the Roman concept of an endowment of "infused grace" which could be employed to align oneself with ecclesiastical rules and regulations, Luther, Calvin, *et al*, objectified righteousness into legal and forensic categories of a declared and imputed placement or status of rightness before God, the heavenly Judge. Such an overreaction to internalized and behavioral righteousness, and the adamant objectification of justification in juridical concepts, has led to a detached concept of soteriological benefits and blessings on which a Christian is encouraged to mentally "reckon" as objective truth. This Protestant emphasis sells short the behavioral implications of God's grace in Jesus Christ, whereby He manifests His righteous character in Christian living.

Included in Paul's understanding of being "justified" (used three times in this verse), are surely both the objective elements of being acquitted and declared righteous by the historically objective righteous acts of Jesus Christ, thus being imputed with right standing and status before God in Christ; as well as the subjective elements of receiving Jesus Christ, the Righteous One (Acts 3:14; 7:52; 22:14; II Tim. 4:8; I Jn. 2:1; Rev. 16:5) in regeneration (Jn. 3:1-6; I Pet. 1:3), thus being "made righteous" (Rom. 5:19; II Cor. 5:21; Heb. 12:23) spiritually in derived identity with Christ, allowing for the expression of the righteous character of God by His grace (Rom. 6:13-20; I Cor. 1:30; Phil. 1:11). Both objectively and subjectively such righteousness is alien to man who is incapable of effecting or generating such, but can only derive rightness and righteousness contingently by the receptivity of Christ's activity, both past and present, by faith. All of these concepts seem to be compressed into Paul's understanding of being "justified."

Paul continues to make his point more personal by noting that ***"even we have believed in Christ Jesus, that we may be justified by faith in Christ, and not by the works of the Law."*** This is not a tautologous repetition, but a progression of thought that brings the point home to Peter, who along with Paul and all other genuine Jewish-Christians (in contrast to the "false brethren" (2:4) of the Judaizers), once thought (and were taught) that they were "Jews by nature, and not sinners from among the Gentiles" (2:15), but now have "believed *into* Christ Jesus" in a personally relational spiritual union. This is not just a general theological tenet or theory of Christianity, but we have personally received the righteous activity of Christ *into* ourselves as a subjective and experiential reality. Such "believing" is not just cognitive assent to historical and theological data, but is a personal reception of the ontological reality of the Righteous One, Christ Jesus, allowing for a righteousness that is both vital, as well as judicial, and can be expressed behaviorally by the grace activity of God in Christ in the Christian. It is not a righteousness "derived from the Law" (Phil. 3:9) by performance of old covenant regulations to earn meritorious favor before God, nor by the specific "works of the Law" in circumcision and food-laws being touted as essential by the Judaizing false-teachers, but a righteousness derived through faith in Christ, as we are receptive to His righteous activity.

As final documentation Paul seems to loosely quote or at least allude to the words of the Psalmist in Ps. 143:2, stating, *"since by the works of the Law shall no flesh be justified."* Later in his epistle to the Romans (Rom. 3:20) Paul would again refer to the words of David that "in Thy (God's) sight no man living is righteous" (Ps. 143:2). No "flesh," no human being from among finite humanity, is capable of generating or effecting righteousness, which is the character of God alone (Ps. 11:7; 119:137,142; I Jn. 2:29; 3:7). No performance of man will make one righteous either objectively or subjectively, forensically or vitally. Paul had tried his hardest to keep the Law in order to be righteous (Phil. 3:4-6), and had to agree with Isaiah (Isa. 64:6) that all such self-effort attempts were futile. The Law (whether in its general Judaic form, or in its more restricted Judaizing form) is "weak through the flesh" (Rom. 8:3), providing no dynamic of grace. It is proposition with no provision, regulation with no resource, document with no dynamic, letter with no life, expression with no energizing – incapable of being the basis of the behavioral expression of God's righteousness; capable only of exposing man's inability and his need to discover such in Jesus Christ.

2:17 Hypothetically rebuilding the argument of the Judaizers in order to refute it, Paul speculates, *"But if, while seeking to be justified in Christ, we ourselves have also been found sinners, is Christ then a minister of sin? May it never be!"* "If we, (Peter, Paul and others) as Jewish-Christians, desiring to be right with God and live righteously by faith in Christ which allows His grace to manifest His righteous character through our behavior, are then mistakenly discovered to be "sinners," as charged by the Judaizers for violating their self-prescribed food-laws and eating with nonconformist Gentiles contrary to what these hard-line conservatives consider acceptable, does this imply that Christ functioning in us is the empowering agency of sinful behavior? Impossible, and absurdly not true!" The character of Christ, as God, is absolute righteousness. Christ was sinless, is sinless, cannot sin, does not sin, and does not lead the Christian to sin (cf. James 1:13). Christ only acts and energizes in accord with His own character of righteousness, so the Judaizing thesis of being "sinners" by acts of nonconformity to their legalistic interpretations must be patently invalid.

2:18 The other side of the argument, in contrast to that proposed by the Judaizers, is that *"If I rebuild what I have once destroyed, I prove myself to be a transgressor."* If Paul or Peter or any other Jewish-Christian should attempt to reconstruct the system of attempted performance righteousness by legalistic Law-observance which they had determined to be broken down and demolished, abrogated and razed by the radical transformation of God's grace in Jesus Christ, then they would be constituted as blameworthy transgressors, walking contrary to the grace of God, the "royal law of Christ" (James 2:8; Gal. 6:2). Paul thought that Peter, by behaviorally suggesting that Law-observances were a test of Christian fellowship, needed to beware of such a reconstruction of a reformed Judaic-Christian religion, which would be a trampling of and trespass of the grace of God in Christ. Paul had thoroughly accepted the demolition of the Law to participate in the dynamic of God's grace in Christ, and was calling on Peter and other Jewish-Christians to make an either/or choice of whether they were going to subscribe to Judaism or Christianity, grace or Law; it couldn't be both for they are antithetical one to the other in their functional operation.

2:19 As for Paul, he knew where he stood, *"For through the Law I died to the Law, that I might live to God."* Paul had made every attempt to find meaning, life and righteousness through the Jewish Law. Such perfunctory performance leaves a person utterly exhausted and frustrated, never able to do enough or do it perfectly enough. The moralistic codifications of religious rules and regulations unrelentingly beat a person to death, for "the letter kills" (II Cor. 3:6). The Law is impotent and sterile in its mandate to produce "dead works" (Heb. 6:1; 9:14); it is inadequate, incapable and powerless to produce any spiritual vitality (3:21). But the Law does play a role in exposing human inability, for "through the Law comes the knowledge of sin" (Rom. 3:20; 7:7) and the awareness of its impotence to forestall such sin and its consequences. The Law had served its purpose in Paul's experience. He realized he could never accomplish righteousness or arrive at spiritual life by keeping the Law, so he chose to "die to the Law" in order to "live to God" by the grace extended in Jesus Christ who is life (Jn. 14:6). The Judaizers still thought they could engage in Christian living by performing the "works of the Law," but Paul had jettisoned all allegiance to the Law, having "died to the Law" by considering the Law as lifeless and inane. The Law no longer had authority or jurisdiction in Paul's life as a religious force that might attempt to dominate, motivate, intimidate, or control by making one feel guilty for failing to live up to the standards. Paul was oblivious to the moralistic performance expectations of the old covenant strictures, including circumcision and the food-laws advocated by the Judaizers.

Paul had discovered "eternal life in Christ Jesus" (Rom. 6:23), being spiritually regenerated unto eternal life (Jn. 3:3-16), and made "alive to God in Christ Jesus" (Rom. 6:10). Such life in Christ was not just a spiritual deposit for futuristic benefits in heaven, but was the vital dynamic whereby "the life of Jesus might be manifested in our mortal bodies" (II Cor. 4:10,11), and we might live to the glory of God by allowing His all-glorious character to be expressed in our behavior. Paul now lived in the jurisdiction of God's grace with the divine dynamic to fulfill all of God's demands, which are nothing more than consistent expression of His character.

2:20 Paul expresses the objective historical basis of his "dying to the Law" by exclaiming, ***"I have been crucified with***

Christ." This concept of co-crucifixion with Jesus when He died on the cross is intrinsic within the biblical and theological explanation of the vicarious and substitutional death of Jesus on behalf of all men. Christ died *for* us. He died in our place. He died *as* us! When Christ died, the old sinful self of every man was effectively put to death. Thus Paul can write that "the old man has been crucified with Christ" (Rom. 6:6; Eph. 4:22; Col. 3:9), and we have become a "new man" (Eph. 4:24; Col. 3:10), an entirely "new creature in Christ, so that old things have passed away and all has become new" (II Cor. 5:17). If the old identity of "sinner" (Rom. 5:19) has been exterminated, then the new identity of Christian "saint" cannot be intimidated or convicted by condemnatory guilt (Rom. 8:1) by the Law after an individual has allowed this spiritual reality to become efficacious in his life by the receptivity of faith. The tense of the verb that Paul employs makes it clear that this co-crucifixion is a matter of historical objectivity, and has nothing to do with the alleged subjective experience of what some have called "dying to self."

Moving from the objectivity of inclusion in Christ's death, Paul proceeds to explain what it means to "live to God" (2:19) by the subjectivity of the indwelling presence of Christ in our spirit (Rom. 8:9). ***"It is no longer I who live, but Christ lives in me."*** The ego-centric "I" of Paul's former spiritual identity as an "old man," struggling to perform righteousness and thereby to live, is dead. It has been replaced and exchanged for the ontological reality of Christ's life, forming the basis of a new identity as a "Christ-one," for Christ by His Spirit (Rom. 8:9) now lives in Paul. The vital dynamic to be and do all that God wants to be and do in expressing His character of righteousness in us is present in the Christian by the presence of the life of the risen Lord Jesus. "Do you not recognize that Jesus Christ is in you?" (II Cor. 13:5), Paul asks the Corinthians. "This is the mystery, ...Christ in you the hope of glory" (Col. 1:26,27), he advised the Colossians.

Avoiding all mystical detachment from time and space, Paul explains that the spiritual condition of Christ's indwelling will inevitably affect one's behavioral expression, for ***"the life which I now live in the flesh I live by faith in the Son of God, who loved me, and delivered Himself up for me."*** As we continue to live in the physical, bodily existence of "the flesh," retaining physical conditions such as race, gender and limitations, as well as psychological conditions of personality and patterned propensities to selfishness or sinfulness, we live behaviorally by the out-living of Christ's indwelling life, and that by the receptivity of His dynamic grace-activity, not by conformity to Judaic Law or any other behavioral performance. As we received Christ Jesus initially in regeneration by the receptivity of His activity, so we continue to walk the Christian life by the receptivity of His activity (Col. 2:6) in faith. Such ongoing faith is the responsibility of each Christian, for it is not Christ's faith (KJV), but our receptivity of His activity. Paul brings his statement full circle by recognizing again the historical objectivity of God's grace in the sacrificial love of the Son of God who substitutionally gave Himself on our behalf in crucifixion and resurrection. Avoiding extremisms of inordinate subjectivity of the expressions of God's grace in Christians, Paul connects the spiritually indwelling Jesus and the behaviorally out-living Jesus with the historical Jesus who lived in Palestine and died to take the death consequences of our sin – "the Christ who loved us and gave Himself for us" (Eph. 5:2,25).

2:21   Paul caps off his argument to Peter and other Jewish Christians by affirming, ***"I do not nullify the grace of God; for if righteousness comes through the Law, then Christ died needlessly."*** What a powerful climactic conclusion to his argument! Under no circumstances will Paul sacrifice the gospel of grace in Jesus Christ. The living Lord Jesus is the essence of the gospel, and grace is the dynamic of His expression. Paul is

2:21

adamant about refusing to set aside the reality of God's grace realized through Christ (Jn. 1:17). He will not accept grace as but an expression of God's historical mercy and election of physical Israel. He will not allow grace to become a theological theory of "undeserved favor" or free benefits derived from Christ. He will not allow grace to be diminished to nothing more than the "threshold factor" of God's redemptive and regenerative work. Paul's conception of grace was inclusive of everything God has done and continues to do in Christ, comprising the singular essential dynamic of the entirety of the Christian life. Paul's assertion was that it was the legalistic Judaizers from Judea who were nullifying the grace of God by advocating that uniformity of thought and conformity of action concerning circumcision and food-laws comprised Christian living and righteousness, and if that be the case then the entirety of Christianity is annulled.

Paul's argument is shockingly conclusive. If righteousness comes through Law-performance as the false Judaizing religionists propose, then the entire message of Christ is a sham and a charade. His death was nothing more than a theatrical "show" – a psychodrama "staged" on the stage of Palestinian history for the psychological effect of appealing to people with the sympathy factor of a martyr symbol – a farce and a fraud. If objective right-standing before God or subjective expression of righteous behavior can be acquired or manufactured by conforming to religious rules and regulations, then Christ's life and death were not necessary – they are a superfluous and trivial irrelevancy; nothing more than the curious blip of a tragic mistake in Palestinian history. If rightness with God or righteous character can result from right principles, right procedures, right practices, other than through the ontological dynamic of the Righteousness of the Person and work of Jesus Christ, then the death of Jesus is an unnecessary redundancy. Or as one person[2] stated it so starkly: "Jesus died for the fun of it!" Such a statement should, and will, assault the spiritual sensitivities of every genuine Christian whose spiritual identity is defined by the living reality of Jesus Christ.

Paul knew that the death of Jesus on the cross initiated and set in motion the "finished work" (Jn. 19:30) of God, whereby Jesus Christ has done and continues to do all that needs doing on man's behalf, functioning in and through receptive Christians to manifest the righteous character of God to the glory of God. If anything else is required other than the simple receptivity of Jesus Christ as the reality of one's life and the basis of one's righteousness, then the death of Jesus Christ was insufficient and does not suffice, for the "finished work" is not finished, necessitating endless acts of moralistic performance on the part of Christians in order to attempt to finish the job. Paul knew by experience the fallacy of such a legalistic system of religious performance. It negates and nullifies the grace of God, and abrogates the efficacy of the cross (5:11). Righteousness will never be achieved by the human effort of legal performance, for man is incapable of generating the character of God. The cross and resurrection were necessitated to allow Jesus to take the death consequences of man's sin and to restore the righteous character of God to man through Jesus Christ, the Righteous One in the resurrection. Righteous in Christians is singularly, exclusively and absolutely the result of the righteous character and righteous acts of Jesus Christ, or there is no such thing as righteousness among men. Yet, so much of both Catholic and Protestant theology to this day continues to view righteousness as either a benefit bestowed or character achieved, ever so subtly detached from the ontological reality and dynamic of righteousness in the Person and activity of Jesus Christ.

There is no doubt that Paul is "straightforward about the truth of the gospel" in contrast to the charge that he makes against Peter (2:14). Intolerant of perfidious perversion of the gospel of grace in Jesus Christ, Paul stood up to Peter and was willing to stand alone with the Gentile Christians of Antioch

2:21

in adamant opposition to any supplemental behavioral requirements considered to be tests of Christian faith or fellowship. Thereby Paul was stating indirectly to the Gentile-Christian recipients of this letter in Galatia that he would stand up against such in their situation also, and they should stand firm in their resolve to allow Jesus Christ to be the totality of the gospel, in like manner as he did against the Judaizers and the Jewish-Christians in Antioch (including Peter and "even Barnabas") who caved-in to their intimidating pressures. "Don't fall into the hypocrisy of Peter and Barnabas," is Paul's message between the lines. "To accept the legalistic thesis of the rigid Jewish-Christian traditionalists is to sell out the truth of the gospel and repudiate the necessity and efficacy of Christ's death on the cross." This was, no doubt, a heavy load of theological implications for the Galatian Christians to consider.

As Christians read these words of Paul today they are prone to project the incident here related completely into its first-century context with its specific issues of Jewish circumcision and food-laws. Many find it difficult to make the application of contemporary issues where behavioral requirements are being added to the singularity of God's grace. Perhaps this is due to the fact that current religious teachers of legalistic behavioral conformity are just as effective as were the Judaizers in imposing and compelling such required actions as essential to the gospel and Christian living. May God grant us the clarity of spiritual discernment to recognize that such issues as alcohol consumption, clothing styles, entertainment options, interracial marriage, church attendance, tithing, and the theological interpretations of baptismal modes, eternal security, eschatology, and spiritual gifts are often posed as mandatory supplements to the gospel. Would that we might see so clearly, stand so firmly, and defend so straightforwardly as did the apostle Paul, the gospel of grace in Jesus Christ as the sole basis of all life and righteousness.

ENDNOTES

1. Ortlund, Bud, sermon entitled "The Politics of Legalism." Preached July 22, 1979 at the Peninsula Bible Church in Palo Alto, California.
2. Author's first pastor-mentor, Kenneth Cable, who later served as president of Manhattan Christian College in Manhattan, Kansas.

God's Blessing Received by Faith

Galatians 3:1-14

In the first two chapters of this epistle Paul *defended* the gospel of grace in Jesus Christ which had been revealed to him. He has been adamant about his unwillingness to allow any additions to the singular reality of the essence of the gospel in the dynamic grace of the spiritual presence of the risen Lord Jesus.

In the second major section of his correspondence, comprising chapters three and four, Paul *documents* that the gospel revealed to him was God's intent from the very beginning. This was necessitated because the intruding teachers in Galatia apparently suggested that Paul had overstepped the bounds of divine propriety by abandoning old covenant performance of the Law and advocating that God now functioned in Christians solely by His grace received by faith. Perhaps their argument was that "this new-fangled gospel of grace that Paul preaches is a traitorous sacrifice of all that God has revealed to His people throughout the centuries of Hebrew history." Paul counters by attempting to document from the old covenant literature (the Old Testament) itself that God's revealed intention was the restoration of all humanity universally in the Person and work of Jesus Christ, responded to in faith.

Paul's argument admittedly requires an acceptance of the progressive revelation of God concerning His intent within a new covenant in His Son, Jesus Christ. The old covenant with its external, physical emphasis of God's actions with His people, Israel, was a pictorial prefiguring of the internal, spiritual realities of the new covenant in Christ. It has been explained that "the Old Testament was the New Testament concealed, while the New Testament is the Old Testament revealed." Only as one understands the new covenant reality of Jesus Christ can he look back and understand how God was preparing and setting the stage for the revelation of His grace in Jesus Christ. The Judaic understanding of the old covenant, complete with self-oriented, exclusivistic and isolationistic interpretations of racial, national and religious preference of God, would require complete reinterpretation. Paul had accepted such a total overhaul of old covenant concepts on the basis of the realization of the reality of the new covenant in Christ, perhaps gained by personal revelation of the Spirit of God (cf. 1:12) in the Arabian desert (cf. 1:17). He could even refer to the old covenant system as being "destroyed" (2:18). Jewish interpretation of the old covenant and the Law, retained for the most part by the Judaizers who were infiltrating the Galatian churches, failed to appreciate the new revelation of God in Jesus Christ, and sought to maintain the functional performance-orientation of the old covenant, resistant to the gospel of grace. Paul found such teaching unacceptable and intolerable, and this letter is his reaction to such.

When Paul received the report of the Judaizing interlopers encouraging the new Galatian Christians to supplement their newfound faith in Jesus Christ with outmoded functional performance of the Law, his ire was riled at such a reversionist distortion of the gospel (1:7). Reading this letter almost two millennia after it was written, we must sort through the polemic of Paul's argument, and attempt to reconstruct, as best we can, the positions and assertions he was attempting to counter. Between the lines we can sometimes detect that Paul was employing particular phrases and lines of reasoning because they were the catchwords or the misrepresentative interpretations of the intruders.

As Paul begins this second section of the epistle he transitions from the indirect instruction of reporting the Antiochan incident with Peter and the consequent theological implications contained in the synopsis of confrontational rebuke, to a direct didactic approach of challenging the consistency of the Galatian Christians. The particular argument of "righteousness by faith" had been set up in his previous comments in 2:16,17 and 21.

3:1 Continuing to be direct and straightforward about the gospel, Paul appeals to the Galatian Christians whom he personally knew and loved. He is not being unkind, nor is he skirting the issue in overly-sensitized sentimentality. To the point, he writes, ***"You foolish Galatians, who has bewitched you, before whose eyes Jesus Christ was publicly portrayed as crucified?"*** Paul was not deriding them as despicable and damnable "fools," as cautioned against by Jesus (Matt. 5:22), but is questioning whether they are using their sanctified common-sense. It is not their IQ that is in question, but whether they are utilizing the spiritual discernment that they should have by the presence of the Spirit in them (I Cor. 2:10-15). They should have been able to see the inconsistent folly of the legalistic strictures being imposed by the Judaizers. Instead, they had gullibly allowed themselves to be misled, as if they had been mesmerized, hypnotized, or put under a magical spell. Though the physical instruments of such hoodwinking were the infiltrating false teachers, the one who (singular in Greek) had bewitched them was actually the Deceiver himself, the diabolic and satanic "father of lies" (Jn. 8:44). This despite the fact that Paul and Barnabas had vividly and clearly spelled out the ramifications of the death of Jesus Christ in graphic detail when they preached "Christ crucified" (I Cor. 1:23; 2:2) among the Galatians. Paul is not implying that the Galatians saw the physical crucifixion of Jesus with their physical eyes, but that metaphorically with the "eyes of their heart" (Eph.

1:18) they understood the meaning of the death of Christ as he had powerfully placarded such to their minds. Christ did not die needlessly (2:21), but His death set in motion the "finished work" (Jn. 19:30) whereby God accomplishes the entirety of His work of redemption and restoration of man. By His death on the cross Jesus took the just consequences of men's unrighteousness in death, to make available His life of righteousness to mankind. The performance of Jesus Christ on our behalf on the cross and the grace dynamic of His resurrection-life in the Christian forestalls any meritorious, rule-keeping performance in the Christian life. If the Galatian Christians had properly understood the implications of the cross of Christ and all that was accomplished and set in motion by that substitutional act, they should not have been so easily entranced by the bedeviling suggestions of the legalists.

3:2 Flabbergasted by their gullibility and lack of spiritual understanding, Paul explains that *"there is only one thing I want to find out from you."* The crux of the matter is contained in their understanding of the centrality of the gospel concerning the receiving of the Spirit of Christ (Rom. 8:9) in spiritual regeneration. If the Galatians clearly understood, as Paul knew they did, that their initial reception of the Spirit of Christ was by faith, rather than by performance of works, then they should be able to see the error of their inconsistency in reverting to such after becoming Christians.

So the single question is, *"Did you receive the Spirit by works of the Law, or by hearing with faith?"* Paul takes them back to the commencement of their Christian lives, asking them to re-evaluate their personal experience and the means by which they received the Spirit of Christ when they were "born of the Spirit" (Jn. 3:3-9). They were not required to perform legally prescribed tasks in accord with rules and regulations, or rites and rituals, in order to meritoriously acquire a spiritual reward for obedient conformity. The spiritual reality of the life of Jesus is never acquired by requisite external actions whereby one must "do this" or "not do that" in order to become a Christian, including the keeping of the Ten Commandments of the old covenant Law. Rather, the Spirit of Christ is freely available to any person willing to receive Him by faith. The apostle John noted that "as many as received Him (Jesus), to them He gave the right to become children of God, even to those who believe in His name" (Jn. 1:12), also linking receiving with believing faith. William Barclay explained that "the first element in faith is what we can only call receptivity,"[1] and James Moffatt added that faith is "the attitude of receptivity towards the gift of God."[2] The essence of the biblical concept of faith is "man's receptivity of God's activity." Paul was reminding the Galatians that every spiritual blessing they had received (cf. I Cor. 4:7), they had received by hearing and listening to the Word of God (cf. Rom. 10:16,17), thus being available to allow the Spirit of God's Son to indwell their hearts by faith (4:6; 3:14). Paul's question did not require an answer, because he knew that the Galatians knew that spiritual regeneration was not based on performance-works, but received in faith.

3:3 In light of the obviated fact of having received the Spirit of Christ by the receptivity of faith, Paul asks, ***"Are you so foolish?"*** "Where is your spiritual understanding and discernment? How can you accept such inconsistent logic that attempts to reverse the premise of God's grace received by faith?"

"Having begun by the Spirit, are you now being perfected by the flesh?" The Christian does not start the Christian life by one means, and then attempt to continue and finish the Christian life by another premise. It is a distorted gospel (1:7) that attempts to jump track or "switch horses in mid-stream." The way one begins the Christian life is the same basis that one must carry on in the Christian life, for there is a consistency in God's grace activity received by faith. To the Colossians (Col.

2:6), Paul wrote, "As you received Christ Jesus (by faith), so walk in Him (by faith)." The beginning of the Christian life was by the active work of the Spirit of Christ in regeneration, and the sanctifying work of Christ throughout the Christian life is likewise the receptivity of Christ's function by the Spirit. The Spirit's presence and work is not a second act of grace subsequent to regeneration as some perfectionist theologies indicate. "He who began a good work in us will perfect it until the day of Jesus Christ" (Phil. 1:6), and that by the dynamic of His grace. It is possible that the Judaizers were using the term "perfected" to refer to an alleged higher level of spirituality which they were offering to lead the Galatians unto via proceduralized performances – a form of legalistic perfectionism. The means and methods of their perfecting of the Christian life was "by the flesh." This could refer to the physical act of male circumcision on the fleshly body, but it more likely refers to the external actions of performance in the body as one engages in the self-reliance of self-effort to accomplish the activity of self-achievement unto self-righteousness. Such was totally antithetical to Paul's concept of "perfecting holiness" (II Cor. 7:1) by the dynamic grace-expression of God's holy character in the behavior of a Christian, thus fulfilling the end-objective of God in man – divine glorification.

3:4 Still prodding the Galatian Christians to consider their initial experience of receiving the Spirit of Christ and the commencement of their Christian lives, Paul asks, ***"Did you suffer so many things in vain – if indeed it was in vain?"*** The word Paul employs sometimes has a broad meaning of "experience," which could refer to the Galatians' receiving of the Spirit and walking in grace; but the word is more often used of "suffering," inclusive of ostracism, harassment and persecution. It is the Greek word from which we derive the English word "pathos." If the Galatian Christians had endured suffering, was this at the hand of the Judaizers? Though we have no record of such, it is more likely that the Galatian Christians suffered at the hands of the Jewish leaders or the Roman provincial authorities. This is not at all unreasonable to assume, given the reaction to Paul and Barnabas in those very communities of south Galatia (Acts 13:50; 14:2,5,19). The Judaizers were offering an avoidance of suffering (6:12), facilitated by identification with the Jews in circumcision and Law-keeping. Could the repeated sufferings of the Galatians have been avoided if they had simply conformed to Judaic performance standards? Was it needless suffering? Paul did not think so, for such would have meant the sacrifice of the gospel of grace and liberty in Jesus Christ. Paul was hopeful that the Galatians would see the folly of reversion to the dead works of legalism, and recognize that their experience of suffering was not in vain. It was worth every painful moment to stand up for the gospel of Jesus Christ.

3:5 Paul asks another question as he continues to remind the Galatians of their regeneration and the subsequent outworking of God's activity in their lives. ***"Does He then, Who provides you with the Spirit and works miracles among you, do it by the works of the Law, or by hearing with faith?"*** "God the Father sends forth the Spirit of the Son into our hearts" (4:6). He abundantly supplies us with the sustained dynamic of His grace in "the provision of the Spirit of Jesus Christ" (Phil. 1:19). The continuing grace of God in the Christian by the ongoing work of the Holy Spirit is "energizing dynamically" in the Christian community. In that sense God is "working miracles" by His supernatural expression and activity, even though such "miracles" may not necessarily take the form of overt sensation. Christian partakers of the Holy Spirit have "tasted the powers of the age to come" (Heb. 6:5), and know that the dynamic of God's grace is active in them and through them as they are receptive to such in faith. Such divine activity is not contingent on religious performance that earns the right to such, but is readily available in the provisional resource of God's Spirit as we are receptive to His activity.

3:6 Paul now begins to document from the Old Testament that this divine method of operation by grace through faith had been God's intended *modus operandi* from the very beginning. The extensive (3:6 – 4:21) documentation is formulated in a well-crafted logical argument that requires spiritual discernment of the new covenant reinterpretation of the old covenant pictorialization and prototypification of God's redemptive and restorative intent in Jesus Christ. The Judaizers, with their Judaic sympathies of race, nation and religion still intact, could not (or would not) recognize the complete fulfillment of the preliminary old covenant in the new covenant of Jesus Christ. In particular, they were appealing to Abraham as their progenitor of lineal and religious descent, claiming that they were the promised blessing of multiplied posterity from Abraham. In support of their emphasis on physical male circumcision, they no doubt referenced Abraham's circumcision as a sign of the covenant (Gen. 17:4-11). Abraham's faithful performance, based on conviction and commitment, and expressed in trusting obedience was evidenced in his willingness to offer up his son, Isaac (Gen. 22:1-19). The Jewish conception of Abraham is clearly stated in the Old Testament Apocryphal book of *Ecclesiasticus*, also known as *Wisdom of Sirach*: "Abraham was the great father of a multitude of nations, and no one has been found like him in glory; he kept the Law of the Most High and was taken into covenant with Him; he established the covenant in his flesh, and when he was tested he was found faithful" (Sirach 44:19,20). Abraham was revered by the Jewish people for his Law-keeping performance and faithfulness. Paul takes the Jewish understanding of Abraham and preempts it by appealing to preceding biblical references to Abraham, prior to those being championed by Jewish religion and the Judaizers. Before Abraham's circumcision (Gen. 17); before Abraham's

3:6

trusting willingness to sacrifice his son, Isaac (Gen. 22); before there was any codified Law to perform (Exod. 20), Paul notes, ***"Abraham believed God, and it was reckoned to him as righteousness"*** (Gen. 15:6).

From the very beginning when God first created man as a receptive and derivative creature, the only human response solicited was receptivity to God's provision. God encouraged man to "eat freely" (Gen. 2:16) from any tree in the garden of Eden including, and particularly, the "tree of life" (Gen. 2:9). God created man as a receptive faith-creature; not as a self-generative actuator.

Abraham responded to God's direction with receptive faith, for "when he was called, he obeyed by going out to a place which he was to receive for an inheritance; and he went out, not knowing where he was going" (Heb. 11:8; cf. Gen. 12:1-4). Abraham did not simply concur with mental consent in a cognitive belief that God could do what He said He would do. Rather, he responded with personal availability to what God proposed to do. That is faith – man's availability to God's ability, or man's receptivity of God's activity. Prior to any examples of Abraham's faithfulness, Paul points out Abraham's response of faith. Abraham was accepting of and receptive to God's promise of an innumerable posterity (Gen. 15:1-6), probably unaware that this applied primarily to a spiritual descendancy of faith. Paul's point to the Galatians is, of course, that the receptivity of faith is historically precedent to, and logically takes precedence over, any performance of faithfulness attributed to Abraham, and used as a Law-keeping incentive as the Judaizers were doing.

The citation from Moses (Gen. 15:6) continues to indicate that Abraham's faith was "reckoned to him as righteousness." The Greek word for "reckon" was an economic accounting term referring to logical calculation that accounts an asset to someone's benefit. Does this mean that in the heavenly bookkeeping department of divine accounting that Abraham was rewarded with an entry in the righteousness column because of his faith? Does this mean that Abraham's faith is regarded as, or constituted as, righteousness? Does this mean that Abraham's faith was sufficient cause to elevate him to a conferred status or standing before God, the divine Judge, in the heavenly courtroom? These would all mitigate against Paul's argument. Consistent with the more extensive treatment of this same Genesis text in Paul's epistle to the Romans (cf. Rom. 4:3,9,22), the Greek text indicates that "Abraham's faith was reckoned unto (or towards) righteousness." Abraham's receptive faith in response to the divine promise of a spiritual posterity of faithful peoples in Jesus Christ was taken into account by God and accounted to Abraham with a view to (towards or unto) the response of receptivity to the righteousness that would be revealed in Jesus Christ, the Righteous One (Acts 3:14; 7:52; 22:14; I Jn. 2:1), whose divine righteousness could be accounted to and enacted in any man receptive to such in faith (cf. I Cor. 1:30; II Cor. 5:21). Whereas the Judaizers reckoned that the faithful performance of old covenant Law-keeping would constitute moral righteousness, Paul denied such by affirming that the human response of receptive faith allows all righteousness to be derived from Jesus Christ, the Righteous One, based on His "act of righteousness" (Rom. 5:18,21) in His death on the cross.

3:7 *"Therefore,"* Paul surmises, based on the premise that all righteousness is derived from Jesus Christ through faith, *"be sure that it is those who are of faith that are sons of Abraham."* The true sons of Abraham are not those who have the heritage of a physical blood-line from Abraham, nor those males who are circumcised, nor those who perform faithfully in Law-keeping, but the true posterity and descendancy of Abraham are Christians who by God's grace derive righteousness from Christ in receptive faith. "It is imperative that you should know and understand this;" Paul wrote to the Galatians,

"It is not those who ascribe to the Law or submit to circumcision that are the sons of Abraham as described by God through Moses in Genesis 12, 15 and 17, but those who continue to exercise the receptive faith that was evidenced in Abraham." This must have been particularly galling to the Judaizers as they heard this letter read in the Galatian churches. For centuries the Jewish claim had been that Abraham was their father based on race, religion and national covenantal privilege. John the Baptist had confronted those who claimed Abraham as their father, contending that God could raise up children of Abraham out of stones (Matt. 3:9; Lk. 3:8). Jesus faced-off with the Jewish religious leaders who alleged that Abraham was their father (Jn. 8:39), and He asserted that spiritually they were "of their father, the devil" (Jn. 8:44). Furthermore He explained that Abraham by his receptive faith "rejoiced to see My day, and he saw it (in faith), and was glad" (Jn. 8:56). The Judaizers, operating as they were in Gentile contexts, were apparently begrudgingly willing to give up the necessity of physical descendancy in order to be sons of Abraham, but were still insisting on the likeness of deeds of performance whereby in doing what Abraham did in circumcision, Law-keeping and faithful obedience persons might qualify to be identified as sons of Abraham. Paul jettisons both physical descendancy and performance-deed as the criteria for identification with Abraham, arguing that the very intent of God in His promised blessing of Abraham's posterity was reference to the spiritual sons of Abraham who looked to Jesus Christ in the receptivity of faith. Thus Paul will later draw the conclusion that "if you belong to Christ, you are Abraham's offspring" (3:29). How regrettable that many Christians to this very day still interpret God's promises to Abraham as physical and external blessings, even denying Paul's statement in this verse by interpreting it to mean that "those who are of faith are like unto, or similar to, the physical sons of Abraham." A bizarre distortion of the gospel, indeed!

3:8 Pressing the documentation of his argument concerning God's spiritual and Christic intent in the promises to Abraham even farther, Paul adduces that ***"the Scripture, foreseeing that God would justify the Gentiles by faith, preached the gospel beforehand to Abraham, saying, 'All the nations shall be blessed in you.'"*** Paul appeals to the graphic writings of the Old Testament scriptures, believing them to be the authoritative reporting of God's actions and words. God foresaw, because it was His foreknown intent from the beginning "before the foundation of the world" (Eph. 1:4), what He was going to do to restore His righteous presence to all mankind, regardless of race, in the Person and work of His Son, Jesus Christ. He facilitated the pre-recording of such in the written revelation of the Hebrew scriptures in the pre-evangelizing good news announced in the promise of blessed posterity to Abraham. Since the gospel is the good news of Messianic redemption restoring divine function in receptive mankind, Jesus could say, "Abraham rejoiced to see My day, and he saw it, and was glad" (Jn. 8:56), and the writer of the epistle to the Hebrews could declare that "Abraham saw the promises (by faith) and welcomed them from a distance" (Heb. 11:13).

Again citing an Abrahamic text from Genesis that preceded those predominantly used by the Judaizers (Gen. 17 and 22), Paul takes the Galatians back to the initial text concerning Abraham, where the divine promise is that "all the nations shall be blessed in you, Abraham" (Gen. 12:3; cf. Gen. 18:18; 22:17,18, 26:4; 28:14). The Jewish interpretation of this Genesis text was that all of the other nations would be blessed indirectly through the kind and well-intentioned generosity of the nation of Israel. This is not just a promise to the Jewish race, nation or religion, Paul argues, but to all ethnic people in all nations, and thus it was a preview of the gospel of Jesus Christ whose divine righteousness would be offered to the Gentiles by the receptivity of faith. In his total reinterpretation of the old covenant literature, Paul was confident that the promises of God to Abraham were fulfilled in the gospel of Christ, and that his apostleship to the Gentiles was a mission that fulfilled the Abrahamic promises. The universality of the availability of the gospel blessing in Jesus Christ would indeed come through Abraham in the Messianic genealogy (Matt. 1:2; Lk. 3:34), but Abraham's receptive faith served as the prototypical paradigm whereby solidarity with Abraham's posterity and blessing could be experienced by all peoples.

3:9 Drawing a logical conclusion from the combined Genesis texts he had just quoted (Gen. 12:3 and Gen. 15:6), Paul wrote, *"So then, those who are of faith are blessed with Abraham, the believer."* In the solidarity of faith comes the solidarity of blessing in Christ for all people. "Those who are of faith," distinct from those who are relying on the legalistic performance of the Law and circumcision (as the Judaizers promoted), are included in the Abrahamic blessing. Such blessing is not a physical or materialistic blessing of prosperity, nor a futuristic utopian blessing in a far-off heaven, but is the comprehensive blessing of God in Jesus Christ presently experienced by Christians. "God has blessed us with every spiritual blessing in the heavenly places in Christ Jesus" (Eph. 1:3). The blessing of God is Christ! The blessing that Christians have in Christ is the very blessing promised to Abraham, and appreciated by Abraham in preview and prospect as he was receptive in faith to the activity of God, including the coming of the Messiah in His redemptive and restorative work. "Those who are of faith," be they Jew or Gentile from any nation in any age, can realize mutual blessing with Abraham in Jesus Christ. Abraham is called "the believer," not because of his credulous conviction of a good outcome (humanism), nor because of his faithful performance (Judaizers' interpretation), but because his receptivity to God's activity was the prototype of Christian faith.

3:10 Some have suggested that verses 10 through 25 are a protracted digression, and that verse 26 could have followed verse 9 with no loss of continuity. But we must remember that Paul was trained as a lawyer who meticulously prepared the details of his logical and legal argument. Examining the other side of the coin by turning the argument to its negation, Paul directed his attention to the concept of curse as opposed to blessing.

"For as many as are of the works of the Law are under a curse," Paul explained. Those who insist upon and are dependent upon observing and performing the behavioral rules and regulations of religion (be they Jewish Law or another form), as the legalistic Judaizers were, are caught in the cursed consequences of disobedience instead of rejoicing in the grace-blessing of liberty in Christ. What a shocking statement this would have been to those sympathetic with Jewish interpretation, for Judaic thought considered God's blessing to be the result of the keeping and performing of the Law. Jewish thought was steeped in the blessing and curse contrast so extensively laid out in the Deuteronomic code (cf. Deut. 11:26-29; 21:22,23; 27:12-26; 28:1-68), which established tangible blessings for obedience to God and destructive curses as consequences of disobedience. The concept of "curse" was not the ultimate anathema of divine damnation, nor was it a vindictive imprecation of harm against another person, but it was the absence of God's protective blessing as a consequence of disobedience. In new covenant reinterpretation God's "blessing" is Christ and the fullness of His grace-activity, whereas "curse" is the absence of that Christic blessing in the frustrating consequences of the inability to perform in accord with God's perceived expectations and demands, or even one's own self-imposed expectations.

To document his shocking declaration Paul cites a verse from Deuteronomy, explaining, *"It is written, 'Cursed is every one who does not abide by all things written in the book of*

the Law to perform them'" (Deut. 27:26). In the Judaic covenant of performance the consequences of disobedience would necessarily come upon those who did not maintain and continue to perform perfectly and completely every detail of the Law. It was "all or nothing." One had to subscribe to the entire performance package. "Whoever keeps the whole Law and yet stumbles in one point, he has become guilty of all" (James 2:10). The legalistic book-religion was unforgiving, inevitably resulting in cursed consequences of disobedience.

3:11 *"That no one is justified by the Law before God is evident,"* Paul continues to reason. No person can perform the rules and regulations of the Law completely and perfectly, in order to be declared or made righteous either objectively or subjectively. This repudiation of Judaic performance-righteousness was stated previously in his synopsis of the rebuke of Peter, where Paul indicated that it was basic Christian knowledge "that a man is not justified by the works of the Law," and they had personally "believed in Christ Jesus, that we may be justified by faith in Christ, and not by the works of the Law" (2:16). Later, to the Philippians Paul would write that he did "not have a righteousness of his own derived from the Law" (Phil. 3:9), and to the Romans he would assert that "by the works of the Law no flesh will be justified in His sight" (Rom. 3:20). Righteousness comes only through Jesus Christ, the divine Righteous One (Acts 3:14; 7:52; 22:14), whose performance of the "righteous act" (Rom. 5:18) of taking the consequences of humanity's sin on the cross made available "His righteousness" (Rom. 3:25,26) that those who were receptive in faith might be "made righteous" (Rom. 5:19; II Cor. 5:21), both in objective status of right-standing before God and in subjective realization of His indwelling presence and character of righteousness. Since Christian righteousness is based only on the performance of Jesus Christ in His redemptive work and in His ongoing sanctifying work, it stands obvious and self-evident that no man can be made right with God or morally righteous by his own performance and achievement of religious rules and regulations.

The aforestated premise is documented by the prophet's statement that *"the righteous man shall live by faith"* (Habakkuk 2:4). In like manner as Jesus Christ, the Righteous Man, expressed the life of God perfectly in human behavior by the receptivity of God's activity in faith (cf. Jn. 14:10; Heb. 10:7-10), so the Christian who has been made a "righteous man" by the presence of Christ's righteousness in him shall live by allowing Christ's life to be manifested in his mortal body (II Cor. 4:10,11), exhibiting His righteous character by the receptivity of His activity in faith. No man is autonomous and independent, capable of generating righteous character by his own performance activity. God created men as dependent and contingent creatures who must derive righteous character from God through faith-receptivity. Christ is our righteousness (I Cor. 1:30); Christ is our life (Col. 3:4); and only by receptive derivation of His righteous life do we live as God intended, expressing His character unto His glory. Paul employed the same quotation from Habakkuk when he wrote to the Romans, stating that "the righteousness of God is revealed from faith to faith, as it is written, 'the righteous shall live by faith'" (Rom. 1:17), and the writer to the Hebrews also quotes the same verse (Heb. 10:38).

Protestant theology from the Reformation onwards has tended to objectify the three elements in this oft-quoted statement into static categories. The "righteous man" is considered to be one who is forensically declared right with God, juridically imputed with Christ's righteousness, and therefore legally reckoned righteous by the redemptive work of Christ. That such a righteous man "shall live" is interpreted as the heavenly imputation and investiture of Christ's life in order to live eternally in heaven. The basis of appropriating such life and righteousness is explained as the cognitive assent of "faith" whereby a man believes and accepts the historical and theological data of Christ's life and work. This tragic over-objectification of the reality of Christianity is woefully inadequate to express what Paul is combating in the false performance-righteousness proffered by the Judaizers. The vital subjective implications of the gospel of Christ must be emphasized to recognize how the righteous character of God indwells the receptive Christian believer in the spiritual presence of the Righteous One, in order to allow the righteous life of Jesus Christ to be lived out behaviorally by the continued reception of faith.

3:12 Only by understanding the subjective and behavioral implications of Paul's argument does the following statement make sense: ***"The Law is not of faith."*** The functional operative of the behavioral directives of the Law are necessarily demanding of personal performance, productivity and the output of behavioral conformity. The rules and regulations of the Law carry with them no inherent or intrinsic provision, resource or dynamic with which to fulfill the divine directives of expressing the divine character. There is nothing in the Law to be receptive to, for there is no dynamic intake of divine activity as there is in the grace-provision of the righteous life of Jesus Christ. Despite the long-held assertion that the old covenant Law was based on the same functional principle of faith as is the new covenant of grace in Jesus Christ, such cannot be legitimately maintained without defining grace and faith in static theological categories. Though there is a continuity with Abraham's receptivity to God, there is also a discontinuity between Law and grace.

"Contrary" to any attribution of righteousness derived from receptivity to the Law, Paul quotes the explicit Old Testament directive of legalistic performance: ***"He who practices them shall live by them"*** (Lev. 18:5). Are the two Old Testament quotations from Habakkuk and Leviticus contradictory? "The righteous man *shall live* by faith" (Hab. 2:4) – "He who practices the regulations of the Law *shall live* by them" (Lev. 18:5; cf. Ezek. 20:11). If understood in the context of Judaic old covenant interpretation they are fully consistent, but Paul has radically reinterpreted Habakkuk from a new covenant perspective, while retaining the old covenant perspective of Leviticus as an argument against the Judaizers. Jesus retained the old covenant premise of this same Leviticus verse when He responded to the Jewish lawyer who asked what he had to do to have eternal life. When asked what the Law advised, the lawyer responded correctly, whereupon Jesus said, "Do this, and you will live" (Lk. 10:28), proceeding to tell the parable of the "wounded traveler" to illustrate the operative of grace. When he wrote to the Romans, Paul again referred to Moses' old covenant perspective "that the man who practices the righteousness which is based on the Law shall live by that righteousness" (Rom. 10:5), noting that the Jewish peoples "sought to establish their own righteousness by performance, failing to recognize and unwilling to submit to the righteousness of God in Jesus Christ, who is the end of the Law for righteousness to everyone who believes" (Rom. 10:3,4).

A closer look at the Old Testament text reveals the point that Paul is attempting to make. God spoke to Moses, saying, "You (the people of Israel) shall keep My statutes and perform My judgments, by which a man shall live if he does them" (Lev. 18:5). Notice the impossible conditional "if" that qualifies the "shall live" based upon the complete and perfect performance of God's statutes, the impossibility of which was already denied by citing Deuteronomy 27:26 in verse 10. Since all religious practice and performance is inevitably imperfect, then the legalistic premise of the Judaizers is therefore invalid, based on the impossibility of fulfilling the Law by human performance and the impotence of the Law to provide any empowering sufficiency that might be received by faith. Although the Judaic and Judaizing incentive was that the performance of the commands of the Law could produce life in accord with

God's intent, Paul will categorically deny such later in the chapter when he states that "if a law had been given which was able to impart life, then righteousness would indeed have been based on law" (3:21). Paul's reinterpretation of the Leviticus statement might be that "he who attempts to keep the works of the Law by performance shall live with the consequences of having chosen that impossible endeavor, the consequences of the impotent inability to keep the Law in the curse-consequences of frustrating failure to live up to the expectations of God, religion and oneself." Paul's objective in citing this verse therefore seems to be to expose the hopelessness inherent in the inability and impossibility of keeping the Law, so that the Galatian Christians should realize that though they could not perform sufficiently, the Spirit of Christ has and does perform sufficiently as the dynamic of all God's demands to express His character. When Jesus Christ enacts the divine character required by the Law which is now written in our hearts as Christians (Heb. 8:10; 10:16), then we do indeed live by His life practiced and expressed in our behavior.

3:13 Turning to that very redemptive and restorative message of the gospel, Paul states that ***"Christ redeemed us from the curse of the Law, having become a curse for us."*** Jesus paid the price of death on the cross to buy us out of the slave-market of enslaving performance in trying to keep the rules of religion, with the resultant cursed consequences of frustrating failure and disobedience due to our inability to perform the commands of the Law completely and perfectly. The death consequences (cf. Gen. 2:16; Rom. 6:23) of human sin, being the failure to align with the righteous character of God, required a vicarious substitute who would become the object of the curse on our behalf. The "iniquity of us all fell on Him" (Isa. 53:6) as He was "made sin on our behalf" (II Cor. 5:21), being constituted as the personification of all sin, incurring all of the death consequences that occurred in Adam at the Fall, in order to give Himself as a ransom for us all (Matt. 20:28). In His death Jesus essentially took all of the curse-consequences outlined in Deuteronomy 28, such as thirst, nakedness, poverty, injustice, etc., upon and within Himself, crying out "My God, My God, why have You forsaken Me?" (Matt. 27:46).

Paul explains that *"it had been written, 'Cursed is every one who hangs on a tree.'"* Though the original reference in Deuteronomy 21:23 had no reference to crucifixion on a cross, Paul is obviously drawing a connection to the Roman execution instrument of the cross, constructed as it was out of wooden cross-beams, and often referred to as a "tree." Jesus was "put to death by hanging on a tree" (Acts 5:30; 10:39; 13:29), and "bore our sins in His body on the tree" (I Pet. 2:24). Jewish execution was enacted by stoning a person to death to reduce evil in the community (Deut. 21:21), and then the corpse was hung in a tree as a public display apparently to serve as a deterrent effect on observers (cf. Josh. 10:26; II Sam. 4:12). Whenever an Israelite saw a dead body hanging in a tree, he was to surely surmise the man whose dead body was thus publicly displayed was receiving the just consequences of disobedience. So the Jewish reaction to Christ's crucifixion, unaware of Jesus' taking the ultimate curse-consequence of death for the disobedient sin of all mankind, regarded the very public display of Jesus on a tree as indicative of a deserved consequence of cursedness. The external, physical evaluation of the crucifixion event totally misses the point of the eternal, spiritual realities that transpired as Christ was crucified on the cross.

3:14 Crucifixion was God's intent for Jesus (Acts 2:23) from the foundation of the world (Rev. 13:8). By the voluntary performance of death on behalf of mankind, the curse of inadequate and disobedient human performance was forever removed *"in order that in Christ Jesus the blessing of Abraham might come to the Gentiles."* God's promised blessing to Abraham (Gen. 12:1-3; 15:1-6; 17:1-8) is fulfilled in the grace-blessing of Jesus Christ (Eph. 1:3), providing God's intended universal restoration of all peoples, Gentile as well as Jew, into an innumerable and unending community of blessedness in Christ. Again, this was a radical reversal of all Jewish thinking, which was retained to some degree by the Judaizers. The exclusivism of Jewish thought attributed the curse of the consequences of disobedient lawlessness upon all Gentiles, who being "without the Law" (Rom. 2:12; I Cor. 9:21) could not be part of the covenant of promise (Eph. 2:12) or the blessing of God. Paul is declaring that the blessing of God promised to Abraham is the very blessing that God has made available to the Gentiles, as well as the Jews, on the basis of Jesus' having taken the curse consequences on behalf of all men. There are not two ways of salvation, one for the Jew and another for the Gentile (as some have indicated), but Jew and Gentile are all united as one family (3:28) of God's sons through faith in Christ Jesus (3:26). There is no intrinsic advantage for the Jews, nor any disadvantage in being a Gentile.

Furthermore, referent to the Judaizing insistence on the performance of the Law for ongoing righteousness, the performance of Christ's death was ***"so that we might receive the promise of the Spirit through faith,"*** thereby negating all performance-righteousness in the Christian life as the Spirit of Christ in the Christian is allowed to express His character of divine righteousness in our behavior as we are receptive to such in faith. The promise of blessing to Abraham (Gen. 12:1-3) is linked to the promise which God gave to Joel to "pour out His Spirit on all mankind" (Joel 2:28; cf. Acts 2:17), and the promise to Ezekiel, promising to "put His Spirit within us to cause us to walk in His statutes" (Ezek. 36:27), which is thus linked to the promise to Jeremiah "to make a new covenant, wherein God's Law is put within men's hearts" (Jere. 31:31-34; cf. Heb. 8:10; 10:16). The promises of Jesus to send "the Helper," "the Spirit of truth" (Jn. 14:16-20,26; 15:26,27; 16:7-14), which the Father had promised (cf. Lk. 24:49; Acts 1:4) are subsequent expressions of the same promise. All the promises of God are fulfilled and affirmed in Jesus Christ (II Cor. 1:20). Jesus Christ is everything that the old covenant pointed to in its pictorial prefiguring, and everything that God has to give by His grace in Jesus Christ is received by faith, the human receptivity of His divine activity. Promises are not delivered on the basis of meritorious performance, but are received by the receptivity of faith.

It should be recognized that the propensity of man to seek moral righteousness and meaning to life by personal performance is indicative of all fallen men in their general pursuits of life, as well as all religion. Whereas religion tends to establish criteria of meritorious performance before God, the orientation of the world-order in culture and society operates on the humanistic premise of utilitarian productivity in order to perform and accomplish successes that allegedly accrue for the betterment and enhancement of mankind. The pragmatic performance of useful activistic performance is regarded as the causal means to utopian progress and perfection. God's intended function for man, having created him as a derivative creature, is that man might accept the dynamic of God's grace in Jesus Christ and be receptive to His activity, allowing for the relational and ontological expression of God's character in man's behavior unto the glory of God.[3] Though the setting for Paul's reactive writing to the Galatian Christians was their tendency to revert to the legalistic performance of the Judaic regulations, Paul's explanation of receptivity to the activity of God in faith is the antidote to all religious performance standards, as well as the human potential incentives for productive performance in the humanistic and activistic orientation of Western society.

Almost everything in the world around us is measured and evaluated by performance and productivity. Students are graded by their test performance and assignment productivity. Employees receive pay increases and promotions on the basis of performance and productivity. Products are marketed on the basis of their sales performance and market-share productivity. This is, no doubt, the way it must be in the world-order. But when the same performance standards are applied within the context of Christianity and the Church, which is supposed to function on an entirely antithetical mode of operation, i.e. receptivity of God's activity – it is particularly appalling. Christians should not be "foolish" like the Galatians in failing to differentiate between performance-activity and faith-receptivity. Christians should know better, especially since Paul expressed the point so adamantly here in the Galatian epistle. Yet we still see the blatant examples of Christian behavior evaluated by such external criteria as clothing styles, cosmetics, entertainment preferences, alcohol consumption, etc. Commitment levels and "spirituality" are measured by active involvement in the church programs, by the performance and productivity of doing and giving. The success of the church itself is often determined by the statistical analysis of the performance and productivity of the three "Big-Bs" – buildings, budgets and baptisms. Is the contemporary church, for the most part, not in the same inappropriate position as were the churches of Galatia?

The need of the hour for the modern church is to hear Paul's forceful argument to the Galatians. We need the cross of Christ vividly portrayed before our spiritual eyes, so that we might understand that the "finished work" of Christ was not only sufficient for redemption, regeneration and a destiny in heaven, but that the risen and living Lord Jesus continues to function in the finishing performance of providing the all-sufficient dynamic of His divine grace for everything in the Christian life. We need to understand that the promises of God's blessing through the patriarchs have all been fulfilled in Jesus Christ (II Cor. 1:20; Eph. 1:3). We are complete in Christ (Col. 2:10), having received everything pertaining to life and godliness in Him (II Pet. 1:3). The manifestation of His life in our behavior (II Cor. 4:10,11) is not in any way based on keeping religious rules, as if by the failure to thus perform we might de-merit the love and efficacy of Jesus Christ which we never merited in the first place. The only Christian response to the all-sufficient blessing of God's grace in Jesus Christ is receptivity to His activity.

ENDNOTES

1 Barclay, William, *The Mind of St. Paul*. London: Fontana Books. 1965. pg. 112.
2 Moffatt, James, *Grace in the New Testament*. London: Hodder and Stoughton. 1931. pg. 12.
3 cf. Fowler, James A., *The Uselessness of Usefulness and the Usefulness of Uselessness*. Fallbrook: C.I.Y. Publishing. 1996.

The Precedence Of God's Promises

Galatians 3:15-29

Imagine a father sitting down at the breakfast table with his children one morning, and saying, "Children, because I love you so much, I am going to take you all to Disneyland in six weeks. You can ride all the rides. You can have all the sodas, hot-dogs and balloons you desire. It will be an enjoyable family day. I promise that we will all go together in about six weeks. What do you think of that, children?"

The children's response would undoubtedly be one of excitement. "Oh Dad, you are such a great Dad. We love you. We can hardly wait until that day comes." Assuming that the children knew that their father was dependable and always kept his promises, there would be much anticipation in that household. The children would be receptive and available to the promise of their faithful father. They would have expectant hope of enjoying Disneyland.

What if that same father were to sit down with his children a couple of days later, and say, "Children, I have a proposition for you. Let's make a deal. If each of you picks up his or her room every day, and puts away all their clothes and toys, and if each one of you will perform this list of chores that I have prepared for you, and if you all come home with good grades on your report cards, then I will take you to Disneyland in about six weeks."

What would be the children's response to such a parental proposition? It would probably be something like: "But,

3:15-29

Daaaad, you already promised to take us to Disneyland in six weeks. That's not fair, Dad, to come back and add those rules and requirements after you already made us a promise!"

Would you agree with the children's reaction?

A promise is a promise! Negotiated performance requirements are something altogether different. Even a child can detect the difference between a parental promise and the contingencies of performance expectations.

What if I were to push this hypothetical scenario beyond all feasible and reasonable limits, and suppose that the children accepted and assented to the reciprocal deal that their father had proposed. (Not likely, but bear with me in this fictional story!) The children become so enamored with performing their duties and getting good grades that they forget the original promise of Disneyland. Or they come to believe that the rewards of good grades and fulfilled duties are, in themselves, better than going to Disneyland. Then, when the Disneyland trip is offered to them, they decline, preferring to maintain the regimen of performance. Or perhaps they accept the Disneyland trip, provided they can retain the self-satisfying, ego-enhancing rules of the home. Granted, this is so far-fetched as to be absurd, but the analogy with the physical peoples of Israel and the Judaizers of the first century plays out in such an outlandish portrayal.

This foregoing analogy is an attempt to picture a contemporary situation that corresponds to some degree with the complicated issues that Paul is dealing with in the Galatian epistle, and to put them in terms that even a child can understand. In fact, Paul begins this section of the letter with just such an analogy of "speaking in terms of human relations," in order to assist in explaining the spiritual relations between God and men. As with all analogies (Paul's and ours included), the story in "human terms" is always inadequate to convey the fullness of divine truth. We know, for example, that God did not promise us a Disneyland, complete with Adventureland, Fantasyland and Tomorrowland. What God promised us is far better both qualitatively and quantitatively – the fullness of His life through His Son, Jesus Christ, both now and forever. And the availability of Christ's life is not acquired by the achievement of performance, but is available in the receptivity of His activity in faith.

3:15 The neophyte Galatian Christians were being influenced by the legalistic Judaizers to misprioritize God's intentions and revert to performance of the old covenant Law in their Christian lives. Though they were gullibly being misled, Paul refers to them as ***"Brothers,"*** regarding them to be "sons of Abraham" (3:7,14,29) together with himself in the family of God.

Paul almost seems to make an advance disclaimer of the inadequacy of the illustrative analogy he is about to employ. ***"I speak in terms of human relations"*** (cf. Rom. 3:5), he writes, recognizing the imprecise parallelism between human contracts and God's covenants. Paul is playing off of the multiple meaning of the Greek word for "covenant," which can refer to (1) a contractual agreement between two human parties in a negotiated settlement with mutual conditions, (2) an individual's last will and testament to be effected after his death, or (3) a covenant arrangement that God as the greater party unidirectionally implements with mankind, the lesser party. ***"Even though it is only a man's covenant, yet when it has been ratified, no one sets it aside or adds conditions to it."*** When human contractual agreements have been ratified, validated and confirmed, i.e. "signed, sealed and delivered," then there is an authoritative definitiveness to the terms of the contract. Once you have "signed on the dotted line" the contract is legally binding, and the obligated parties cannot arbitrarily disregard, reject or nullify the contractual terms they agreed to, nor can they determine after the fact to individually or arbitrarily modify, alter or add contingencies to the agreement. There is a certain permanence and irrevocability to human contracts, but that is not to say that there are not arrangements for mutual modifications, amendments, and addendum.

The popular interpretation which suggests that Paul is specifically referring to an individual's last will and testament is based on the synonymous usage of "testament" and "covenant." References to "promise" (16,17,18,19, 21,22,29), "inheritance" (18) or "heirs" (29), and "descendants" (16,29) also seem to correlate with this death-contract thesis. In this case the ratification of the "last will and testament" is effected irrevocably upon the death of the testator, and no one else is allowed to annul the will or add codicils. The analogy seems to break down in the recognition that God who effected the covenant of promise with Abraham cannot die, but then again, the death of Jesus Christ (cf. 2:21;3:1,14) and the "finished work" of Christ on the cross could suffice as the death ratification of the promised inheritance.

It is obvious that Paul is attempting to make an analogy between a human contract or testament and the covenant of promise that God made with Abraham. But the Jewish response to Paul's legal argument of contractual irrevocability and inalterability would undoubtedly have been that God's covenant (Gen. 15:18; 17:2-21) with Abraham was indeed subsequently supplemented or replaced by the covenant of Law at Sinai (Exod. 19:5; 24:7,8; Deut. 4:13; 23:1,21). They would have been unconvinced by Paul's legal argument in the analogy of semantic variability in the word "covenant," and even more aghast at the semantic and grammatical variability that Paul employed as the basis of his next tenet.

3:16 Specifically identifying his analogy, Paul explains that *"the promises were spoken to Abraham and his seed."* He is referring to the promises of God to Abraham in Genesis 12-24, specifically cited in vss. 6 and 8 above, and linked with the promises of the Spirit (3:3,14) in Joel 2:28 and Ezek. 36:27.

Paul viewed all of the promises of God to be fulfilled in Jesus Christ (cf. II Cor. 1:20; II Tim. 1:1; II Pet. 1:4).

The startling part of Paul's interpretation of the promised "seed" (Greek word *spermati*), offspring or descendants of Abraham (Gen. 13:15,18; 17:7,8,19; 21:12; 22:18; 24:7) was his narrow focus on the singular number of the Hebrew noun for "seed." ***"He does not say, 'and to seeds,' as to many, but to one, 'and to your seed,' that is Christ."*** As in English and Greek, the singular Hebrew noun can refer to an individual "seed," or serve also as a collective singular of plurality. It can refer to a single offspring of Abraham (ex. Ishmael, Gen. 21:13), or all of the offspring of Abraham, both physically and spiritually (3:29). Despite the obvious references to innumerable multiplicity (Gen. 13:16; 15:5; 16:10; 22:17) of descendants, thus obviating the collective singular interpretation of "seed," Paul chooses to focus on the individual singular interpretation in order to link such with Christ as the promised descendant of Abraham.

Jewish theology would have found Paul's hermeneutic appalling and indefensible. The Jews prided themselves in their physical and racial ancestry from Abraham to form a multitudinous nation linked to "father Abraham." But even within Jewish interpretation Paul could have cited the precedent of God's covenant promise to David to "raise up your seed who will establish his kingdom forever" (II Sam. 7:12,13), which was interpreted within Jewish theology as the Messianic "son of David," and was thus used by Paul himself in his preaching in the southern Galatian city of Antioch of Pisidia, noting that "from the seed of David, according to promise, God brought to Israel a Savior, Jesus" (Acts 13:23). Paul could also have referred to the earlier Messianic promise of the "seed of the woman" (Gen. 3:15) defeating diabolic descendancy. Paul was certainly not out of line to employ this interpretation of the individual singular "seed," even though some have considered his argument as a weak diversionary documentation of semantic hair-splitting, or as a "spiritualizing" tendency.

Paul's objective was not to engage in grammatical or semantic technicalities, but to reveal that the promised descendancy of Abraham was fulfilled in Jesus Christ, and therefore in all who are identified with Christ as Christians. It is the Christological fulfillment of the Abrahamic promises that is important, not the physical and biological fulfillment in the Jewish race. Much Judaizing eschatology today could be put to rest by consistency with Paul's inspired Christological interpretation. In the physical genealogical lineage Jesus was the ultimate and preeminent descendant of Abraham (Matt. 1:2; Lk. 3:34), but as the promised individual Messianic "seed" He fulfilled the divine promises to Abraham, to allow the collective singular of Abrahamic "seed" to apply, as God intended from the beginning, to all Christians "in Christ" (3:29; Rom. 4:13-18). The ultimate intent of God's promises to Abraham was Christological rather than biological.

3:17 Apparently recognizing that his argument is somewhat convoluted, Paul attempts to clarify by writing, ***"What I am saying is this:"*** – the point I am trying to make is that of precedent priority alluded to in the analogy of human contract (15). ***"The Law, which came four hundred and thirty years later, does not invalidate a covenant previously ratified by God, so as to nullify the promise."*** The Judaizers in Galatia retained the Judaic perspective that exalted the Mosaic Law even above the Abrahamic promise. Although they appealed to Abraham as their racial father, the patriarchal period was viewed primarily as a preliminary prelude to the Mosaic receipt of the Law. The tablets of the Law were tangible and concrete, giving definitive parameters of obligatory performance and providing a distinctive national identity as "the people of the Law." The Law was primary and preeminent in Jewish theology, regarded as eternal and immutable, and thus elevated as a deified idolatrous end in itself. That is why Jesus said to the Jewish leaders, "You search the scriptures because you think that in them you have eternal life; and it is these that bear witness of Me" (Jn. 5:39,40).

Paul seeks to establish the precedence and priority of the Abrahamic covenantal promises in relation to the Mosaic covenant of Law. The promises preceded the giving of the Law on Mt. Sinai by a chronological period of four hundred and thirty years according to Paul's calculation. Though many have debated the precise number of years, it is probably impossible and unnecessary to seek exact calculations. God told Abraham that his descendants would be "enslaved and oppressed four hundred years" (Gen. 15:13), as quoted by Stephen (Acts 7:6) in his recitation of Hebrew history. Exodus records that "the sons of Israel lived in Egypt four hundred and thirty years" (Exod. 12:40). The imprecision of annual calculations results from not knowing where within the series of God's promises to Abraham (Gen. 12-23) the calculation should commence. The interval of time is not the important issue, however, for Paul is emphasizing the precedence and priority of the divine promise to Abraham rather than the period of time between the promise and the Law. Since the "covenants of promise" (cf. Eph. 2:12) were duly ratified and validated by God unto Abraham, the later introduction of the Law covenant with Moses did not sever (5:4), abolish (5:11) or nullify (cf. Rom. 4:14) the earlier promise. Such illegitimacy of covenant practice (3:15) would cast God as a dishonest covenant-broker, willing to break His fiduciary relationships through chicanery or sleight-of-hand by altering His agreements or conditioning His covenants, thus reneging on His promises and untrue to His Word. Paul obviously considered such contrariety of the character of God unthinkable.

3:18 Continuing his argument of the precedence, priority and primacy of the promises of God over the subsequent Law of God, Paul explains that *"if the inheritance is based on Law,* *it is no longer based on a promise: but God has granted it to Abraham by means of a promise."* This is Paul's first introduction of the theme of "inheritance," which in correlation with the concept of "heir" will later become a prominent emphasis in the epistle (3:29; 4:1,7,30). Within God's promises to Abraham there was the promise of "heirs" (Gen. 12:7; 13:15,16; 15:15; 17:8,19) and "inheritance" (Gen. 12:7; 13:15; 15:7,8; 17:8), but these were based on the unidirectional promise of God, not on performance requisites from the Law. The promises were not contingent on keeping the Law which was introduced later. Inherent in the very concept of "inheritance" is the idea of promised giftedness. Inheritances are not earned. If something is inherited, then it is not merited. Inheritances come by way of promise, whereas merits are earned through performance. Since God's character is that of absolute faithfulness, His promises to Abraham were completely fulfilled when by His grace He redeemed and restored humanity in His Son, Jesus Christ, making available the inheritance (cf. Acts 26:18; Eph. 1:11,18; Col. 1:12) of all things (I Cor. 3:21-23; Eph. 1:3; II Pet. 1:3) in Christ, that Christians might be the heirs of God's promises (Rom. 8:17; Gal. 3:29; Eph. 3:6; Titus 3:7; James 2:5; I Pet. 3:7). True to His promises – true to His Word – God freely gave (the Greek word is the verb form of "grace") the promised blessings and inheritance to Abraham by faith, even though the spiritual fullness of Christ was "seen from a distance" (Heb. 11:9-16). The fulfillment of God's promises is not conditioned on legal performance merit, but solely on receptivity to the promised blessings and inheritance in Christ.

3:19   With the foregoing emphasis on the precedence and priority of promise over Law, Paul recognizes that some will inevitably question, *"Why the Law then?"* Contrary to the Jewish perspective, retained in large part by the Judaizers who had infiltrated the Galatian churches, Paul did not regard the Law to be preeminent and primary in the over-all plan of God.

In reaction to what they regarded as denigration of the Law, the Jewish leaders in Jerusalem later accused Paul of "teaching against the Law" (Acts 21:28). But in promoting the primacy of the Abrahamic promise, was Paul implying that the Law was impertinent, irrelevant, superfluous or redundant? No. The Law was an essential part of the Torah (as was the promise), and Paul was not advocating that Exodus through Malachi be expunged from the Old Testament record. The Law had a legitimate purpose in the complete economy of God that was not inconsistent with the purpose of the promise, though it was incidental, auxiliary, subsidiary and subordinated. Paul had previously pointed out that the purpose of the Law was not justification (2:16; 3:11), or righteousness (2:21), or life (2:19; 3:11), or receipt of the Spirit (3:2,5), or Christian perfection (3:3), or blessing (3:10,13), or the energizing dynamic of God (3:5). What then was the purpose of the Law? In verses 19 through 25 Paul will explain that the Law was devoid of divine immediacy (20), devoid of divine vitality (21), devoid of divine righteousness (21), and devoid of divine salvation (22); but it did serve as a temporary treatment of transgression (19), a temporary custodial confinement (23), and a temporary disciplinary directive (24,25).

Paul begins by noting that "***It was added because of transgressions.***" At least four hundred and thirty years (17) subsequent to the promises to Abraham, the Law was introduced through Moses as an extra, though not extraneous, work of God. The Law was implemented within the gracious purposes of God to deal with the persistent Israelite propensity to transgress the character of God in sin. This does not appear to mean that the Law had a *preventative* purpose to prevent people from sinning, to keep them in check and prevent them from getting "out of hand," even though law can have such a moralistic purpose of social constraint (I Tim. 1:8-10). Nor does Paul mean that the Law had a *promotional* purpose to promote, produce and increase sin, for God has no desire to promote that which

3:19

is contrary to His character. It has been suggested that the Law had a *provocative* purpose to provoke frustration at the human inability to avoid sin and its continued increase (Rom. 5:20), but such an interpretation does not seem to derive from Paul's words in this verse. Perhaps Paul is indicating a *prescriptive* purpose of the Law whereby the character of God in human behavior is clearly prescribed and clarified, making transgressions obvious in order to awaken and acknowledge the guilt of sinfulness (Rom. 4:15). Or Paul may be positing the *provisional* purpose of the Law, whereby God provided a pictorial pre-figuring of His intent to deal with the sin of man in Jesus Christ, and provided a temporary means of atonement in the Hebrew sacrificial system which pointed to the sacrifice of Christ. The Law, however, during its provisional period of jurisdiction over the Israelites, did not provide the provision of God's dynamic, enabling grace necessitated to express His character and avoid sin. In addition, Paul will subsequently add the *protectional* purpose (23) and *preparational* purpose (24,25) of the Law.

In another apparent thought-digression, Paul notes that the Law **"has been ordained through angels by the agency of a mediator."** That the Law was ordained, arranged, appointed or administered by God through angels is a fact not recorded in the original records of the Law's introduction in Exodus 19. It was a well-established Rabbinical interpretation, however, derived from such texts as Deut. 33:2 and Ps. 68:17. Stephen obviously accepted such, for before the Jewish Council in Jerusalem he said, "You received the Law as ordained by angels, and did not keep it" (Acts 7:53), and the writer of the Hebrews refers to "the word spoken through angels" (Heb. 2:2). How the hosts of angels served God in the transmission of the Law is not known. It is certainly a fallacious interpretation, though, that denies the origin of the Law in God, and ascribes its origin to demonic angels.

That the Law was "by the agency of," or more literally "by the hand of," a mediator, no doubt refers to Moses who served as the human intermediary, the "middle-man" who stood between God and the Israelite people (cf. Deut. 5:5) and received the tablets in his hands (Lev. 26:46; Exod. 32:19). The point Paul is making, as amplified in vs. 20, is the secondary and indirect transmission of the Law, as compared to the primary and direct revelation of the promise.

Paul continues to explain the temporal historical parameters of the Law, added (19) four hundred and thirty years (17) after the Abrahamic promises, and valid only *"until the seed should come to whom the promise had been made."* Luke's record that "the Law and the Prophets were proclaimed until John the Baptist" (Lk. 16:16) is entirely consonant with Paul's chronology of the terminus of the Law. The Law, though not essential to the fulfillment of the promise, served as an expedient and instrumental means to enhance the implications of the promise within the temporal and transitory period between Moses and the Messiah. The Law was designed as an interim arrangement with planned obsolescence to serve only during the provisional period of Israelite history before Christ (B.C.); only until the singular, individual "seed" of Abraham "that is Christ" (16) would come "in the fullness of time" (4:4) in the incarnation and fulfill His redemptive purposes. The temporality of the Law (cf. II Cor. 3:11; Heb. 8:13; Rom. 10:4) is being emphasized by Paul to reveal to the Galatian Christians the preposterous illegitimacy of reverting back to legalistic performance standards which have been terminated. The "Seed of Abraham," Jesus Christ, was the One concerning whom the promise had been made to Abraham, serving as the eschatological terminus of the Law, the "Last Adam" (I Cor. 15:45) inaugurating the final solution of God for man in the "last days" (Acts 2:17; Heb. 1:2; I Pet. 1:20). If there was an historical parenthesis in God's plan, as some have maintained, the historical parameters of the Law age would be parenthetical rather than the "Church-age," as often indicated.

3:20 Returning to the previously mentioned idea of the Mosaic mediator (19), Paul attempts to explain that ***"a mediator is not for one; whereas God is one."*** The ambiguity of his explanation has confounded commentators through the centuries. A mediator by definition is a go-between who stands in the middle of the negotiations between two other parties. When a mediator serves as a third-party negotiator he is an indirect intermediary link between the other parties. Paul's argument is apparently based on the fact that when Moses served as the mediator between God and the Israelites in the introduction of the Law, the indirect and secondary mediation of creaturely agencies (angels and man) posits the inferiority of the introduction and administration of the Law as compared to the promise. The promises were introduced by direct revelation of the one God to Abraham (Gen. 12:1; 13:14; 15:1; 17:1), and the fulfillment of the promises in Jesus Christ was a demonstration of the monotheistic oneness of God (cf. Deut. 6:4) expressing the divine unity of God's promise and action, the direct *homoousion* unity and immediacy of God's Being in His action. Indeed, the man, Christ Jesus, was the "one mediator between God and man" (I Tim. 2:5; Heb. 8:6; 9:15; 12:24), but God is one with the mediator since Jesus is one with the Father (Jn. 10:30). Jesus was not a separated mediator, nor a substitute or surrogate for God, but God Himself incarnate functioning singularly (yet distinctly) and directly in the ontological dynamic of divine grace. The underlying Trinitarian presuppositions must be recognized for any legitimate understanding of this verse, as the old Mosaic covenant of Law is being contrasted to the new covenant in Christ in fulfillment of the Abrahamic promises.

3:21 Paul has been contrasting promise and Law, thus indicating some sense of disjunction and discontinuity between promise and Law, but he does not want to leave the impression that promise and Law are antagonistic or antithetical. He poses the expected questioning of his thesis by asking, ***"Is the***

Law then contrary to the promises of God?" And his answer to his own question is, *"May it never be!"* The one God (20), immutable and faithful, is the source and origin of both the promise and the Law. He cannot contradict Himself, or violate His singularly absolute consistency of Being and character. The Law was not contradictory to the promises, but concomitant. The Law was not inconsistent with the promises, but incidental to the promises. The Law was not antithetical to the promises, but ancillary. The Law was not competing against the promises, but was complementary. The Law was not an antagonist of the promises, but was auxiliary to the promises. The Law did not subvert the promises, but was subsidiary to the promises. The Law did not stand opposite to the promises, but had a parallel and provisional objective in the Christological purposes of God. The one ultimate objective of God was fulfilled in Jesus Christ in accord with the Abrahamic promises, and the Law served a subordinated objective to reveal more precisely the character of God, to reveal man's inability to produce the character of God, and to reveal the coming Messiah who would be the divine dynamic of expressing the character of God. When understood within the parameters of its historical contingencies to the ultimate fulfillment of the promises in Jesus Christ, the Law is not contrary or contradictory to the promises. But when the Law is interpreted outside of its temporal and supplemental purposes within the context of the old covenant, and when the performance of the Law is superimposed supplementally as an incentive to Christian vitality and holiness subsequent to the receipt of God's grace in Jesus Christ (as the intrusive Judaizers were advocating to the Galatian Christians), then such abuse and misuse of the Law is contrary and contradictory to God's grace-fulfillment of the promises.

The promise and the Law had different functional purposes, and the Law was incapable of providing what God had promised to Abraham. The Law was not a variation of the promise, nor was it a vehicle to implement the promise, but it was, nonetheless, a valid and valuable diversion orchestrated by God in the provisional interim period of the old covenant, intended to cause the Israelites to recognize their sinfulness so that they could appreciate God's grace fulfillment of the promise in Jesus Christ. The inadequacy and inferiority of the Law compared to promise is noted in Paul's statement: ***"For if a law had been given which was able to impart life, then righteousness would indeed have been based on law."*** If God had given a law that had the power or dynamic to activate divine life in man, then the righteous character of God which is entirely implicit in His own Being and character could have been derived out of legal performance of the law. But this is impossible, because God's life and righteousness can only be derived out of Himself by the dynamic of His grace — never in detachment from His own Being in action. Paul later explained to the Corinthians that "the letter of the Law kills" (as man dies trying to perform perfectly, only to be condemned all the more), but "the Spirit gives life" (II Cor. 3:6). To the Romans he explained that the Law was an instrument of death (Rom. 7:9,10,13), whereas "the Spirit of God Who raised Jesus from the dead gives life to the Christian as the Spirit of Christ indwells us" (Rom. 8:11). This obviates Paul's repeated contrasting of Law and Spirit (3:2-5; 4:4-6; 5:13,16,18). There was no inherency of life in the Law. It was impotent. The Law carried with it no dynamic, no provision, no resource to perform its demands, much less restore and invest divine life in fallen man. It could not regenerate, and because it could not enliven man with the life of God it could not justify or impart God's righteous character to man either objectively or subjectively. Paul's point? Though the Abrahamic promises and the Mosaic Law are not contradictory, there is nevertheless an impotency and inferiority of the Law in reference to the promise. Old covenant Law was unable to provide what fallen man needed, unable to fulfill the divine promises, able only to expose man's need and the inability of man to acquire or achieve such, thus setting mankind up for the life (Jn. 1:4; 14:6; 10:10; I Jn. 5:12) and righteousness (I Cor. 1:30; II Cor. 5:21) that are derived from Jesus Christ alone in fulfillment of the Abrahamic promises.

3:22 Eliminating any possibility of self-justification for any person, Paul adds that ***"the Scripture has shut up all men under sin."*** As in 3:8 the "Scripture" is seemingly personified as it represents the written revelation of God's activity. God's actions as recorded and presented in the scriptures have consigned and confined all men universally, both Jew and Gentile (Rom. 3:9), in the consequences of their sin, stemming as it does from their Adamic solidarity in the Fall. "God has shut up all in disobedience that He might show mercy to all" (Rom. 11:32). Paul does not seem to be referring to any particular passage of scripture, but may be referring to the collective whole of the Old Testament scripture message, or to a general collection of scripture citations similar to those he later quoted in Romans 3:10-18. The solidarity of humanity's sin with the choice of Adam (Rom. 5:12-21) and the universality of man's condemnation (Rom. 5:16,18; I Cor. 11:32; II Cor. 3:9) "under sin," being "made sinners" (Rom. 5:19) in spiritual condition, and locked into sin as "slaves of sin" (Jn. 8:34; Rom. 6:6) behaviorally, serves to demonstrate that "all have sinned" (Rom. 3:23) and "all the world is accountable to God" (Rom. 3:19). The entirety of the human race in their fallen spiritual condition are under the condemnation of sin objectively before God, and under the power of sin subjectively, which includes imprisonment in the bondage of religious and humanistic performance standards.

    This plight and predicament of mankind in the condition and consequences of sin allows God's purposes to be served, ***"that the promise by faith in Jesus Christ might be given to those who believe."*** Not that God predestined man's sin, but He certainly foreknew the occasion of such and His solution for such in His Son. His promises to Abraham of a blessed solution to the stalemate of sin in His own action of redemptive and restorative grace in Jesus Christ, made known the only antidote to the universality of man's sin. Jesus Christ as the Redeemer, Deliverer, Savior and Lord sets the human prisoners of sin free from their bondage and imprisonment, allowing them the liberty (5:1,13) to function as God intended. The promised blessings of divine life and righteousness can only be received by faith, as was prototypically portrayed by Abraham (3:6-14). They are not earned by meritorious performance of the Law. They are not detached benefits dispensed by a deistic benefactor. But everything that God has to give to man is in the ontological dynamic of the Person and work of Jesus Christ by His Spirit. Christian faith is not a singular and punctiliar event of consent, but is the continuous dynamic process of our receptivity of His activity, as we "keep on believing."

3:23   Returning to the explanation of the purpose of the Law, Paul states that *"before faith came, we were kept in custody under the Law, being shut up to the faith which was later to be revealed."* Prior to the coming of the availability of the life of Jesus Christ received by faith, Paul and all of the Jewish peoples were guarded by a guard (the Greek word contains this repetition) under the jurisdiction of the Law for a prolonged period in the past (imperfect tense in Greek). The negative sense of being held under the custody of a guard would imply that the Jews were held in subjection under the sentence of condemnation. But in the positive sense in which the Greek word is used elsewhere in the New Testament (cf. Phil. 4:7; I Pet. 1:5), Paul's meaning is probably that the Jewish people were watched over and kept in God's protective custody. The Law was not an oppressive and abusive jailer, but it did serve a custodial purpose of providing moral parameters which kept the physical peoples of God corralled and thus guarded and protected from the ramifications that could have befallen them in rampant and unrestrained rebellion.

Remaining "shut up under sin" (22), the Hebrew peoples were also "shut up to the faith," the availability of Jesus Christ, which was yet to be revealed. Contained within God's protective custody, they were still constrained from all the promised blessings of God in Jesus Christ, until God "in the fullness of time" (4:4) would reveal the fullness of His redemptive and restorative purpose in His Son. The advent of Jesus Christ, the fullness of the revelation of God in the new covenant fulfillment of the Abrahamic promises, was at the same time the terminus of the old covenant arrangement allowing for the liberation of the physical Israelites from the protective custody of the Law in order to participate in the grace-provision of the Lord, Jesus Christ.

3:24 Employing a correlative metaphor that transitions from the protective to the preparational purpose of the Law, Paul explains, *"Therefore the Law has become our governor until Christ, that we may be justified by faith."* The thought moves from the protective custody of a guard to the preparational custody of a child-attendant during the provisional period of the Law's purpose. The Greek word that Paul uses (*paidagogos*) has been employed in English as the pedagogical discipline of education and teaching. Various English translations have translated Paul's reference to the Law in this verse as a "schoolmaster" (KJV) or "tutor" (NASB). However, the Greek word that Paul used did not refer to a schoolteacher, but to the first-century practice of a slave who served as a supervisory guardian to attend to and escort minor children in their upbringing. After the wet-nurse in infancy and the nanny for young children, the male children in particular were served by a governor who attempted to govern their behavior, made sure they were escorted to school, and directed them in the development of adult social skills. In the process of preparing these adolescent children for adulthood the governor often had to use corrective discipline to enforce the guidelines and keep the young boys in line and on schedule. This discipline was often stern, harsh and oppressive. The *paidagogos* is depicted in ancient drawings with a rod in his hand, meting out abusive corporeal punishment. He was often like a dictatorial drill-instructor using physical force to direct the young boys into manhood. The importance of understanding the first-century meaning of *paidagogos* becomes clear when the analogy to the Law is interpreted. The Law did not serve as an educatory instructor teaching the Jewish people how to perform morally and religiously so they could live better Christian lives after the Messiah came. (That would have been consistent with the Judaizers' emphasis.) Rather, the Law served as a corrective and disciplinary governor over the Hebrew peoples during the adolescent phase of their history prior to the availability of full adulthood privileges as "sons of God through faith in Christ Jesus" (26). The Law did not prepare Israel educationally or tutorially for the Messiah, nor was its purpose primarily to escort them to Christ, but it was an oppressive disciplinary measure that was designed to make the promised blessings of adulthood in Christ all the more desirable. It served such a purpose until Christ came, at which time it was revealed that righteousness, both objectively imputed and subjectively imparted, could only be experienced by faithful receptivity of the activity of the Righteous One, Jesus Christ.

3:25 *"But now that faith has come, we are no longer under a governor."* The availability of Jesus Christ as the fulfillment of the Abrahamic promises meant that the Hebrew people no longer required a disciplinary governor. They no longer needed a baby-sitter, a child-escort, or a disciplinary drill-instructor. The slavish purposes of the Law were no longer required. They could go beyond the restrictive supervision of childhood immaturity by receiving the ontological presence of Jesus Christ in their spirit, in order to enjoy the full privileges of adult sonship in the Christian family of God. No longer were they to be led around by the legal guardian, but they could be "led by the Spirit" (Rom. 8:14) as mature sons. "If you are led by the Spirit, you are not under the Law" (5:18). "Christ is the end of the Law for righteousness to everyone who believes" (Rom. 10:4). Paul was affirming the cessation, the historical terminus of all the instrumental purposes of the Mosaic Law, and advising the Galatian Christians of the impossibility of going back to adolescent discipline when the age of mature adulthood had been made available by the grace of God in Jesus Christ. To even attempt to revert to legalism as the Judaizers were encouraging, would be to deny all the privileges of God's promised grace.

3:26 The reason why no one in the Galatian churches needed a legal governor was *"because you are all sons of God through faith in Christ Jesus."* Verses 15 to 25 were a digression that considered the precedence of the promises and the purpose of the Law, and now Paul draws that premise together with the conclusion to the point he was making in verses 6 to 14 about Christians being the sons of Abraham by faith. It must be remembered that the Jewish peoples claimed to be the exclusive "sons of Abraham" by physical descent, as well as the exclusive "sons of God" in special relationship with God. Paul counters such exclusivism by indicating that all of the Galatian Christians, whether of Jewish or Gentile heritage, are completed sons of God with a direct, spiritual relationship with God through the receptivity of Christ in faith. While emphasizing the universality of the availability of the gospel in Christ, Paul is not espousing the universal inclusivity of universalism, for such a personal relationship with God is conditioned by the receptivity of faith. Such faith is not just the cognitive assent of believism, but is the ontological reception of the Spirit of Christ whereby a spiritual union is effected with His divine life. In this new covenant fulfillment of the divine promises, the physical connections of the Jewish claim to be the "sons of

Abraham" and the "sons of God" have been superseded by the privileges of all Christians to participate in the spiritual "family of God," as the "chosen race, the holy nation, the people of God" (I Pet. 2:9,10).

3:27 In additional explanation of such a relationship of spiritual union "in Christ Jesus," Paul writes, *"For all of you who were baptized into Christ have clothed yourselves with Christ."* The contextual setting of his argument disallows any sacramentalistic interpretation of baptismal regeneration which might imply that being "sons of God" was essentially contingent on the external act of water baptism. Paul had no intent to replace the external rite of circumcision with the performance of the external rite of water baptism. Instead, Paul affirms that every genuine Christian who has been overwhelmed into, and identified with, Jesus Christ is now encompassed, enveloped, enclosed and enclothed with His life and character. Notice, there is no reference to being "baptized into water," but only the figurative concept of being "baptized into Christ," i.e. into His name (cf. Matt. 28:20), His Person, His Being, His presence, His nature, His life, His character, His family relationship. To the Romans, Paul would later write that "all of us who have been baptized into Christ Jesus have been baptized into His death" (Rom. 6:3); overwhelmed in identification with His death, "buried with Him in baptism, raised up with Him through faith" (Col. 2:12). The overwhelming of the human spirit by the Spirit of Christ in regeneration enacts a spiritual union that creates an entirely new spiritual identity as a "Christ-one," a Christian. "If any man is in Christ, he is a new creature; old things have passed away, behold, all things have become new" (II Cor. 5:17). This regenerative spiritual overwhelming is the spiritual baptism that Paul refers to when he writes that "by one Spirit, we were all baptized into one Body, whether Jew or Gentile, slaves or free, being made to drink of one Spirit" (I Cor. 12:13). The physical act of water baptism has always been regarded by orthodox Christianity as the external, visible, public representation and expression of the internal, spiritual reality of being overwhelmed into Christ and the Spirit's overwhelming of the human spirit. That being true, the Galatian Christians might well have remembered their water baptism as pictorially representative of their overwhelming into Christ.

When we use such language of being "baptized into Christ" or "clothed with Christ" in "spiritual union," there is no implication of becoming "little Christs" or of being absorbed into Christ to the extent that there is no distinction between Christ and the Christian. Such mystical absorption theories extract Christianity from the time and space actualities of human life on earth. Spiritual realities are admittedly difficult to express in human language, but Paul uses the metaphor of being enclothed or invested with Christ, in consonance with the concept of "putting on the new man" (Eph. 4:24; Col. 3:10). This should not be conceived of in terms of theatric role-playing by the putting on of a costume, but instead as the investiture of Christ in order to express the character of Christ in Christian behavior. Many commentators have mentioned the Roman practice of *toga virilis*, the occasion when a Roman boy put on a toga to indicate that he had "come of age" and entered manhood. Though the picture corresponds with Paul's reasoning about becoming mature sons in Christ, there is nothing in the text that would indicate that he had this in mind as he wrote these words to the Galatians.

3:28 Continuing to emphasize the universality of the gospel in contradistinction to Jewish exclusivism, Paul declares that ***"there is neither Jew nor Greek, there is neither slave nor free man, there is neither male nor female; for you are all one in Christ Jesus."*** If all Christians have put on the same Christ-clothing, the same Christ-investiture, the same Christ-identity, then all human class distinctions have been transcend-

3:28

ed and superseded in Christian unity. The major physical differentiations that create divisive segregation among men are (1) racial, ethnic and cultural differences, (2) social and economic differences, and (3) sexual gender differences. Paul indicates that all exclusivism and discrimination based on these three major areas of race, money and sex are eliminated for those who are overwhelmed in Christ and clothed with Christ (27).

Racism, culturalism, and nationalism have no part in the kingdom of God, for all Christians comprise a "chosen race" and "a holy nation" spiritually (I Pet. 2:9). Though Christians may be of different races having diverse ethnic heritage, such differences have no significance before God.

Likewise, the differences of social class or economic privilege should have no bearing on value and worth within the interactions of Christian peoples. There should be no sense of personal superiority or inferiority; no sense of elevation or condescension; no sense of pride or embarrassment. It doesn't matter if one Christian is a blue-collar worker and another is an aristocrat, if one is a minimum-wage worker and another is a millionaire stock-broker. The identity of every Christian is found only in Jesus Christ. That is why slaves and masters could function together in the early church (Eph. 6:5-9; Col. 3:22-4:1; Philemon).

Even the gender discrimination so unfairly imposed by religion and cultures through the centuries is to have no place in the kingdom of Christ. God created mankind as "male and female" (Gen. 1:27), and husbands and wives are "joint-heirs of the grace of life" (I Pet. 3:7) in Christ. There are to be no second-class citizens in the kingdom of God, and it is a sad fact indeed that women have often been relegated to such in male-dominated ecclesiasticism.

Paul is not advocating the annihilation of human differences, but is emphasizing the integration and interdependence of Christian people. His is no argument for absolute egalitarianism that refuses to recognize racial, social and gender differences. There are blacks and whites, wealthy and poor, men and women in the Church of Jesus Christ. Paul is not promoting the extremisms of social egalitarianism, "liberation theology" or the feminist agenda that espouses an androgynist uni-sex. Paul's point is the interpersonal integration and cooperation of Christian people.

The restoration of man in Jesus Christ restores the individual to a spiritual condition of union and relationship with God, but also creates the restoration of collective interpersonal relationships among Christians that constitutes a "new creation" (6:15), a "new humanity" (Eph. 2:15) as a "holy nation" (I Pet. 2:9) within the singular Body of Christ (Eph. 2:16; 4:4). This radical and revolutionary integration of people wherein "Christ is all in all" (Col. 3:11) was such a contrast to the predominant Jewish perspective expressed by the daily prayer of a Jewish male: "Thank you, Lord, for not making me a foreigner, a slave, or a woman." Such attitudes were probably retained to some degree by the Judaizers who had come to Galatia. Paul did not want the young Galatian Christians to be swayed into thinking that Jewish blood, free birth, or male gender constituted any advantage in the kingdom of Christ.

Paul reminds the Galatian Christians that they "are all one in Christ Jesus." This spiritual unity is established by God in Christ, and is not necessarily a structural unity of ecclesiasticism achieved through ecumenism (cf. Eph. 4:4-6). Christ in each Christian creates a collective identity and unity in the Body of Christ (Rom. 12:4,5; I Cor. 12:12-27; Col. 3:15).

3:29 In conclusion to his careful argument that ties the blessing of Christ to the promises to Abraham, Paul writes: ***"If you belong to Christ, then you are Abraham's offspring, heirs according to promise."*** He wanted the Galatian Christians to know, beyond a shadow of a doubt, that they did not have to submit to male circumcision or perform the requirements of the Jewish Law in order to participate in all that God intended for man, as expressed in His earliest promises of restoration. "As many as are the promises of God, they are affirmed and enacted in Jesus Christ" (II Cor. 1:20). If (since) you are "in Christ" (26,28), "of Christ" (29), "overwhelmed into Christ" (27), or "clothed with Christ" (27) – in other words, if you have received the Spirit of Christ and are identified as a "Christ-one," a Christian, then you are part of the promised offspring of Abraham. Abraham's descendants are no longer determined by the physical procreation of the Hebrew blood-line. Christians who are spiritually incorporated into the singular individual "Seed" of Abraham (16,19), i.e., Jesus Christ, are the collective spiritual "seed" of Abraham, and heirs of all that God promised to mankind in Abraham. "Those who are of faith are sons of Abraham" (3:7). The promised blessings of God are inherited by the grace of God, not merited by legalistic performance. This concept of Christians being the "heirs" of the promised "inheritance" will become the springboard for Paul's argument in the following chapter.

The importance of Paul's argument in these verses cannot be over-estimated. Despite the difficulty of following the intricacies of his reasoning, and the danger of "missing the forest for the details in the trees," Paul was a master logician and a meticulous lawyer who crafted his arguments with precision. Using the same old covenant documents that the Judaizers were no doubt using to bolster their position of performance, Paul cites prior references to the Genesis promises employing a radical reinterpretation of Old Testament history from a new covenant perspective "in Christ," which he maintains was God's intended perspective from the beginning. He preemptively poses the questions (19,21) that might be raised by those of a different persuasion, and answers the questions before his opponents can ask the questions. Brilliant debate technique!

His argument is for the "precedence of the promises" to Abraham over the Mosaic Law, arguing that the Abrahamic promises (1) precede in time or sequence, (2) have priority of importance or significance, and (3) have preference of superiority or supremacy. Though the promises and the Law are not contradictory, they do have contrasting purposes. The objective of the promises to Abraham reveal the comprehensive and essential purpose of God to restore mankind to His created intent by a direct and immediate expression of grace whereby the divine blessing of the inheritance of life and righteousness in Jesus Christ might be received by faith. The temporary and limited purposes of the Mosaic Law were subsidiary and supplemental, incidental and instrumental, serving to expediently enhance Israel's awareness of the need of God's grace, and thus to develop appreciation for such grace when it was historically incarnated in Christ. The Law prescribed behavior consistent with God's character, provided temporary atonement procedures for the failure to live perfectly in accord with God's character, protected the nation of Israel from the repercussions of total lawlessness, and prepared the physical people of God for the full blessings of God in the Messiah, as promised to Abraham. It is imperative that Christians in every age recognize the subordinated and auxiliary purposes of the Law within the context of the greater restorational purposes of God. Failure to understand the distinct and varied objectives of promise and Law impinges upon the character of God, making Him unfair and inconsistent like the hypothetical father who promised his children a visit to Disneyland and then reneged by attempting to implement a program of performance standards. Failure to understand the provisional parameters of the interim arrangement of the Law within the primary purpose of the Christological promises to Abraham allows Christian people to be susceptible to the performance incentives of the Judaizing legalists, who were not only present in the first-century world, but have spawned myriad religious relatives in every age.

From an historical perspective, it is important to note that God did not say to the Israelites, "If you do not keep the Law, you will not get the blessings of the promises to Abraham," i.e.,

Jesus Christ. The fulfillment of the promises was not contingent on Israel keeping the Law. Thank goodness! God did not threaten the abolition of the promises based upon the Jewish failure to keep the Law. That would have been unfair and inconsistent of God. He did indicate that the failure to keep the Law would incur individual and national consequences, but despite their failures God was committed to keep His promise to send His Son, who would "become the curse for us" (3:13), incurring upon Himself all the consequences of human disobedience and sin, taking our deserved death consequences that we might have His life.

The problem that precipitated this letter was that the Galatian Christians had received the complete fulfillment of all the promises of God in Jesus Christ. They were cognizant of the grace-dynamic of Christ's life and righteousness. Why, then, were they prone to fall for the Judaizing insistence on performance of the Law? The Galatians still had the fallen, fleshly propensity to revert to the fallacious idea of human ability to perform and produce in order to please God. That temptation is always presented to Christians, contrary to the Spirit's grace motivations (5:16,17). In addition, the content of Paul's letter would indicate that the Galatians (and obviously the Judaizers) failed to apprehend the temporary purpose of the Law, terminated as it was in the advent of Jesus Christ, and failed to appreciate the complete restorational purpose of God in Jesus Christ. When one has received everything that God has to give in Jesus Christ (cf. I Cor. 3:21-23; Eph. 1:3,10; Col. 2:10; II Pet. 1:3), it is ludicrous to listen to the religious legalists and their preposterous propositions of performance in order to acquire what one has already received. Why would the Galatians go backwards to that which was obsolete and superseded? Why would they submit to the demands of a dead religious system of "dos and don'ts" and "dead works" (Heb. 6:1; 9:14)? Paul explains that such reversionism is a distortion of the gospel (1:7), a denigration of the cross (2:21), and a denial of the all-sufficient grace of God in Jesus Christ. Yet, to this day we observe innumerable forms of legalists advocating the experiential behavioral benefits of the Law for Christians, focusing, as they do, on sin-consciousness, brokenness, confessionism, suppressionism, crucifixionism ("dying to self"), and submission to moral and ethical guidelines. Many well-meaning teachers are inadvertently playing the role of the Judaizers as they teach so-called "Christian ethics" based on the Ten Commandments, and explain that everyone must first submit to the Law in order to understand grace.

Christians in every age are obliged to ask, "Does the old covenant Law have any behavioral application to Christians? Are Christians expected to keep the Ten Commandments?" Despite the attempts of theological interpreters to arbitrarily subdivide the Law into ceremonial, civil and moral categories in order to make some requirements applicable to Christians and eliminate others, the specifically defined historical parameters of the Law between the time of Moses and John the Baptist (Lk. 16:16) or Jesus (3:19) explicitly indicate that the behavioral incentives of the Old Testament Law are not applicable to Christians. The Law, expressive of the character of God, is now "written in the hearts" (Jere. 31:33; Heb. 8:10; 10:16) of Christians, with all the provision, resource and sufficiency of the grace of God in the ontological dynamic of the life of Jesus Christ.

Should the Law be utilized and incorporated into civil law to create moral and legal guidelines which serve as a social deterrent to lawless anarchy (cf. I Tim. 1:8-10)? Human government has an obligation to do so, but Christians must understand that such legal and ethical formulations serve no purpose in the function of the Kingdom of God. Should parents establish parental laws with defined parameters of expectation for their children? They are obliged to do so, but Christian parents should not expect such to be the conduit whereby their children become Christians and evidence Christian conduct. The failures of the children will be made evident to them by the consequences of their failure to abide by parental guidelines, governmental guidelines, or moral, legal and logical guidelines, and God will draw them to Himself by His grace. It is always illegitimate for Christians to attempt to extract the old covenant Law from its historical context, and attempt to implement the Law experientially and behaviorally in the Christian life.

Allow me to conclude with another illustrative analogy "in human terms" (15). Who in his right mind (only a fool) would want to go back to "basic training" or "boot-camp," when he has already enjoyed the privileges of his rank as a soldier? Boot-camp is that horrible process of being pushed to one's limits, screamed at by the drill-sergeant, and humiliated until one's impudence and pride are quashed. It is a rigid, unforgiving and depersonalizing process. But it serves a temporary and expedient purpose in subduing a brash young man or woman, until they discover their identity and purpose as a soldier in the Armed Forces. There are, no doubt, a few militaristic masochists and sadists who think that real soldiers should function in boot-camp regimen all the time, but the majority of soldiers appreciate the fact that they do not have to do so. Despite the obvious limitations of this analogy, it serves to demonstrate the pathological perplexity of the Galatians reverting to the burdensome rules and regulations of the Law after having enjoyed the blessings of the fulfilled promises of God in Jesus Christ.

The Privilege of Sons

Galatians 4:1-20

Paul continues his extended argument documenting that the gospel of grace in Jesus Christ was God's intent from the beginning. Presenting his argument in response to the reasonings of the infiltrating Judaizers in Galatia, Paul has explained that the promise to Abraham preceded the Law (3:15-29), and the promises of blessing are received by faith rather than by the performance of Law-observances (3:1-14).

The legalistic Judaizers advocated that the neophyte Galatian Christians needed to connect with the legacy of Abraham and become "sons of Abraham" by the performance of the demands of the Law, thus achieving a full status and stature of spiritual maturity as "sons of God." Paul, on the other hand, wanted to reiterate to the Galatian Christians that by God's grace in Jesus Christ received by faith they were already "sons of God" (3:26), Abraham's spiritual progeny (3:7,29), and heirs of all the blessings and promises of God (3:9,14,22,29). The period of immature childhood and adolescence was historically past. As Christians, the Galatians were "complete in Christ" (Col. 2:10), having received "all the things of God" (I Cor. 3:21-23), including "every spiritual blessing" (Eph. 1:3) and "everything pertaining to life and godliness" (II Pet. 1:3). Paul wanted the Galatians to recognize how spiritually rich (Eph. 3:8,16) they were as the heirs of God's promised blessings, so that they might enjoy their privileges as mature sons of God in Christ. That did not mean that they could not "grow in grace"

4:1,2

(II Pet. 3:18), allowing for a more adequate representation of Christ's character in their behavior by faithful receptivity of His activity, but the maturity of sonship could not be meritoriously achieved through performance. Employing slightly altered metaphors comparing sons and heirs with slaves, Paul emphasizes the privilege of being full-fledged, adult sons of God in Jesus Christ.

4:1 Continuing the word-pictures of "sons" (3:26) and "offspring" who are "heirs" (3:29), Paul presents a variation of his analogous theme by writing, ***"Now I say, as long as the heir is a child, he does not differ at all from a slave although he is owner of everything."*** "Let me explain it this way," he begins. During the period of time when an heir to the estate is still a minor child, he has no functional advantage over a slave in the same household. Though the minor child may be "master" and "lord" of the entire estate *de jure* (by law), he is deprived of any independent function over the estate, being *de facto* (in fact) subject to the supervisory restrictions of designated guardians. The actions of both a minor child and a slave are determined by another.

Keying off of the previous figures that Paul has used to explain the historically progressive revelation of God, i.e. the protective custody (3:23) and the custodial oversight of the *paidagogos* (3:24), Paul is making the point to the Galatian Christians that they are not minor children waiting or striving for the *de facto* realization of all the divine inheritance in Jesus Christ. The privilege of mature, adult sonship is theirs, both *de jure* and *de facto* in Jesus Christ.[1]

4:2 A minor child ***"is under guardians and managers until the date set by the father,"*** Paul explains. The minor child, like the slave, is subordinated to other decision-makers and authority-figures. He is not free to make his own decisions concerning the utilization of the estate. The "guardians" and the "managers," distinct from the *paidagogos* (3:24), are the legal controllers both of the child and the estate, serving as legal guardians and governors of the child and administrators or trustees of the property and finances.

The chronological parameters of this arrangement were previously ordained and appointed by the father of the child. He laid down a fixed time or age that would serve as the terminus of this condition of subservience, at which time the child would be regarded as having reached adulthood with the full functional privilege of enjoying all of the assets of the estate *de facto*. The commentators have long speculated whether Paul had in mind a father, still living, who had established a "trust fund" for an under-aged child which could be possessed at a certain age of majority, or whether Paul was picturing a father who had died leaving a "last will and testament" with details concerning the welfare of the son and the administration of the estate. If the latter was intended, which seems more reasonable, the concept might correspond with the "ratified covenant" mentioned in 3:15, with the analogous difficulty being that God cannot die, though the death of Jesus Christ could serve as the death of the testator if the figure were pressed into an allegory.

Either way, it should be noted that the timing was determined "by the father." Likewise, Paul will point out in verse 4 that the Father, God, made the timing arrangements for the Son to move into the new covenant era of Lordship in control of the divine estate, the Kingdom. The point that Paul is making to the Galatians is that the time of full appreciation and enjoyment of the inheritance of God has come, and they should recognize the privilege of living in God's grace as sons.

4:3 Explaining the pictures he has painted in verses 1 and 2, and seeking to make application to the Galatian believers, Paul reminds them, ***"So also we, while we were children, were held in bondage under the elemental things of the world."*** Comprehensively it is true both of Paul and the Galatians, both for

Jews and Gentiles, that we have all endured a childhood period of restrictive subservience to "the powers that be." In our pre-regenerate period we were all enslaved to performance-oriented principles and premises that controlled and dominated the way we walked in the world. The world-system is comprised of such cause and effect principles based on humanistic premises of how man can exert his self-effort to "get ahead" and be productive in life. Such performance incentives always involve a slavery to self-effort as we strive to reach a utopian goal that is neither attainable or satisfactory.

Commentators have long debated the meaning of "the elemental things of the world" that Paul mentions in this verse. Suggestions have included (1) the cosmic material substances or components of earth, water, air and fire, which were regarded by some ancient peoples as the constitutive elements that dictated events, (2) the astrological alignment of heavenly bodies which many through the centuries have relied on for the fate of all circumstances, and (3) the spiritual and demonic powers of the cosmos that have generated fear and superstition which have held many peoples in bondage and enslavement. The latter of these three categories, relating to the spiritual rather than the physical, is broad enough to include all religious activity and all the utilitarian endeavors promoted by the natural humanistic objectives of fallen mankind. As Satan is "the god of this world, blinding the minds of unbelievers" (II Cor. 4:4) and "holding them captive to do his will" (II Tim. 2:26), he energizes "the powers, the world forces of darkness, the spiritual forces of wickedness" (Eph. 6:12) that are contrary to God's intent, inclusive of all religious disguise (II Cor. 11:13-15). The bondage of Judaic religion "under the Law" served as the childhood restrictions and temporary time of minority for the Jewish peoples (3:19), while the Gentile peoples had their own variations of "weak and worthless elemental things" (4:9) in the restrictive regulations of their pagan religions. Writing later to the Colossians, Paul asked, "If you have died with

Christ to the elementary principles of the world, why do you submit yourself" (Col. 2:20) to those restrictive regulations again? "See to it that no one takes you captive, according to the elementary principles of the world" (Col. 2:8). It was that same tendency of reversionism that Paul was cautioning the Galatians about, asking, "How is it that you turn back to the weak and worthless elemental things, to which you desire to be enslaved all over again?" (4:9). Jesus' prayer was that Christians might function "in the world," but not be "of the world" (Jn. 17:11,16).

Paul is reminding the Galatian Christians of the "bondage" of performance-oriented religion and humanistic human-potential incentives that are contrary to the gospel of grace in Jesus Christ. The word "religion" in the English language is even derived from the Latin word *religare* which means to "bind up" or "tie back." Religion binds a person to ethical rules and regulations and ties them to rituals of devotion that enslave them in the performance of such duties. In the natural, preliminary stage of our pre-regenerate lives, we were all enslaved like minor children and slaves to the elements of worldly induced behavior patterns. But Paul's argument is that Christians have already reached the age and stage of adult sons of God who need no longer submit to the enslaving bondage of the performance standards such as those that the Judaizers were seeking to impose, but are free to enjoy the privileges of spiritual inheritance in Christ by God's grace.

4:4 The "date set by the father" (4:2) was that ***"when the fulness of the time came, God sent forth His Son"*** in order to provide for mankind the privileges of full spiritual sonship in Jesus Christ. The historical terminus of the restrictive times of having to perform in accord with legal determinations and external decision-makers is marked by the incarnational advent of Jesus Christ and the availability of God's grace-dynamic. In His sovereign determination of time and human history, un-

4:4

regulated by necessity or social setting, God completed what He intended to do in the preliminary era of the Law, and "sent forth His Son" at a definite point in time which was to become the dividing point of all history (His-story). "What the Law could not do, God did by sending His Son in the likeness of sinful flesh" (Rom. 8:3). A proper philosophy of history does not commence with predetermined dispensational segments of time complete with cyclical patterns of divine activity, but must begin with the focal point of Christ's advent and interpret all events from the perspective of His Person and work, both antecedently and subsequently. The Christ-event is the center-point of human history. At that time the eternal God at His own initiative and appointment "sent forth" His Son *ek theos*, "out of Himself," and out of His pre-existent eternal state to be invested in time, space and humanity. In the Christological formulation of the God-man, God acted out of His Triune deity to invest His life in His Son (cf. Jn. 5:26) in order to redeem and restore created humanity. This was no unforeseen event or secondary plan of God, but constituted "the fulness of the times" (Eph. 1:10) and "the ends of the ages" (I Cor. 10:11) as Jesus Himself indicated when He said, "The time is fulfilled and the Kingdom of God is at hand" (Mk. 1:15).

The pre-existent Christ was *"born of a woman"* as "the Word became flesh" (Jn. 1:14). Though conceived supernaturally by the Holy Spirit (Matt. 1:20; Lk. 1:35), Jesus was delivered by natural childbirth to Mary, "a descendant of David, according to the flesh" (Rom. 1:3). The incarnational begetting of "the man, Christ Jesus" (I Tim. 2:5), being "born of a woman," completely human, emphasizes the humanity of the Son of God. Though some have attempted to push the meaning of the phrase "born of a woman" to imply that it means "born without human paternity," and thus seek to provide additional documentation of His supernatural conception (often called "virgin birth"), the uniqueness of conception is not implicit within these words, though not diminished or denied by these words.

Paul's words simply indicate that Jesus was born a human being in the context of time.

Additional context of time and humanity is provided by the notation that He was *"born under the Law."* Though the historical parameters of the Jewish Law were terminated by His redemptive and restorational work (3:19), He was born a Jewish male in the context of the old covenant Judaic Law jurisdiction. Jesus was circumcised according to the Law (Lk. 2:21), was taught the Torah, and went to synagogue. He knew from personal experience the bondage of that performance-based system of Law, even though He lived perfectly "without sin" (II Cor. 5:21).

4:5   The purpose of the Son of God being sent as a Jewish man by God the Father was *"in order that He might redeem those who were under Law."* The Christology of Jesus' Person was the basis of the soteriology of His redemptive mission. The Being of the God-man acted with saving significance as the Savior.

Employing the language of the *agora*, the marketplace, which was often the location where slaves were sold and purchased in the first-century Roman world, Paul explains the Messianic mission as that of purchasing mankind out of slavery. Enslaved to sin (Jn. 8:34; Rom. 6:6,17), to Satan (II Tim. 2:26), to idols (Gal. 4:8), to corruption (II Pet. 2:19), to the elementary principles of the world (Gal. 4:9), and to the Law (Gal. 3:13,23), mankind needed to be delivered and redeemed. The price that was paid to buy man out of his miserable, fallen condition of spiritual solidarity with Satan was the death of Jesus Christ which alone could vicariously and substitutionally satisfy the just consequences of sin (cf. Gen. 2:17; Rom. 6:23). By Jesus' death we were "bought with a price" (I Cor. 6:20;7:23), and the death consequences were "paid in full" (Jn. 19:30) on our behalf.

4:6

    As slaves in the first-century were often purchased and redeemed from slavery in order to be set free, in like manner the redemptive action of Jesus Christ sets men free to function as God intended. Not only are we delivered from slavery, but that with the express purpose *"that we might receive the adoption as sons."* When we receive Jesus Christ we receive the glorious privilege of instatement as "sons of God." All human adoption procedures, be they ancient Roman practices or modern Western legalities, are inadequate to portray the spiritual union (I Cor. 6:17) and solidarity that the Christian has in being placed and appointed as a "son of God." Being the "first-born among many brethren" (Rom. 8:29), the redemptive purpose of God in Christ was "to bring many sons to glory" (Heb. 2:10) as "fellow heirs with Christ" (Rom. 8:17). This adoptive placement as a "son of God" is both objective in the sense of a reconciled relationship with God that replaces the previous estrangement and alienation, as well as subjective in the vital internal emplacement of the life of God in regeneration, whereby we share the life of our Father as sons. Paul wanted the Galatian Christians to understand the ontological intimacy that was their spiritual birthright as "sons of God" in Christ Jesus, based not on performance but only on the spiritual reception of Jesus Christ in faith.

4:6   Sons of God are only sons because the Spirit of the Son of God, Jesus, dwells in them. *"Because you are sons, God has sent forth the Spirit of His Son into our hearts, crying, 'Abba! Father!'"* Contrary to what the English translation seems to indicate, Paul is not advocating a cause and effect sequence whereby in becoming a Christian one first becomes a "son of God" and then receives the Spirit of Christ. These spiritual realities are concomitant rather than consequential. "In that," or "since," you are "sons of God through faith in Christ Jesus" (3:26), this is evidence that God has sent forth the Spirit of Christ into your heart, your "inner being" (Jn. 7:38; II

Cor. 4:16; Eph. 3:16), your "spirit" (Rom. 8:10,16; Gal. 6:18). The parallel in Paul's epistle to the Romans reads, "You have not received a spirit of slavery leading to fear again, but you have received a spirit of adoption as sons by which we cry out, 'Abba! Father!' The Spirit Himself bears witness with our spirit that we are children of God" (Rom. 8:15,16).

Once again, Paul's concern was that the Galatian Christians might recognize the privilege they had as completed sons of God, allowing for the intimate relationship with God wherein they might passionately and affectionately solicit the Father-God with a Spirit-prompted cry of the heart. First-century Palestine was a bilingual society, so the Aramaic *Abba* and the Greek *pater* are duplicated for intensity in this passionate plea, which was quite possibly a Christian tradition based on Jesus' importunate prayer in the garden of Gethsemane (Mk. 14:36). This is not to be regarded as the cry of infancy calling for "Daddy," but rather the solicitation of intimacy that recognizes the ontological spiritual relationship that we, as Christians, have with God the Father. This was a radically new and uniquely Christian concept of God, which viewed God not as an intimidating and powerful authority-figure or Judge (as in many religions), but as an intimately personal Father. Whereas the Jewish religion tended to view God as somewhat distant and "wholly other," reverencing the name of *Yahweh* as unpronounceable and unspeakable, Paul was advocating that Christians could address God with familial intimacy — a practice the Jews rejected as irreverent familiarity.

Theological consideration recognizes the distinct Trinitarian reference in this verse to "God," "the Spirit," and the "Son." The unity of the Three-in-One must be recognized, as the indwelling presence of Christ in the Christian (cf. II Cor. 13:5; Gal. 2:20; Col. 1:27) is also the presence of God the Father in the Christian (cf. Jn. 14:23; II Cor. 6:16; I Jn. 4:12,15,16), as well as the presence of the Holy Spirit (cf. Rom. 8:11; II Cor. 1:22; James 4:5; I Jn. 3:24). The Holy Spirit, the Spirit of God, and the Spirit of Christ are all one in Being (cf. Rom. 8:9). On the other hand, Paul's reference to "God sending forth the Spirit of His Son" evidences the distinct functional procession among the three personages of the Deity, consideration of which led to the *filoque* formulation and the unfortunate division of the Eastern and Western churches.

4:7 Paul's objective was not to formulate precise Trinitarian theology, but to impress upon the Galatian Christians the privilege that was theirs in their intimate spiritual union and communion with God as sons. In summary of the slave/son contrast that he has drawn (4:1-6), Paul draws the conclusion that *"Therefore,"* since the Spirit of Christ dwells in you, *"you are no longer a slave, but a son."* Whether Jew or Gentile, we were all previously enslaved to some form of law or performance standard, which may have been religious rules and regulations, or simply the elemental principles of linear cause and effect unto utilitarian productivity. In Jesus Christ, by the dynamic of God's grace activity the bondage of performance expectations are removed. We have new identities as "sons of God" with full privileges in the "family of God." That means we are not minor sons (4:1,2) still awaiting maturity and full privileges, but we are fully completed sons, *"and if a son, then an heir through God."* All the inheritance that God promised to Abraham (3:18,29) has been granted to every Christian in Christ. "Every spiritual blessing in heavenly places is ours in Christ Jesus" (Eph. 1:3). We are "fellow heirs with Christ" (Rom. 8:17) of everything that God intends for and bestows upon mankind. But it all comes "through God" by the dynamic of His grace, incapable of being added to or amplified by the performance of man. Thus Paul counters the argument of the Judaizers who were demanding legal performance to become fully mature sons of God.

4:8 Paul seems to backtrack in order to reiterate that the Galatian Christians who had Gentile backgrounds were equally enslaved to their pagan performance standards as were those of Jewish heritage who were "under the Law" (4,5). In the midst of doing so, he will also point out the absurdity of reverting back to such enslaving performance after having entered into an intimate relationship with God (vs. 9) as Christians – the primary theme of this epistle.

Reference to *"that time when you did not know God"* most likely refers to pre-regenerate Gentiles, especially in conjunction with the subsequent allusion to idolatry. Writing later to the Thessalonians, Paul mentioned "the Gentiles who do not know God" (I Thess. 4:5). To the Ephesians he wrote of the Gentiles who "were without God in the world" (Eph. 2:12). These were consistent with the Old Testament references to "the nations that do not know God" (Ps. 79:6; Jere. 10:25). Although all peoples are spiritually ignorant of God apart from Jesus Christ (cf. I Cor. 2:14; Jn. 14:7), the Gentiles were regarded as particularly estranged from God in their paganism.

The additional mention of their being *"slaves to those which by nature are not gods"* further serves to indicate that Paul was probably referring to pre-Christian Gentiles and their superstitious devotion to idols. Writing to the Corinthians, Paul explained "that when you were pagans, you were led astray to the dumb idols" (I Cor. 12:2). While the Jewish peoples were instructed by God to avoid idols (Exod. 20:4; Deut. 4:25;5:8), the Gentile nations were known for their superstitious reliance on the pantheon of Greek and Roman false-gods. It was an enslaving bondage indeed trying to perform what they perceived to be the whims and desires of the idolatrous deities. But Paul indicates that these idolatrous images were not essentially or constitutionally gods. Elsewhere Paul asserts that behind every idol there is a demon (cf. Acts 17:22; I Cor. 10:19-21), but here he denies that an idol is in reality, by nature, a god. Certainly they cannot be compared to, or classified in, the same sense as

God, who is by nature the essence of all goodness, righteousness, love, etc., with the absolute singularity of being all-powerful and holy.

It must be admitted that since no one can "know God" except through Jesus Christ (Jn. 14:7; 17:3), and since the Jewish religion had essentially deified the Law and its interpretations in idolatrous adoration (cf. Jn. 5:39), being thus enslaved to those things "which were by nature not gods," this verse could be interpreted as inclusive of both Gentiles and Jews, even though the more probable reference is specifically to those who were Gentiles. The primary emphasis of Paul, regardless of his ethnic intent, is upon the universally enslaving factor of all religious performance, which is not conducive to the Christian life lived by God's grace.

4:9   Encouraging the Galatians to recall the radical spiritual exchange that transpired in their regeneration and conversion, Paul writes, *"But now that you have come to know God."* In contrast to the idols which are "not gods," the Galatians had come to know the one and only living God in a personal relationship through Jesus Christ (cf. Jn. 14:7). "This is eternal life, to know God, the only true God, and Jesus Christ whom He has sent" (Jn. 17:3). Within the context of highlighting the intimacy of the Father/son relationship, Paul is obviously not referring to epistemological knowledge about God. He is not asserting that the Galatian Christians have arrived at more accurate ideological information about God by intellectual assent to a theistic belief in a monotheistic God. Rather, it is obvious that Paul is referring to an ontological knowing wherein the very Being of God is received by the believer in the intimacy and intensity of personal relationship.

Paul's recollection that the Galatian Christians "have come to know God, *or rather to be known by God,"* obviates that this is the knowing of a personal relationship, and emphasizes that it was God who took the initiative to know us through His

Son Jesus Christ. "God so loved the world that He gave His only begotten Son" (Jn. 3:16). "Not that we loved God, but that He loved us and sent His Son to be the propitiation of our sins" (I Jn. 4:10). Consistent with the theme of God's grace throughout this epistle, Paul is noting that the initiative of action and performance is accomplished by God, and cannot be supplemented by any human performance. We did not take the initiative to know God; He took the initiative to know us through His Son. We do not take the initiative to perform in a manner that we think will please Him; He takes the initiative of grace to provide the dynamic to manifest His character and to "do His works" (cf. Jn. 14:10) in our behavior, unto His own glory.

In light of all that God in Christ has done and continues to do, ***"how is it that you turn back again to the weak and worthless elemental things,"*** Paul asks the Galatians. It is incomprehensible to Paul that a Christian who had experienced God's grace in Christ should want to revert back to the restrictive regulations of religious performance. In fact, as the root word that Paul uses for "turn back" is the word for "convert" (Matt. 18:3; Acts 26:18,20), he could be intimating that to revert back to the former functionality is a "reverse conversion." Such reversion had a dire warning in Jewish history when God said, "If you or your sons shall indeed *turn away* from following Me, then I will cut them off and cast them out of My sight" (I Kings 9:6,7). It seems that the Galatian Christians were in danger of the apostatizing reversionism proverbially illustrated by "a dog returning to his vomit" (Prov. 26:11; II Pet. 2:22). Contrary to the forward progression unto maturity that the Judaizers held out as an incentive for engaging in legalistic "works," Paul indicates that what they were doing was a backwards regression to "the weak and worthless elemental things" of religious bondage. As noted previously in verse 3 the "elemental things" are probably best understood as the performance-oriented principles that promote self-effort under the guise of human potential. These are the core of religious inculcation to obey and keep the divine Law or ecclesiastical law in order to please God, as well as general humanistic premises of pragmatic utilitarian productivity – thus equally applicable to Jewish and Gentile backgrounds. They both focus on man's activity, rather than on receptivity of God's activity, and are based on the fallacious premise that "doing constitutes being." Paul calls all such "works" agendas "weak and worthless," having no power and no value before God. The power and the value are only derived from what God does by His grace in manifesting His character through His people.

If we, as Christians, "have died to the elementary principles of the world, why then would we submit ourselves" (Col. 2:20) to "be taken captive again to such elementary principles" (Col. 2:8), *"desiring to be enslaved all over again?"* The "desire" for such seems to be the natural, fallen tendency of man to seek pre-set parameters of performance which he can try to attain and credit himself with any visible progress. In conjunction with such, it is attractive to many people to have programmed rituals that do not require any thought or decision, allowing the authority-figures to make all the decisions for them (like the minor children mentioned in vss. 1,2). But such determined procedures of human activity constitutes slavery to "the powers that be," be they religious, fraternal, or the pressures of social philosophy. They ultimately culminate in the enslaving idolatry of worshipping man and his ways.

4:10 Specifically, the Galatian Christians were being enslaved by reverting back to *"observing days and months and seasons and years."* The Judaizing intruders were undoubtedly advocating Jewish observances, but some of the Gentile believers may have been lapsing back into pagan social customs, surmising that they could be mediums through which God might be pleased with their devotional efforts. Writing to the Colossians, Paul explained that "a festival or a new moon or a Sabbath day were things which are but a shadow, for the substance belongs to Christ" (Col. 2:16,17). Religion inevitably has the tendency for programmed scheduling of rituals in order to allow for visible expression of human activity. This was certainly true of the Jewish religion and its observances of Sabbath days (Exod. 20:8-11; 31:16,17), monthly festivals (Numb. 10:10; 28:11; II Kgs. 4:23), seasonal feasts (Exod. 23:14-17; 34:22,23), and year-long observances (Exod. 23:11; Lev. 25:4-17). It was also true of the pagan observances of astrological "new moons" and the "signs of the seasons" among the Gentiles. But what about the observances of "holy days" in the ecclesiastical calendar of Christian religion? To the extent that they are attributed with having any merit or favor before God for participation therein, they, too, can become "elemental things" that enslave and hold people captive to superstition and performance. But that is not to say that certain days (cf. Acts 20:7) and seasons cannot be utilized to celebrate the grace of God in Christ Jesus (cf. Rom. 14:5,6).

4:11 Paul expresses his personal concern for the Galatian Christians by writing, *"I fear for you, that perhaps I have labored over you in vain."* From deep within his pastor's heart Paul had a heartfelt fear that his personal involvement with the Galatians might come to naught with no lasting effects, if the Galatians would not see the error of their ways and repent, recognizing once again the grace of God. If they failed to appreciate the grace and liberty extended to them in Jesus Christ, there was the real possibility that they would apostatize against grace (5:4), and the fruit of Paul's labors of ministry would not remain in the cities and churches of Galatia. This was similar to Paul's appeal to the Thessalonian Christians, when he wrote, "I sent to you to find out about your faith, for fear that the tempter might have tempted you, and our labor should be in vain" (I Thess. 3:5). Paul's mention of his "labor" should not be misconstrued as self-effort, for to the Colossians he explains that "I labor, striving according to His power, which mightily works within me" (Col. 1:29). Paul was quite cognizant of the source of his endeavors, as he wrote to the Romans, "I will not presume to speak of anything except what Christ has accomplished through me" (Rom. 15:18).

4:12 Continuing his personal appeal to the Galatian Christians, based on the spiritual bond they had with him as their spiritual father, Paul writes, ***"I beg of you, brethren, become as I am, for I also have become as you are."*** Despite his masterful logical ability, Paul's emotional empathies shine through as he implores and beseeches those whom he still regards as his "brothers in Christ" to reconsider what they are doing.

His request that they "become as he is" is not a request that they become imitators of him, for such smacks of self-effort, but is an appeal to the Galatians to adopt his stance toward law and grace. Paul had "died to the Law, that he might live to God" (2:19), and his prayer for the Galatians was that they might likewise reject the Judaizers' coercive persuasion to keep the legalistic observances of the Torah, and instead enjoy the freedom of living by grace in all the blessings of the promises to Abraham. Paul knew from experience the frustrating misery of legalistic bondage, having been a meticulous Jewish Pharisee (cf. Phil. 3:4-10). But he rejected and broke free from all the Jewish conventionalities of religion and culture, disregarding all their legalistic performance standards of the Law, in order to become like most of the Galatians were, "living like a Gentile" (2:14). This was more than just cultural accommodation (cf. I Cor. 9:21), for it involved a repudiation of the Law so as to live solely by the grace of God in Christ, which was exactly what Paul wanted the Galatians to do.

Paul's statement, ***"You have done me no wrong,"*** is extremely difficult to interpret contextually. While some have suggested that Paul was advising the Galatians that it was not him whom they had wronged by their reversion to Law-performance but the Lord Jesus Christ, the word-order of the original

Greek does not seem to place the emphasis on the pronoun "me" to elicit such a meaning. Others have suggested that the Judaizers were using this argument with the Galatians, that there was "no wrong done to Paul" by their continuing on in the Christian life in adherence to the Law, but that is speculative at best. Since this phrase seems to be contextually linked to the following verses, perhaps the best interpretation is to understand Paul to mean that, "When I was with you in Galatia, you did me no wrong. You received me warmly and with respect despite my limitations (13-15). That is why I find it so inexplicable that your attitude has changed so radically from empathy (15) to enemy (16). But, still, I will not hold that against you, and simply appeal for what is for your own best interest, that you not be used by others (17), but allow the character of Christ to be formed in you (19) by God's grace."

4:13 Almost reminiscing, Paul reminds the Galatians, saying, ***"You know that it was because of a bodily illness that I preached the gospel to you the first time".*** Although Paul was providentially directed in his ministry – "sent, went and put" by the Lord into the particular circumstances that he encountered – this does not mean that his evangelizing ministry in Galatia was not secondarily occasioned by or enacted through the physical limitations of a "weakness of the flesh." The particular health problem that Paul suffered from is probably impossible to ascertain. But some have suggested that it was the effects of the physical violence that he encountered in Galatia (cf. Acts 14:19; II Tim. 3:11). Others have linked his "weakness of the flesh" to the "thorn in the flesh" (II Cor. 12:7) that Paul refers to in his epistle to the Corinthians, but that affliction cannot be definitively identified either. Further speculations of Paul's infirmity have abounded including malaria acquired in the swampy regions of South Galatia, epileptic seizures, diabetes, hyperthyroidism, and ophthalmological eye diseases. These latter suggestions (including diabetes and hyperthyroidism which can have direct effects on the eyes) find some contextual support in Paul's references to their willingness to "pluck out their eyes and give them to him" (15) and the "large letters he writes with his own hand" (6:11), but the exact nature of his physical problem remains inconclusive. All we know is that on his original visit to the region of Galatia, probably on the first missionary journey (and we have no specific record of his having visited there subsequently prior to the writing of this letter), Paul was bothered by some physical ailment.

4:14 In continuation of his sentence, Paul notes that *"that which was a trial to you in my bodily condition you did not despise or loathe"*. Apparently the physical infirmity that Paul had in his fleshly body was repulsive and abhorrent, either symptomatically, aesthetically or behaviorally. We do not know whether there was deformity or disfigurement, or whether his physical limitation caused aberrant behaviors (as with epilepsy), but Paul admits to the Corinthians that his opponents indicated that "his personal presence was unimpressive" (II Cor. 10:10). In light of the fact that both Jews and Gentiles had a tendency to identify physical infirmities or adversities as the penalty of God's displeasure (cf. Jn. 9:2; Acts 28:4), it is indeed remarkable that however piercing Paul's problem was the Galatians did not react with disgust, disdain, contempt or scorn. The Greek word translated by the English word "loathe" is particularly graphic, for it literally means "to spit" or "to expectorate." Paul was appreciative that the Galatians were not so repulsed by his condition that they wanted to spit, gag, barf, or vomit; indirectly indicating that his appearance or actions were particularly repulsive.

Rather than despising what you observed in me, Paul continues, *"you received me as an angel of God, as Jesus Christ Himself."* The Galatians had graciously welcomed Paul as their guest, treating him as a messenger or envoy sent from God, even as an angel. The writer to the Hebrews encouraged such "hospitality to strangers, for by so doing some have entertained angels without knowing it" (Heb. 13:2). The Galatians received Paul "as Christ Jesus," as though he were Jesus, which if we understand the indwelling presence of the risen Lord Jesus living in Paul (2:20) would rightfully make Paul an incarnational representative of Christ. Jesus Himself said that "he who receives whomever I send receives Me" (Matt. 10:40; Jn. 13:20).

4:15 Based upon their reception of Paul and the gospel he shared, he now asks, *"Where then is that sense of blessing you had?"* The "blessing" referred to here is not the same as that mentioned previously (3:8,9,14), though the two Greek words are both translated "blessing" in English. Here Paul is alluding to the sense of appreciation, satisfaction and joy that the Galatians had for Paul's having shared the gospel with them. They felt blessed and favored by God for having heard of His revelation in Jesus Christ. They were enthused and excited about the liberating message of grace and liberty in Christ. This experiential "blessing" that the Galatians had is well expressed in the poetry of William Cowper:

> Where is the blessedness I knew
> When first I sought the Lord?
> Where is the soul-refreshing view
> Of Jesus and His Word?
>
> What peaceful hours I once enjoyed!
> How sweet their memory still!
> But they have left an aching void
> The world can never fill.[2]

"For I bear you witness," Paul continues, *"that if possible you would have plucked out your eyes and given them to me."* The Galatians were so appreciative of Paul's having shared the gospel of Jesus Christ with them, that they would have done

anything for him. Perhaps this is simply figurative language, signifying that their appreciation knew no bounds. On the other hand, it might imply that Paul's physical problem was related to his eyes. Was he "bug-eyed" with the protruding effects of hyperthyroidism (Graves disease)? Was he going blind with the effects of diabetes? Did he have grotesque pus-filled eyes due to some other ophthalmic disease? We do not know! Whether this statement is completely figurative or has physical reference, either interpretation employs the language of hyperbole just as did Jesus' pronouncement about "plucking out one's eyes and throwing them away" if what one sees causes offense (Matt. 5:29). The hyperbolic nature of the statement is evident by Paul's allusion to the physical impossibility of such an ocular transplant (at least at that point in time).

4:16 In an abrupt shift based on his awareness of the Galatians' shift from open-heartedness to opposition, Paul asks, ***"Have I therefore become your enemy by telling you the truth?"*** Paul does not regard himself as an enemy of the Galatians, but as their spiritual parent (19). The projection of being an enemy was coming from other quarters. The Judaizers may have been attempting to paint Paul as an enemy, perhaps by implying that Paul was "an enemy of the Law" (Acts 21:28), and by insinuating that a real friend would have told them that they needed to keep the Law in order to be all they could be before God. In some sense the Galatian Christians seem to have transitioned from hospitality to hostility, from empathy for Paul to regarding him as their enemy. Paul questions how this change could have come about since he had simply told them the truth, both previously when he shared the gospel with them in Galatia and on the present occasion of this letter. The "truth of the gospel" (2:5,14) is, of course, Jesus Christ (Jn. 8:32,36; 14:6), and Paul only wanted the Galatians to experience the reality of God's grace and liberty in Jesus Christ.

4:17 Paul knew who the culprits were who were poisoning the relationship he had enjoyed with the Galatians by painting him as an "enemy." Attempting, now, to reveal their true colors, Paul writes, ***"They eagerly seek you, not commendably."*** "The Judaizers who came to visit you after I left are very zealous for you," Paul admits. "They pay attention to you, and make a 'play' for your sympathies and confidence. They woo you. They fuss and fawn and flatter in order to court your favor. But their motives are not good and pure, seeking your highest good before God. They have dishonorable intentions of selfish ends."

Their real agenda is that ***"they wish to shut you out, in order that you may seek them."*** The Judaizers sought to isolate the Galatian Christians from the greater community of grace in the Body of Christ, in order to indoctrinate them with their legalistic demands. In so doing, they sought to drive a wedge between the Galatians and their founding father, Paul. If by casting Paul as the Galatians' "enemy," they could create an estranged and alienated attitude toward Paul, they could perhaps exclude the Galatians from any additional influence of the renowned "apostle of grace," and his gospel of grace. Their attempts to segregate and sequester the Galatians was ultimately an attempt to exclude them from the living Lord Jesus and the freedom of enjoying His life by God's grace.

Like so many religious teachers throughout history, the Judaizers wanted to count the Galatians as their "disciples," and in order to do so they zealously sought to create dependency attachments upon themselves. Such religious personality cults wherein followers seek after human religious teachers are so contrary to the Christocentric gospel that advises believers to "seek Christ alone" and live by the grace-dynamic of His life as "Christ-ones."

4:18 Recognizing that zealous actions are not wrong in themselves, for he himself was probably zealous in his presentation of the gospel to the Galatians, Paul adds, ***"But it is good always to be eagerly sought in a commendable manner, and not only when I am present with you."*** If the motives behind the zeal are godly motives, seeking only the highest good of the people to serve God's purposes, then zeal can indeed be the expression of the passion of God. The concerned Christian will not be indifferent, apathetic or dispassionate, but his motivations must be aligned with and derived from God's loving intentions. Paul wanted the Galatians to know that his desire for them was only that God's objective might be manifested in their lives as they were faithfully receptive to the grace of God expressive of the life of Jesus. Such motivation was true "not only when he was present with them" during his initial ministry, but remained true even in his absence, despite what the Judaizers might have been intimating.

4:19 The affectionate passion of Paul's concern for the Galatians is revealed in his appeal, ***"My children, with whom I am again in labor until Christ is formed in you".*** Surprisingly it is not as a spiritual father that Paul expresses the intimacy of his concern for the Galatian Christians, but as a spiritual mother, for he employs the metaphor of childbirth. This is amazing imagery for a Jewish male to use. Remember that Jewish males looked down upon women condescendingly, thanking God that they were "not born a woman." For a Jewish male to cast himself in the role of identification with a woman was almost unheard of in Jewish thought, and reveals the extent to which Paul recognized the dissolution of gender barriers (3:28). But then again, Jesus Himself made a similar passionate appeal for the Jewish peoples, likening His concern to "a hen who gathers her chicks under her wings" (Matt. 23:37; Lk. 13:34). Later Paul would liken himself and his co-workers to "a nursing mother tenderly caring for her own children" (I Thess. 2:7). Desiring to explain the pain and anguish he was feeling for the Galatian Christians, Paul identifies with the labor pains of a pregnant mother facing delivery. Paul's figurative remarks were not intended to be a discourse on spiritual embryology, and we should not generate speculative allegories as some have attempted to do by suggesting that although Paul thought he had birthed and "delivered" the Galatians to regenerated new life in Christ, by their defection and reversion it was apparent that they were "still-born," so Paul is experiencing the travail of labor again with the hope that they will come to "full-term" in genuine regenerative spiritual birth. Others have suggested that Paul was desirous that Christ might be impregnated as an embryo in the womb of expectant Galatian Christians, being formed there in order to give birth to others. We must remember the limitations of a metaphorical allusion, and not press such into detailed allegories. Most likely, recognizing that Paul regarded the Galatians as having received the Spirit (3:2; 4:6) in regeneration and having received the life of Christ as "sons of God" (3:26; 4:6,7), Paul was simply expressing his anguished desire that the life of Christ might be formed into a living, behavioral formation of His character expressed in the soul and body of the Galatians. Being thus "transformed by the renewing of their minds" (Rom. 12:2) "into the same image, from the Lord the Spirit" (II Cor. 3:18), the Galatians would be "conformed to the image of Christ" (Rom. 8:29), allowing the "life of Jesus to be manifested in their mortal bodies" (II Cor. 4:10,11). Such a behavioral formation of Christ living in (2:20) and through the Galatians was Paul's passionate desire.

4:20 Breaking off in mid-sentence, Paul writes, *"but I could wish to be present with you now and to change my tone, for I am perplexed."* Paul's desire was to meet with the Galatians person-to-person, for the straightforward and aggressive approach he was having to take in this letter could easily be misinterpreted. Serious discussions are often tempered by face-to-face interaction and explanation. But apparently Paul was not able to travel to Galatia at that time, possibly because he was actively engaged in putting out the fires that the incendiary Judaizing arsonists were enflaming in the hearts of young Christians in Antioch and Jerusalem, as well as Galatia. Perhaps he was at that time preparing to travel to Jerusalem (Acts 15:2) in order to attack the issue at its source. Regardless of the reasons, Paul admits that he was baffled and bewildered, worried and at his wit's-end, to understand why the Galatian Christians were rejecting God's grace for legalistic performance. Though "perplexed, he was not despairing" (II Cor. 4:8), for he still had hope that the Galatians would rely solely on God's grace.

Paul's message of the privilege of functioning as sons of God and the foolishness of reverting to the religious restrictions of slaves and minor children is a much-needed reminder in every age. Christian religion today is mired in legalism and addicted to Judaizing tendencies; ignorant of and impervious to the liberty of God's grace in Jesus Christ. The message of Paul's epistle to the Galatians impinges upon the religious legalism and the Christianized forms of Judaism that are so prominent in Christian religion today. Many religious leaders want to avoid Galatians because they do not want their religion called into question. They prefer the status-quo of keeping the programs functioning by advocating loyalty to the ecclesiastical organization through pre-set ritualistic religious performance. Divine grace is beyond their human control, so they resist the unknown effects of encouraging Christians to live in the freedom of the spiritual dynamic of God's grace in Jesus Christ by His Spirit.

Admittedly, there is a constant natural tendency among Christians, and men in general, to revert to performance-orientation in religion and life. When there are pre-set parameters of expected performance, people feel comfortable in knowing the rules and exerting themselves in self-effort to perform in accord with the expectations. Believing in themselves, that they can indeed perform and produce, people appreciate the cause and effect paradigm wherein they can see the results of their visible progress, and then take personal credit for what they have achieved and attained. In addition, it is attractive to many people to have religious authority-figures who will oversee and evaluate their progress. Like minor children under guardians and managers (4:2), they do not have to think or make decisions, but simply allow the authority-figures to make the decisions for them as they continue to do what they are told.

The genuine Christian life, on the other hand, does require personal decision-making in the moment-by-moment choices of faith whereby we choose to allow for the receptivity of divine activity in our lives. Freedom always entails responsibilities! Granted, grace is full of unknowns, since we never know what God might do (always consistent with His character, however!). Operating by grace through faith is like depending on Someone to lead you into unknown areas. It is as risky as walking across a swinging-bridge without handrails, trusting Another to keep you on. Yes, the slavery of religious performance can be difficult, but at least it is predictable! And the freedom to function as sons of God in grace is gloriously unpredictable! Many, like the Galatians, opt for the slavery of programmed religious performances, unwilling to trust God in the receptivity of His activity. They thereby miss the fulfillment of restored humanity – the freedom to be man as God intended man to be by allowing the dynamic of God's grace in Jesus Christ to be all and do all in them.

Paul would remind the Christians of Galatia and the Christians of every age in every place of their glorious privilege as "sons of God" through faith in Christ Jesus (3:26) – the privilege of functioning in the freedom of God's grace. He would caution all Christians of the absurdity of returning to the slavery of "elemental principles" of performance criteria, since God has given us all that He has to give by His grace in Jesus Christ.

4:20

ENDNOTES

1   cf. Fowler, James A., *Christianity de facto*. Fallbrook: CIY Publishing. 1997.
2   Cowper, William, unknown source.

Sons of Promise

Galatians 4:21-31

Throughout chapters three and four of this epistle, Paul has been documenting that the gospel revealed to him (cf. chapters one and two) was God's intent from the beginning, documented by repeated references to the priority of the promises to Abraham. Although the Judaizers were apparently appealing to the Galatian Christians to identify with the heritage of Israel as the people of God by submitting to male circumcision as initiated in Abraham (and thus to become true "sons of Abraham"), the predominance of their admonitions involved submitting to the performance regulations of the Mosaic Law. Utilizing his Jewish heritage and knowledge of the Torah, Paul attempted to direct the thinking of the Christians in Galatia back to the prior and superior promises of God to Abraham, indicating that the divine promises of blessing and inheritance were all fulfilled in Jesus Christ (3:14,16,22), constituting Christians as the intended "sons of Abraham" (3:7,29), "sons of God" (3:26), and the "heirs" (3:29; 4:1,7) of all that God intends for His people. In so doing, Paul employed a radical reinterpretation of the events of Judaic history which the Jewish peoples had always understood in the exclusivism of physical fulfillment in Jewish privilege. Having been taught the gospel of Christ by the revelation of the Holy Spirit (1:11,12,16), Paul abandoned all of the prejudiced, traditional Jewish interpretations in order to view all of history and all of scripture from a Christocentric interpretation which regarded Jesus and His work to be the focal point of all

4:21-31

God's activity. Challenging the foundational tenets of Jewish interpretation, Paul recast biblical history as the prototypical prefiguring of the spiritual fulfillment of God's promises in Jesus Christ. As Abraham had responded to God's promises in faith, the blessing of God in Christ (Eph. 1:3) is received in Christians by faith, rather than by performance (3:6-14). The promises of Abraham take precedence in sequence, significance and supremacy over the performance standards of the Mosaic Law (3:15-22), which had a subsidiary purpose of custodial constraint until the reality of Christ's life was revealed (3:23-29). Christians, therefore, have the privilege of being the true "sons of God" and "sons of Abraham" who inherit all that God has for mankind in Jesus Christ (4:1-20). These previous reinterpretations that Paul had recorded would have been a bitter pill for the traditionalist Judaizers who had invaded Galatia to swallow, for these reinterpretations knocked the props from beneath the Judaizers' religious house of cards, but the argument that Paul makes in this final documentary portion of his letter (4:21-31) is the "clincher" that seals the case. The little Jewish lawyer "pulls out all the stops" as he builds his case to a climax that decimates all the arguments of his Judaizing opponents. James D.G. Dunn refers to this passage as Paul's "*tour de force*," his ultimate feat of ingenuity and strength.[1]

Many commentators have complained that these verses are the most difficult or puzzling passage in Galatians, or even in the entirety of the New Testament. Such complaints are usually due to prior misconceptions based on faulty presuppositions which do not correspond with what Paul has written. Without a doubt this passage will be difficult and baffling to those unwilling to accept what Paul has written at face value, because they are attempting to protect invalid premises and impose a grid of biased theological interpretation upon the scriptures. On the other hand, those who honestly accept what Paul writes will find his argument totally consistent with his Christ-centered emphasis throughout all of his writings. The Christocentric reinterpretation of old covenant history that Paul employs in this initial epistle becomes foundational for a proper understanding of all the rest of the Pauline literature, as well as for understanding the full spectrum and panorama of God's activity and intent in all of history and scripture, contextualized as it is in Jesus Christ alone.

4:21 Returning to the objective documentation of Old Testament scripture, Paul challenges the Galatian Christians with another question (cf. 3:1-5; 4:9). ***"Tell me, you who want to be under Law, do you not listen to the Law?"*** The Judaizers, like many teachers of religion, probably utilized many biblical quotations from the Old Testament to support their premises, and Paul knew that the best way to combat such was to respond with accurate biblical exegesis that explains God's spiritual intent in Christ. Since the religious infiltrators were appealing to the Mosaic Law, Paul begins by asking the Galatians whether they have any spiritual comprehension of the Torah and the Old Testament scriptures. As Spirit-indwelt Christians, they should have had spiritual discernment (I Cor. 2:10-16) to differentiate between legalistic conformity to behavior standards and the grace-dynamic of the Spirit of Christ in Christian living. By listening to, tolerating, and sympathizing with the Law-based message of the Judaizers, the Galatian Christians were evidencing how undiscerning they really were about the *modus operandi* of the Christian life. They were reverting back to that natural and religious tendency to desire prescriptive performance guidelines of legislated behavior, thinking that they could please God thereby and achieve the status of "sons of Abraham" or "people of God." Paul had already explained that the time of being "under Law" was historically past (3:23) for Jesus Christ redeemed the Jewish peoples who were enslaved "under the Law" (4:5), and the same was true experientially for the Gentiles who had become Christians and were no longer enslaved to "elemental things of the world" (4:3,9). To desire to be under legalistic rules and regulations was to deny God's all-sufficient grace in Jesus Christ.

4:22 If the Galatians had been willing to listen to the Old Testament scriptures with spiritual discernment, they should have been able to detect the Christocentric prefiguring of the historical events. As a case in point, Paul writes, ***"For it is written that Abraham had two sons, one by the bondwoman and one by the free woman."*** Actually, Abraham had eight known sons, six additional sons from his wife, Keturah, after Sarah had died (Gen. 25:1,2), but these are not pertinent to Paul's argument.

Let us review the pertinent historical narratives: God promised Abraham that he would have a son (Gen. 15:4). Abraham's wife, Sarah, was barren, so she suggested to Abraham that he do the next best thing (a logical alternative to trusting God's promises, that was culturally moral and acceptable), and take their Egyptian slave girl, Hagar, as another wife, in order to have a child. Abraham took his wife's advice, married Hagar, and she conceived and bore a son, Ishmael. Sarah was jealous (Gen. 16:1-4). God again promised Abraham that he would have a son through his wife, Sarah, but Abraham laughed because he was 100 years old and Sarah was 90 years old. Abraham appealed to God to accept Ishmael as his promised heir, but God refused (Gen. 17:15-20). Three messengers of God came to Abraham to confirm that he was going to have a son within a year. Listening through the tent-flap, Sarah laughed within, but subsequently denied that she had done so, and was corrected. "Is anything too difficult for the Lord?" was the question asked of Abraham and Sarah (Gen. 18:9-15). As promised by God, Sarah conceived and bore a son despite her advanced age. They called his name Isaac, meaning "laughter" (Gen. 21:1-8).

By returning to the events of Abraham's life, Paul retains the continuity of his documentary argument (3:6 – 4:20), wherein he addresses the question, "Who are the true sons of Abraham?" The Jewish peoples had always proudly considered themselves the true sons of Abraham through physical lineage and religious heritage. Reacting to their boast, John the Baptist had warned that such connection would not suffice, for "God is able to raise up sons of Abraham out of stones" (Matt. 3:9). Also reacting to their boast, Jesus explained that instead of Abraham being their father, they were "of their father, the devil" (Jn. 8:33-44). So Paul's denial of Jewish privilege through physical heritage had its precedents in earlier teaching, allowing him to assert that those who have received Jesus Christ in faith are the real "sons of Abraham" (4:7,29). The Judaizers, on the other hand, retaining certain ideas of Jewish privilege, were reluctantly allowing that Gentile converts who had received Jesus as the Messiah could somehow be identified as "sons of Abraham," provided the males received the physical mark of circumcision as was initiated with Abraham (Gen. 17:9-14), and they all conformed to the Mosaic Law of Judaic religion. Paul is now prepared to turn the tables on the entire issue of the "sons of Abraham" by arguing that the connection of physicality with either Isaac or Ishmael is irrelevant, for it is the spiritual connection with the sons of Abraham that determines the difference.

Commencing to lay out his argument, Paul notes that one of Abraham's sons, Ishmael (meaning "God has heard"), was born out of the slave-girl, the maidservant, the Egyptian bondwoman, Hagar, who served in Abraham's household (Gen. 16:1). The other son, Isaac (meaning "laughter" – both incredulity and exultation), was born out of the free woman, Abraham's first wife, Sarah, who was thenceforth regarded as "the mother of Israel" in Jewish thought which stressed their physical linkage to Abraham through Isaac and Sarah. By portraying the two mothers in this manner Paul is constructing a variation on the freedom vs. slavery theme previously alluded to (2:4; 3:23;

4:1-9), which will be amplified more fully later in the letter (5:1-13).

4:23 Proceeding to note the context of the births of the two sons of Abraham, Paul writes, ***"But the son by the bondwoman was born according to the flesh."*** Ishmael, born of Hagar, came into being "according to the flesh." The phrase "according to the flesh" has been variously interpreted. It cannot mean natural, physical generation, because both sons were born through Abraham's physical intercourse with a woman, and the subsequent conception, gestation and birth. Neither does "according to the flesh" mean "according to sexual desires," for we can safely assume that Abraham had sexual desires both for his wife, Sarah, as well as Hagar. The most feasible explanation, then, is to recognize that Paul was not referring to physical action or desire, but to the behavioral motivation that prompted Abraham to accept Sarah's suggestion and consent to the cultural capitulation of using a young slave-maiden as a proxy for child-bearing. God had made a promise to Abraham that he would have a son with his wife, Sarah. God keeps His promises; He cannot lie (Numb. 23:19; Titus 1:2; Heb. 6:18). And what He promises, He is quite capable of performing (Gen. 18:14; Lk. 1:37; Rom. 4:21). When man takes matters into his own hands and attempts to help God out by trying to bring about God's promises by the human means and devices of self-effort, then he has acted "according to the flesh." A promise from God is not a challenge to man to assist God in bringing the promise to pass, despite the abominable religious clichés that say, "God helps those who help themselves;" "Do your best, and God will do the rest;" or "Just do something, and God will bless it." Religion is always replete with such encouragement to human planning and performance; human activity and attainment. The hallmark of religion is utilitarian human productivity, instead of ontological receptivity of God's activity in faith. Abraham acted "according to the flesh" when he listened to his wife instead of God, and chose what W. Ian Thomas has called "the reasonable alternative to faith",[2] by thinking that he could perform and enact what could only be accomplished by God in fulfillment of His own promise.

By contrast, *"the son by the free woman* (was born) *through the promise."* Isaac was born to Sarah in fulfillment of God's promise, without any self-orchestrated assistance on the part of Abraham. God's promises can only be enacted by His own activity. To illustrate that truth, God acted against all odds to bring about the birth of Isaac from Sarah. God took Abraham who was "as good as dead" (Rom. 4:19) at one hundred years of age and Sarah with the "deadness of her womb" (Rom. 4:19) at ninety years of age, and supernaturally caused them to conceive Isaac in accord with His own promise. God's work done God's way by God's grace is the only way that God is glorified in His creation. What God desires from man is simply the dependent and contingent reliance of receptivity to His divine activity, allowing Him to be and do what He desires to be and do in each person. This is the faith that Abraham exemplified as the prototypical "father" of faith (Rom. 4:16; Gal. 3:7,26) for all Christians. Abraham's receptivity of faith that allowed God to "bring life out of death, and call into being that which did not exist" (Rom. 4:17) in his son, Isaac, was a pictorial prefiguring of God's promised regeneration and restoration of mankind in Jesus Christ, which can only be effected by the receptivity of His activity of life and Being in the individual. So Isaac, as the promised son received by faith by Abraham, was the type of the Promised Son, Jesus Christ, in Whom all Christians become the promised "sons of Abraham" by faithful receptivity of the grace-dynamic of God in accord with His promise, which was intrinsic in the Abrahamic promises. Isaac was born "through the promise" as Abraham and Sarah were receptive by faith to the extraordinary act of God enacted through ordinary people and procedures.

4:24 Paul now explains that *"this contains an allegory,"* or more accurately translated, "this is being allegorized" (the verb is a present, passive participle). Paul takes the historical narrative of Abraham's two wives (Hagar and Sarah) and two sons (Ishmael and Isaac), and without denying or diminishing their historicity, he posits that the persons and events have instructional value and meaning beyond the particulars of the incidents themselves. There are truths that go beyond the *prima facie* (first view) reading of the historical facts. Under the surface and between the lines of the historical narrative there are spiritual truths which prefigure God's spiritual intent in His Promised Son, Jesus Christ, and His "promised sons," Christians.

The legitimate use of figurative language and interpretation has been hotly debated. The linguistic word-doctors have attempted to define figurative, pictorial and illustrative language into rigid categories of allegory, analogy, typology, parable, metaphor, simile, hyperbole, etc. Based on their definitions, some commentators have alleged that Paul was not employing allegory but typology. Others have accused Paul of "spiritualizing" the historical events and the scriptural text. Still others would charge that Paul used faulty rabbinical methods of hermeneutics, using the methodology of *eisegesis* instead of *exegesis*. Operating on the premise that Paul wrote by the inspiration of the Holy Spirit, we must recognize the legitimacy of his figurative interpretation, all the while cautioning against additional allegorizing or spiritualizing that is not explicitly thus interpreted in scripture. Men can take figurative images and make them apply to anything they choose, so the foregoing caution is necessary for human hermeneutics.

The figurative comparison and contrast that Paul draws from the historical details is that *"these women are two covenants."* Hagar and Sarah, along with their two sons, Ishmael and Isaac, are illustrative or representative of two disparate covenants of God. They pictorially prefigure two contrasting covenant agreements or arrangements that God has "put through" (the meaning of *diatheke,* cf. 3:15,17) with mankind. The covenant of promise that God made with Abraham concerning his promised son, Isaac, has already been identified with the new covenant promise of Christ and Christians (3:15-19,29). The Jewish people, on the other hand, identified themselves as the "covenant-people" of God, based primarily on the Mosaic Law-covenant given to Israel on Mt. Sinai. Paul's argument is that the promise-covenant given to Abraham finds its eternal fulfillment in the new covenant of Christ, while the Law-covenant given to Moses found its temporary fulfillment in the interim period of the old covenant leading up to Christ – the external religious vestiges which were disappearing (II Cor. 3:7-11) and becoming obsolete (Heb. 8:16) in Paul's world of the first century. Though arbitrary human interpretation of history has often attempted to divide time into numerous segments of covenantal arrangements, the biblical perspective divides God's dealings between two primary covenants, the "old covenant" and the "new covenant" (I Cor. 11:25; II Cor 3:6; Heb. 7:22; 8:6-13; 9:15-20; 10:16,29; 12:24; 13:20), which Paul has figuratively identified with the Mosaic Law-covenant and Abrahamic promise-covenant, respectively. This verse effectively serves as a negation of both the Dispensational theological thesis of Jewish privilege with its overemphasis on discontinuity of several covenants, as well as the Covenant theology thesis of singular covenant with its overemphasis on continuity of covenant, for Paul refers to the contrast of "two covenants."[3]

The real bombshell of radical reinterpretation of Jewish history was dropped when Paul explained that the *"one"* covenant, the Mosaic Law-based old covenant, *"came from Mount Sinai bearing children who are slaves; she is Hagar."* This was the Hiroshima of Paul's battle with the Judaizers! Nothing would have been more unexpected and shocking to Judaic interpretation than to identify the old covenant Jewish religion

4:24

with Hagar and her son, Ishmael. Jewish interpretation regarded the Jewish people as the chosen people of God, physically related to Abraham through Sarah and her son, Isaac; recipients of the Mosaic Law on Mount Sinai in a unique and special covenant with God; and thus properly related religiously with "the God of Abraham, Isaac, and Jacob." The Jews were proud of their physical heritage and descent from Abraham through Isaac. They regarded the despised Gentiles, and more particularly the Arab peoples of the Middle East (Gen. 25:13-18), as the physical descendants of Ishmael and Hagar, having no viable relationship with God apart from the Law (cf. Ps. 147:19,20), but languishing in the bondage of ignorance and sin; enemies of God's people (I Chron. 5:10,19,20; Ps. 83:6). The Arab people accepted their identification with Ishmael and Hagar, at least from the seventh century A.D. onwards, after Mohammed identified Muslims and Islam as descending from Abraham through Ishmael in the *Koran*. The Jewish interpretation was clear-cut: A person was either a Jew with physical and religious connection with Abraham through Isaac and Sarah, or a person was a Gentile (or an Arab) with physical and religious connection with Abraham through Ishmael and Hagar.

But Paul turns the tables, inverts the argument, and stands the Jewish interpretation on its head. He identifies the Sinaitic covenant of Law received by Moses, by which the Jewish peoples identified themselves as "the people of the Law," as having been brought into being in spiritual connection with Hagar and the context of her bearing Abraham's son, Ishmael. The Judaizers, who retained much of the physical and legal interpretations of the Jews, must have been aghast and appalled when they heard Paul's reinterpretation in the reading of the Galatian epistle. It was almost inconceivable that a person of Jewish heritage could or would promulgate the imagery that Paul develops in these verses. It was akin to denying one's heritage! Indeed, only by God's supernatural grace placing the "mind of Christ" (I Cor. 2:16) in Paul and giving him spiritual discernment by the Spirit, could Paul have jettisoned everything he had been taught about his background wherein the Jewish peoples considered themselves the unique, special, blessed and chosen people of God through Abraham and Isaac; repudiate the Jewish prejudice of exclusive privilege; and relegate Jewish religion with all of its regulations and rites to the realm of Hagarian bondage.

In fact, Paul was dumping all human religion, whether Jewish religion, Arab religion, Chinese religion, Christian religion, etc., into the same hopper of enslaving performance. (It has already been noted that the English word "religion" is derived from the Latin word *religare*, meaning "to bind up," or "to tie back," thus enslaving a person to rules and regulations and rituals of devotion.) Hagar was a slave-girl in the household of Abraham and Sarah, with whom Abraham joined himself in performance "according to the flesh" (23). Slave-girls always gave birth to little slaves, delivered into the condition of slavery. In like manner, the Mosaic Law brought forth performance slaves to the Law, as the self-effort performance of religious bondage serves as "the logical alternative to faith."

Paul's radical reinterpretation of Jewish connection is totally consistent with his previous statements in the epistle, identifying Christians as "the sons of Abraham" (3:7,29) enjoying the privileges of divine promise, and correlates precisely with all the rest of the new covenant literature. Paul interpreted everything from a Christological perspective rather than from the biological perspective of Judaism, from a spiritual perspective rather than from a physical perspective. But the religious belief of physical, Jewish privilege is still present today in the Zionist interpretations that posit an inherent right of Jews to occupy Palestine and to rebuild the dead Jewish religion.

4:25 Paul goes on to make the figurative connection more explicit, stating, *"Now this Hagar is Mount Sinai in Arabia."* "Now," either in the chronologic present point in time or in the

4:25

logic of the present point of argument, Paul links Hagar with Mount Sinai. This is a connection that no traditional Jewish interpreter would ever have made. The Law given to Moses at Mount Sinai (Exod. 19:1,2,19; Lev. 7:28; 26:42) was regarded as having set the Jewish people apart from all Gentiles as "the people of the Law." Hagar was regarded as the "mother of the Gentiles." So, Hagar and Mount Sinai had no connection, but were regarded as antithetical in Jewish thought. Paul, however, links Hagar and Mount Sinai in the commonality of slavery – Hagar was a slave-girl and Mount Sinai was the location where the slavery of Law-performance commenced. Some have attempted to avoid the religious link of bondage that Paul draws between Hagar and Mount Sinai by suggesting merely a geographical connection between Hagar and her Ishmaelian descendants and the Sinai wilderness (cf. Gen. 21:21), but such is to miss the express point of Paul's argument.

That Paul locates Mount Sinai in Arabia creates an interesting geographical footnote. With Paul's previous reference to going away to Arabia after his conversion (1:17), these are the only two references to Arabia in the New Testament. There are numerous references in the Old Testament to the region of Arabah between the Gulf of Aqaba and the Dead Sea, as well as mention of Arabia, the general region to the southeast of Palestine now occupied by the countries of Jordan and the northwest part of Saudi Arabia. Several attempts have been made throughout history to locate Mount Sinai in this area, rather than in the traditional location of the southern part of what came to be called the Sinai Peninsula. Regardless of the geographical location of Mount Sinai, this does not alter Paul's argument connecting Hagar and Mount Sinai with the bondage of slavery.

Even more explicitly, Paul continues by explaining that Hagar *"corresponds to the present Jerusalem."* This stands to reason because the city of Jerusalem was the capital of Judaic religion, the center of Law-observance, and the location of the

Jewish temple and its worship. Mount Sinai and Jerusalem are inseparably linked by reference to Jewish Law. Paul even uses the Hebraic form of the Greek place name, *Ierousalem,* in this verse, rather than the Hellenized form, *Ierosoluma,* which he had used previously (1:17; 2:1), apparently in order to emphasize the religious significance of the Jewish capital. The physical "City of Peace" remains to this day as a focal-point of religion, having ironically become the site of violent religious conflict as Jewish religion, Christian religion and Islamic religion battle over the site for the external performances of their rites and rituals.

But it was the identification of the first century capital of Judaism with Hagar, joining them in the context of slavery, that is the point Paul seeks to make as he concludes, ***"for she is in slavery with her children."*** "She" – both Hagar and Jerusalem are nouns of feminine gender. Paul is emphasizing the mutuality of the slave condition of Hagar and Judaism and their descendant peoples. Hagar and the Judaic Law could produce nothing but slaves – slaves to the "elemental principles" of performance "according to the flesh." The Jews adamantly protested that "they had never been enslaved to anyone" (Jn. 8:33), but at that very time they were physically enslaved in Roman occupation, religiously enslaved to Law-requirements, and spiritually enslaved to the Evil One (Jn. 8:44; II Tim. 2:26). Despite their disavowals of denial, those involved in Jewish religion were slaves in like manner as was Hagar.

When Paul wrote that Hagar "corresponds" to Jerusalem, the Greek word he used means "to walk together with," or figuratively "to line up with," "to parallel," "to place in the same category or column." The related concepts that Paul is comparing and contrasting can indeed be placed in parallel linear columns to illustrate what Paul is picturing, and this is probably what Paul intended by the previous use of the word "allegorizing" (24) also:

Hagar (24,25)	Sarah
bondwoman (22,23,30,31)	free woman (22,23,30,31)
son of bondwoman (23,30,31)	son of free woman (23,30,31)
Ishmael	Isaac (28)
born of flesh (23)	born through promise (23)
slave children (24,25,31)	free children children of promise (28) children of Jerusalem above (26)
slavery (24,25,31)	freedom (26,31;5:1)
covenant of Law (24)	covenant of promise (24)
old covenant (24)	new covenant (24)
Mt. Sinai (24,25)	Mt. Zion
Law (21)	Grace
physical Jerusalem (25)	Jerusalem above (26)
Jews, Judaizers	Christians
religion	Christianity
not heirs (30)	heirs (3:29; 4:30)

4:26 With the "***But***" of contrast, Paul switches his correspondence to the other column to figuratively explain that ***"the Jerusalem above is free; she is our mother."*** Paul envisions the ideal city or community of Peace wherein the "Prince of Peace" (Isa. 9:6), Jesus Christ, reigns as Lord. Jewish apocalyptic thought and literature (II Baruch 4:2-6; II Enoch 55:2; 4 Ezra 7:26; 8:52; 10:25-59; 13:36) had long anticipated a greater city and temple, recognizing that the physical city of Jerusalem and its temple were temporary, provisional and perishable. Prophetically and eschatologically they sought a "heavenly Jerusalem above" where God dwelt more fully (cf. Jn. 3:3,7; 8:23). But the external and physical emphases of popular Jewish religion in the first-century were so caught up in legal bondage and material place that they no longer sought spiritual and heavenly realities.

4:26

Paul is advising the Galatian Christians that the spiritual reality of the heavenly City of Peace is already available as the community of Christians in Christ. He does not refer to a "Jerusalem that is to come in the future," but to "the Jerusalem above that is free at the present time." That city and land (Gen. 12:7; 13:15) that was promised and anticipated is now realized in Jesus Christ. The Abrahamic promises did not refer only to Middle Eastern geography, but to a spiritual geography of a spiritual city and land for spiritual inhabitants and descendants. Abraham was "looking for the city, whose architect and builder is God" (Heb. 11:10), for the "better country, a heavenly one" (Heb. 11:16), and such is now realized for Christians who have "come to Mount Zion, to the city of the living God, the heavenly Jerusalem, and the church of the first-born who are in heaven, and to God." (Heb. 12:22,23). As Christians, we have "citizenship in heaven" (Phil. 3:20), even though there is a "not yet" realized expectation of the consummation of such a new covenant community in "the holy city, Jerusalem, coming down out of heaven from God" (Rev. 3:12; 21:10). This serves to evidence that the "Jerusalem above" is not to be strictly identified with the physical, visible and institutional church on earth.

Paul wants the Galatian Christians to understand that "in Christ" they are already participating in the new covenant community of Peace. It is a spiritual and heavenly city that is not restricted by physical time and space. It is not a city of slaves, but a free city wherein Christians are free to function as God intended in the freedom of God's grace, living in the "peace that surpasses comprehension" (Phil. 4:7) under the Lordship of the "Prince of Peace." The "Jerusalem above" wherein we live in the presence of God by His Spirit is not confined and restricted to physical parameters, nor is it bound up in religious rules and regulations. Paul's argument is aimed at convincing the Christians in the Galatian churches that Christ has set them free (5:1), and they should not cross over in reversion to the religious column being advocated by the Judaizers.

Whereas the Judaic religion regarded Sarah as the "mother of Israel" by physical lineage, and the physical city of Jerusalem on Mount Zion as the place that engendered and gave birth to their religion and nation (Ps. 87:1-6; Isa. 51:17,18), Paul switches the maternal identification from physical to spiritual, having already noted Hagar as the figurative mother of Judaic religion, and now indicating that "the Jerusalem above" (connected with God's intent through Sarah) is the engendering source of Christianity. Heaven has given birth to Christians in Christ!

4:27 The corresponding imagery of the new Jerusalem on Mount Zion correlating with Abraham and Sarah in connection with the Messianic promise brought the passage in Isaiah 51-54 to Paul's mind (cf. Isa. 51:2,3). Immediately following the Messianic "suffering servant" passage of Isa. 53:1-12, Paul notes that *"it is written, 'Rejoice, barren woman who does not bear: Break forth and shout, you who are not in labor: for more are the children of the desolate than of the one who has a husband.'"* To reconstruct Paul's connecting thoughts and rationale for citing this verse, Isa. 54:1, is not a simple task. The greater context of the Isaiah passage is dealing with the fruitfulness (51:3) of Zion, Jerusalem, the holy city (52:1), which Paul had just referred to in the previous verse. The peoples of the physical Jerusalem were held captive (52:2) and would be redeemed (52:3) by the Messiah who would bring good news (52:7), but be despised (53:3), oppressed (53:7) and die for the sin of many (53:12). The heavenly Jerusalem/Zion, the spiritual Israel of the real people of God, had not travailed in the labor of childbirth and had not borne a child – the Messiah had not yet come and was still anticipated in the time of Isaiah. So the "Jerusalem above" was still desolate – dry, unoccupied and lifeless – and barren. But when the promised Messiah would come the desolation would be turned to fruitfulness, the lamenting to joy, and the barrenness to innumerable progeny. Judaic religion which was "married" to external, physical relationships and the performance of the Law "according to the flesh" would be overshadowed by the spiritual sons of God in Christ.

It is not difficult to see how Paul connected Genesis 11:30, "Sarah was barren; she had no child," with the similar statement concerning Zion in Isaiah 54:1. The passage readily, if not explicitly (cf. 51:2), allowed for the corresponding imagery. Zion, like Sarah, was not to feel humiliated or be disgraced (54:4), for with great compassion (54:7,8) God would call her, like a wife forsaken and grieved in spirit (54:6), providing redemption (54:5,8), and turning her sorrow into the joy of exultation (Gen. 21:6) by His divine action (54:5). According to His "covenant" (54:10; Gal. 3:17; 4:24) God would provide the "seed" (54:3; Gen. 13:15,18; Gal. 3:16,19,29) of descendancy within the heavenly city of Jerusalem (54:11,12; Rev. 21:10,11,18-21). Sarah's true child, typologically illustrated by Isaac as the "son of promise," was the "Seed" of Abraham in Jesus Christ, the Messiah (Gal. 3:19). Through Jesus Christ the heavenly city of Jerusalem, God's community of Peace, would eventually have more children than the old, physical Jerusalem whose Judaic religion of Law did not produce or accept the Messiah. Judaism produced many adherent sons "according to the flesh," Ishmaelian "alternatives to faith" preoccupied with the physical performance of self-effort in a physical city with its physical temple, priesthood and sacrifices, but the spiritual fulfillment of the heavenly Jerusalem in Christ would produce far more numerous descendants than were ever numbered in the religion of Judaism. Jesus Christ, the "first-born among many brethren" (Rom. 8:29) would "bring many sons to glory" (Heb. 2:10) in identification and union with Himself, creating a "holy nation, a people for God's own possession" (I Peter 2:9,10), and this would indeed be the intended spiritual fulfillment of God's promises to Abraham in the beginning when He promised innumerable descendants in many nations (Gen. 13:16; 15:5; 16:10; 17:5; 22:17).

4:28 Bringing direct application to the Galatian Christians (and all Christians), Paul writes, ***"And you brethren, like Isaac, are children of promise."*** The promised children of Abraham are Christian peoples. Isaac and the ethnic Jewish people of Israel were the physical pre-figuring, the pictorial prototype of the "sons of promise," but Christians comprise the spiritual fulfillment of the Abrahamic promises as the sons (3:7) and offspring (3:29) of Abraham, the "sons of God" (3:26) born into the intimacy of God's family and community. Later, to the Romans, Paul would write, "It is not the children of the flesh who are children of God, but the children of the promise are regarded as descendants" (Rom. 9:8,9) in fulfillment of the promise to Abraham. "As many as may be the promises of God, in Jesus Christ they are fulfilled and affirmed" (II Cor. 1:20). God's intent from the beginning was to have innumerable children in a spiritual community, a heavenly city, based not on physical acts "according to the flesh," but the spiritual action of His Spirit; not on biological connection, but on Christological connection with Christ; not by ethnicity, but by the eschatological acts of His own grace. Paul is driving home the point to the Christians of Galatia that they are already children of Abraham, children of promise, children of God by spiritual union with Jesus Christ, and they do not need the performance of male circumcision and Law-observances in order to become or attain such, as the Judaizers were encouraging.

4:29 Paul also wanted to warn the Galatian Christians that the spiritual "children of promise" have not been promised a utopian existence without problems or persecution. ***"But as at that time he who was born according to the flesh persecuted him who was born according to the Spirit, so it is now also."***

Recalling the interactions of Abraham's two sons, Ishmael and Isaac, Paul notes that Ishmael, the son born "according to the flesh" (23), persecuted the younger son, Isaac, the son born "according to promise" (23) by the work of the Spirit of God. Genesis 21:9 records that Sarah observed Ishmael "playing with" his half-brother, Isaac, who was fourteen years his junior. Many interpretations of this phrase have been proffered, from "making sport of," "mocking," "aiming his bow at as if to scare or kill," as well as more sinister Jewish interpretations of homosexual activity or the introduction of idolatrous practices. Whatever the activity, Paul identifies it as a form of persecution that usually implied some harassment or threat.

"As at that time, so it is now," Paul warns the Galatians. The historical incident alluded to serves as a prototype of two categories of people in spiritual conflict. Ishmael, representing Judaic religionists as Paul has already explained (24,25), engaged in the self-effort of performance and defending their physical privilege, persecuted Isaac, representing Christians (26,28). Much evidence exists of first-century Jewish persecution of Christians (Acts 4:1; 5:17; 7:57-60; 8:1; 12:3,4; 13:50; 14:2,19; II Cor. 11:24; Gal. 1:13; 5:11; 6:12; I Thess. 2:14-16), as well as the more indirect ostracism that disallowed Christian converts in Jerusalem and Judea the freedom of vocational enterprise that led to their poverty.

In a more general sense, Paul's statement can be expanded to include the persecution that religion as a whole has brought against Christians. The religious half-brothers in their legalism and exclusivism are unwilling to tolerate those who view Christ as the singular Redeemer and who would live in the grace and liberty of the singular dynamic of Christ. It can be said generally that "all who desire to live godly in Christ Jesus will be persecuted" (II Tim. 3:12).

Particularly, Paul was warning the Galatian Christians that the actions of the religious Judaizers who had infiltrated their fellowship was a form of persecution that was "playing with," "making sport of," "mocking," and harassing the freedom they had in Christ to live "according to the Spirit" by the grace of God. We could, of course, note that the hostility of Jewish religion remains to this day in carefully coordinated offensives against Christians, especially Jews who accept Jesus as the Messiah, but also in legal actions against Christian symbols and holidays, as well as the nation of Israel attempting to deny residency, citizenship and the right to worship to Christians in their country. "As at that time, so it is now" still applies!

4:30 Paul now comes to the point of the specific action that he is encouraging the Galatian Christians to take, in response to the Judaizers. To do so he retains the allegorical imagery that he employs throughout this passage, and cites Sarah's response to the persecuting harassment of her son, Isaac, by his older half-brother, Ishmael. *"What does the Scripture say?"* Paul asks. Sarah's original response, as recorded in Genesis 21:10, was, *"Cast out the bondwoman and her son."* Sarah would not tolerate the persecution of her son, Isaac, and commanded that Hagar and her son, Ishmael, be thrown out of the camp. Jewish interpretation of this verse regarded Sarah's action as God's rejection of the Gentiles, maintaining the privileges of the physical people of God, the Jews. The Judaizers in Galatia might have used this verse as an encouragement to the Galatians to, "Cast off Paul, for he is not a true Jew anyway, because he does not advocate circumcision and the keeping of the Law." If so, Paul turns the tables 180 degrees, consistent with the imagery he has used throughout, encouraging the Galatian Christians to expel the Judaizing religionists from their midst: "Run them off!" "Throw them out!" "Send them on their way!"

As a general principle, this can be understood as an inculcation of imperative necessity for Christians to take deliberate and definite action that refuses to tolerate the religionizing harassments of those who reject the dynamic of God's grace in Jesus Christ alone. Though there is much latitude for diversity in Christianity, as Christians "agree to disagree" over differing opinions, practices and styles, the singularity of the gospel of Jesus Christ, centering in God's grace through the risen Lord Jesus and the dynamic of the Spirit of Christ, must be stood up for, just as Paul opposed Peter (2:11-14) and was now berating those who would distort the gospel (1:7) in this epistle. The bondage of legal performance and the freedom of God's grace in Jesus Christ are incompatible and at odds with one another. There are times, as previously noted in the exegesis of 2:11-21, when Christians are obliged to stand firm (5:1) in defense (I Pet. 3:15) of the singular gospel of grace in Jesus Christ.

Sarah's continued response indicated that ***"the son of the bondwoman shall not be an heir with the son of the free woman."*** Having been "cast out," Ishmael would not be regarded as a legitimate heir of the physical estate of Abraham, but Isaac would be the sole heir of the estate created by the union of Abraham and Sarah. In Jewish interpretation, of course, this was regarded as God's repudiation of the Gentiles to give exclusive privilege to ethnic Israel as the heirs of God's blessings. In Paul's inspired reinterpretation it means that Jews, Judaizers and religionists in general do not inherit the spiritual fulfillment of the promises of God in Jesus Christ, because the singularity of the gospel demands the presence and dynamic of Jesus Christ alone. This would have been a major blow to the Judaizers, denying and excluding them from the inheritance of the promised blessings of God to Abraham. British commentator J.B. Lightfoot wrote, "The apostle confidently sounds the death-knell of Judaism."[4] But we must be careful to note that Jewish individuals (whether so designated by race, religion or nationality) are not excluded from being spiritual heirs of God's promises, any more than peoples of any other race, religion or nationality. That would be abhorrent anti-Semitism or abominable religious exclusivism, whereas the Christian gospel is universally extended to all men who will individually receive

4:31

the singular Son of God, Jesus Christ, as the sole basis of their standing and fellowship with God.

Paul essentially denies the inheritance of any divine blessing to all religion (including Judaism), and asserts that Christians alone are the spiritual heirs of God's promises by the reception of Jesus Christ by faith. This is the basis of designated sub-theme of this epistle: "The Gospel *versus* Religion." There is a definite dichotomy in the corresponding columns that Paul draws pictorially in these verses (cf. 25), positing that Christianity and religion are mutually exclusive. It must also be noted that this verse is an explicit denial of the Dispensational thesis of a divided blessing of double means and dual paths of salvation for Jews and Gentile Christians. Adherents of Jewish religion, identified as sons of the bondwoman (24,25), shall not be heirs with the sons of promise, the sons of the free woman, Christians.

4:31 After lengthy documentation of his "case," Paul, the former Jewish lawyer, deduces and draws a summarizing conclusion, not only to this allegorical distinction of Hagar and Sarah, but also to the entire section of the letter that seeks to document Christianity as the fulfillment of the promises to Abraham (3:1-4:30). *"So then, brethren, we are not children of a bondwoman, but of the free woman."* Identifying himself in the same spiritual family of God with the Galatian Christians, Paul reiterates that Christians are not related to the bondwoman, Hagar, in the slavery of religious performance. Therefore, they should not be listening to the Judaizers who would lead them back into the slavery of "elemental things" (4:3,9) and the slavery of Law-observance. They should not be "bewitched" (3:1), hoodwinked or mesmerized by the deceitful scheming of the Judaizers who would "shut them out" (4:17) from the blessing of grace in Christ and entrap them in religious dependency attachments. Paul wanted the Galatians to understand their true identity in Christ as "sons of Abraham"

(3:7,29), "sons of promise" (4:28), "sons of God" (3:26), "sons of the free woman," Sarah, who bears children intended to operate in the freedom of God's grace activity. That is why this verse leads right into the next verse (5:1), where Paul begins the practical description of the behavioral implications of living by grace, by declaring, "It was for freedom that Christ set us free." Paul was so keen that the Christians of Galatia should understand that they were free to be man as God intended man to be, by the dynamic grace of God's function within receptive humanity; i.e. by the life of the risen Lord Jesus living and reigning in them as Christians.

This paragraph (21-31) serves as the culminating and climactic argument of Paul's case to document that Christians are the "sons of promise," the "sons of Abraham," thus giving a perspective of God's over-all intent for mankind from the beginning, centered in His Son, Jesus Christ. This passage is the very "heart" of the message of Paul's epistle to the Galatians, and it is utterly amazing that it is so often avoided, glossed over, or misinterpreted by those who would seek to protect Jewish sympathies and preserve exclusivistic religious tendencies.
When this letter was first read in the Galatian churches, this portion was, no doubt, the most shocking part of the correspondence. What a shock it must have been, particularly for the Judaizers who were listening, to hear Paul's radical Christocentric reinterpretation of Hebrew history, which, in essence, stood all Jewish interpretation of those same events on its head. It was absolutely inconceivable for them to think that Paul could identify the Jewish religion, the Judaizing half-brothers, and all religion with Hagar and Ishmael. Paul was not singling out the Jewish religion for more severe censure than others, but since that was the context out of which Christianity emerged, and since the Judaizers in Galatia retained a variation of that religion's legal performance-orientation, Judaism and the Juda-

4:31

izers become the focal point, though indicative of all religion in general. When Paul, the zealous Jewish Pharisee (Phil. 3:4-6), was converted from Judaism on the road to Damascus (Acts 9:3-8; 22:6-11; 26:12-18), and the gospel of Christ was revealed to Him by the Spirit of Christ (Gal. 1:11,12), the revelation of Jesus Christ as the Messianic fulfillment of all God's promises (II Cor. 1:20) demanded that he abandon all of his ingrained Judaic prejudice of divine privilege for the physical Jewish peoples, and all benefit of Jewish Law-observance (Phil. 3:7-9). Paul saw and realized that Christians, those who are "in Christ" (II Cor. 5:17), regardless of ethnicity, economy or gender (Gal. 3:28), are the spiritual heirs of all the promises of God.

In order to express the point in the most overt and obvious way, as well as the most striking and shocking way, Paul identifies the physical Judaic religion with Hagar and Ishmael, knowing full well that it was a major premise of Jewish interpretation that their enemies, the despised Arab/Gentiles, were physically connected to Ishmael. Paul was not referring to physical heritage, though, but to the spiritual connection of all performance-based religion "according to the flesh," in order to assert the spiritual connection of Christianity with Sarah and Isaac, "according to the promises" of God to Abraham. Without a doubt, Paul's denial of Jewish privilege and legal religious benefit would have been taken as a terrible insult, a slap in the face, by those Judaizing religionists who were without spiritual understanding (cf. I Cor. 2:14). But Paul felt compelled to make the point that the gospel is comprised of Jesus Christ alone; not Jesus Christ plus Jewish privilege, Jewish performance, Jewish sympathies, or Jewish expectations – a point that many Zionist religionists to this very day have failed to appreciate.

Additionally, Paul notes that just as Ishmael persecuted Isaac, the one through whom the singularity of God's promise was to come, so the Jewish religionists persecuted Christians in the early centuries, as illustrated by the Judaizers' harassment of the Galatian Christians. Religionists, in general, are a prosecutive, persecuting bunch, accepting only those who conform to their predetermined parameters of thought and action. The history of the institutional Christian religion is, likewise, replete with crusades, inquisitions, persecution, ostracism, scorn and derision, even against Christians who simply wanted to live in the freedom of God's grace through faith (ex. Anabaptists, Puritans, Pietists, Evangelicals, etc.). Despite how sincere Christians might attempt to live in peace with traditionalists and religionists, the half-brothers of the religious "establishment" and the denominational hierarchy will inevitably resist the singularity of Jesus Christ as the basis of the Christian life, and insist that we live by their rules, conform to their traditions and ceremonies, and assent to their creedal belief statements. The religious Ishmaels cannot tolerate the Isaacs of God's promised grace. They never have! They never will! "As it was then, so it is now."

That does not mean that Christians are to "cave in" and capitulate to such persecutive religion. As Sarah "cast out" Hagar and her son, Ishmael, Paul urges the Galatians to expel the Judaizers, and in its broadest application this is a call to Christians of all ages to, "Repudiate and expel religion and its reasonable alternatives to faith!" Christians have an obligation to take resolute action in "standing firm" (5:1) in defending the gospel of grace in Jesus Christ. This may involve exposing and opposing legalistic religious tendencies in our midst, as Paul did to Peter (2:11-14) and as Paul was doing to the Judaizers in this letter. This does not mean that Christians should ever take offensive violent action, but we must stand up in defense of our faith and freedom. If we will not affirm our right and desire to live in the freedom of God's grace, allowing the living Lord Jesus Christ to live out His life through us, then, in essence, we are saying that His action in setting us free on the cross of Calvary was not worth doing – "Christ died needlessly"

(2:21). God forbid! "It was for freedom that Christ set us free; therefore keep standing firm and do not be subject to a yoke of slavery" (5:1).

ENDNOTES

1. Dunn, James D.G., *The Epistle to the Galatians*. (Black's New Testament Commentary series). Peabody: Hendriksen Publishing. 1993. pg. 245.
2. Thomas, Maj. W. Ian, *The Mystery of Godliness*. Grand Rapids: Zondervan Publishing House. 1964. pg. 20.
3. Fowler, James A., *Dispensational Theology, Covenant Theology, or Christocentric Theology*. Fallbrook: C.I.Y. Publishing. 1994.
4. Lightfoot, J.B., *The Epistle of Paul to the Galatians*. Grand Rapids: Zondervan Publishing House. 1969. (first printed 1865). pg. 184.

Stand Firm in Freedom

Galatians 5:1-12

Paul transitions to the third major section of his epistle in these verses. First, he *defended* the gospel revealed to him (chapters 1 and 2). Then, he *documented* that the gospel revealed to him was God's intent from the beginning, tracing his documentation back to the promises of God to Abraham (chapters 3 and 4). Now, he begins to *describe* and *demonstrate* the practical behavioral implications of how this revealed gospel is lived out in freedom and love and interpersonal Christian relationships (chapters 5 and 6).

The reality of the Person and work of Jesus Christ is not just barren theology, as so often explained in the juridical and forensic categories of an imputed righteousness that effects a right standing or status before God. The doctrine of "justification by faith," so adamantly defended by Protestantism, has been so objectified in logical and legal categories that the practical behavioral implications of the righteous character of Christ, the Righteous One, lived out through the believer have been neglected. Paul, on the other hand, always brings his readers to the practical implications of the Christ-life lived out in everyday behavior.

In this passage (5:1-12), Paul focuses on the freedom that is the privileged birthright of every Christian. H.D. Betz explains that "freedom is the central theological concept which sums up the Christian's situation before God as well as in this world. It is the basic concept underlying Paul's argument throughout the

5:1

letter."[1] In these verses, Paul is making a passionate appeal to the Christians of Galatia to recognize the freedom they have to live by God's grace.

The situation was critical! If the Galatian Christians would not respond to Paul's appeal to live in the freedom of God's grace, they would likely be lost to religious slavery. Paul seems to have regarded this letter as a last chance, "now or never" opportunity to explain the "either/or" choice between religious performance and God's grace received by faith. The dichotomy of the alternatives is clearly delineated — either Christ is all, or Christ is nothing! T. L. Johnson remarks that "this is one of the most strident passages in the entire letter, echoing the either/or language of Paul's opening blast in 1:6-9."[2]

So keen is Paul that the Galatians should see the importance of the decision they needed to make and the action they needed to take, that his rhetoric becomes heated and vehement. His statements are short, choppy and pointed, like the thrusts of a sword (especially in verses 7 through 12). These words were uttered in the heat of passion as Paul engaged in a last-ditch effort to convince the Galatians to reject the Judaizers.

5:1 This verse serves as the concluding summary to Paul's contrast between the slavery of the bondwoman, Hagar, and the freedom of the free woman, Sarah (4:21-31), as well as the climactic call to action that culminates from all that Paul has previously written in the letter. At the same time it is the transition to the practical implications of the Christian life (chapters 5 and 6), and more specifically to the appeal to freedom in 5:1-12. This could be called the key thematic verse of the entire epistle.

Picking up the theme he had alluded to earlier when he referred to "our liberty which we have in Christ Jesus" (2:4), Paul now affirms that, *"It was for freedom that Christ set us free."* He will follow this theme throughout the paragraph to his assertion that "you were called for freedom, brethren"

(5:13). Freedom can be a very abstract concept, but Paul is referring to the specific Christian freedom gained for us by the action and performance of Christ, the Liberator, when by His death and resurrection He "set us free" from sin, death, law, etc., in order to be free to function as God intended. Notice that freedom entails both a freedom *from,* as well as a freedom *unto.* By the death of Jesus Christ the Christian is set free *from* all self-effort of performance and productivity to please God, since Christ in His "finished work" on the cross performed everything necessary to take the death consequences of man's sin. By His resurrection to life out of death, Jesus made available in Himself everything necessary to enjoy the freedom *unto* the functional humanity that lives by the grace-dynamic of the Christ-life. Paul wanted the Galatians to recognize that they were free *from* the legalistic and moralistic expectations of behavioral conformity that were being foisted upon them by the Judaizers, and free *to* manifest the character of God by the grace of God unto the glory of God.

Religion often views freedom predominantly as freedom *from* governmental restriction or the consequences of sin in a sulfuric hell. Like the Jewish leaders surrounding Jesus, they seldom recognize that "if the Son shall make you free, you shall be free indeed" (Jn. 8:32,36). By the dynamic of the life of the risen Lord Jesus, Christians function by the "perfect law of liberty" (James 1:25), for "where the Spirit of the Lord is, there is liberty" (II Cor. 3:17). Christian freedom is the freedom *to* be man as God intended man to be; the freedom *to* love and serve others (5:13,14,22).

Based on the freedom gained for us by Christ and inherent in Christ alone, Paul admonishes the Galatian Christians to **"keep standing firm and do not be subject again to a yoke of slavery."** What Christ did, and Who Christ is, is too valuable to be exchanged for the burdens of religious performance. With an imperative command, Paul calls on the Galatians to act on and by the reality of Christ's action. "Continue to stand firm in the grace-dynamic of His Life. Do not capitulate to the religious legalism of the Judaizers." There comes a time when resolute action is required (cf. 2:5,11,14; 4:30), a time to tenaciously defend the freedom we have in Christ, firm in our resolve to live by His grace. This does not imply that we should take violent offensive means of conflict, but that we "stand firm" in the Lord (Phil. 4:1; I Thess. 3:8), in the faithful receptivity of His activity (I Cor. 16:13), and against all diabolic schemes (Eph. 6:11,13,14). Christians are not called to fight, but to "stand firm."

Christians should not allow themselves to be rounded up in the corral of religion, as the Judaizers were attempting to do to the Galatians. Paul commands the Galatians to avoid being confined, loaded down, and oppressed by the burdensome restrictions of performance regulations. He employs the metaphor of a yoke being placed upon a beast of burden in order to restrict its freedom and cause it to perform as desired. "Don't be a dumb ox, and let those religious slave-drivers put the religious yoke upon you in order to drive you to perform according to their expectations," Paul seems to say. That, indeed, is a binding slavery. It is interesting that the same metaphor was used when Paul went to Jerusalem soon after writing this letter. There it was Peter who asked the gathering of predominantly Jewish-Christian conferees (many of whom were demanding circumcision and Law-observance - Acts 15:5), why they insisted upon "placing upon the neck of the disciples a yoke which neither our fathers nor we have been able to bear?" (Acts 15:10,11). It was determined that these should not be restrictive requirements placed upon Gentile believers, but that did not seem to stop the Judaizing traditionalists from dogging Paul's steps wherever he went, intent on implementing their agenda to impose Jewish traditions on Gentile Christians. There is, indeed, a sense in which Christians are yoked to Jesus Christ, for freedom must always have a context, but our connection with Christ is not oppressive or burdensome, as He provides the all-sufficient dynamic of His life. "Take My yoke upon you, and you shall find rest for your souls, for My yoke is easy, and My load is light" (Matt. 11:29,30).

5:2 Going directly to the specific issue at hand, Paul declares, *"Behold I, Paul, say to you that if you receive circumcision, Christ will be of no benefit to you."* "Look," Paul says, "open your eyes, listen up, and take note of this important point." Directly and emphatically, he appeals to them as an apostle (1:1), as a spiritual parent (4:19), and as a brother in Christ (3:15; 4:31; 5:11) – "I, Paul, say to you." Thereupon he attacks what was a major tenet of the Judaizers' platform, the demand for the circumcision of all male believers in order to have the identifying physical mark of God's covenant people, and merit God's pleasure. It was the same attitude as displayed by those who came from Judea to Antioch at about the same time as Paul was writing this letter to the Galatians, proclaiming, "Unless you are circumcised according to the custom of Moses, you cannot be saved" (Acts 15:1). The Judaizers in Galatia were apparently advocating the circumcision of male Gentile believers in order to identify with the Jewish heritage as the people of God. It became the foremost and ultimate physical action, symptomatic of the entire Judaizing platform of external performance.

Male circumcision was inaugurated as a physical sign of God's covenant agreement with Abraham. God declared, "You shall be circumcised in the flesh of your foreskin; and it shall be the sign of the covenant between Me and you. An uncircumcised male shall be cut off from His people" (Gen. 17:11,14). The Judaizers wanted to bring Gentile Christians back to identification with Abraham, but what they failed to understand was that physical circumcision (like so many activities in the old covenant) was merely a pre-figuring of that which God would do in Jesus Christ to fulfill His promises to Abraham. It was repeatedly emphasized that what God really desired was to cut

5:2

away the sin from man's heart (Deut. 10:16; 30:6; Jere. 4:4), and the prophet Jeremiah explained that one could be circumcised physically and yet be uncircumcised of heart, charging all the house of Israel with such (Jere. 9:25,26). The fulfillment of the Old Testament circumcision picture was effected when Jesus Christ made it possible for sin to be cut away from man's heart by the acceptance of His death and resurrection-life. Paul explains that "in Christ you were circumcised with a circumcision made without hands, in the removal of the body of the flesh by the circumcision of Christ" (Col. 2:11), a "circumcision that is of the heart, by the Spirit" (Rom. 2:29), constituting Christians as "the true circumcision, who worship in the Spirit of God" (Phil. 3:3). The identifying mark of the Christian is not a physical circumscribed seal, but the seal of the Spirit of Christ (II Cor. 1:22; Eph. 4:30).

The Judaizers of Paul's day were so preoccupied with physical circumcision that they were identified as "the party of the circumcision" (2:12). For many Jewish people of the first century, it was not so much a concern for being identified with God's covenant people receptive to God's promises, as it was a mark of superior distinction from the Gentiles, marking racial superiority, nationalistic privilege, religious exclusivism, and ideological imperialism. The Judaizers were willing to admit that God would include Gentiles, but not unless the males engaged in the performance of receiving this physical mark as an essential element of righteousness before God. This was the premise that Paul would not tolerate, for the gospel that he received and preached was that all righteousness came through Jesus Christ alone, by the performance of Christ's "finished work" alone.

That Paul couches his comment in the hypothetical structure, "if you receive circumcision," seems to suggest that he had reason to believe that some of the male Christians in Galatia had not yet submitted to the demands of the Judaizers, and he was hoping that what he was writing could forestall such.

Again, it was not the physical action of receiving circumcision that was the issue, for Paul will indicate that "circumcision or uncircumcision mean nothing" (5:6), but when such is received with the belief that it is a spiritual act that has significance before God, meritoriously supplementing or enhancing one's relationship with God, or making one more "spiritual," then one indicates that the work of Christ is insufficient in itself, requiring performance supplementation. If a male receives circumcision on the grounds of health, hygiene or cultural conformity such is irrelevant to Paul, but if it is regarded as having spiritual benefit before God, then Paul draws the "either/or" dichotomy: either Jesus Christ is of sole spiritual benefit before God, or circumcision (or any other action) is of some benefit before God, in which case "Christ will be of no benefit."

Essential to the understanding of the Christian gospel is the realization that the Person and work of Jesus Christ, His Being and His doing, are singularly and entirely efficacious for the redemption, regeneration, salvation, righteousness, and sanctification of mankind. Christ will be no part of an equation that adds circumcision or anything else to His Person and work. Christianity is Christ! Christ plus circumcision amounts to nothing of any spiritual significance before God. There can be no amalgamation, admixture or assimilation; no combination, merging or supplementation. To add anything to Christ's Being and activity does not merely lessen or diminish His benefit; it eliminates, negates, nullifies and voids the singular benefit of Christ. Any addition logically implies that Christ's sacrifice and saving life are inadequate, insufficient, incomplete and unfinished. Paul does not indicate that consent to the benefit of circumcision means that one will retain His redemptive and regenerative benefits, but will lack the experiential sanctifying benefits of His saving life. He categorically explains that Christ will be of no benefit whatsoever. Why? Because Jesus Christ is not a benefactor who distributes certain spiritual benefits! The benefit, worth and value of Jesus Christ is solely in His own

Being. There can be no benefit of Jesus Christ apart from His Being expressed in His action. There is no profit in Christ apart from His personal presence and dynamic performance. There is no value of Christ apart from the viability of the vitality and visible expression of His own life. The Being and presence of Christ cannot be detached from His benefits. To attribute spiritual reality and value to anything other than Jesus Christ and His activity alone is to deny Christianity. Christianity is either Jesus Christ singularly and completely, or not at all. Using the economic terminology of "benefit, value, worth or profit," Paul presents the either/or equation: circumcision or Christ, which will you "bank on?" If you put stock in circumcision (or any other act of performance), then the "finished work" of Christ is not finished; He did not really set us free (5:1) from performance; and He died needlessly (2:21). In that case, who Christ is and what Christ did is worthless, useless, and of no benefit or value.

5:3 Paul proceeds to reiterate his thesis by showing the reverse, flip-side of his argument. ***"I testify again to every man who receives circumcision, that he is under obligation to keep the whole Law."*** Drawing on the legal terminology of his background as a Jewish lawyer, Paul indicates that he "testifies, witnesses, and is willing to lay down his life" (cf. Acts 20:26; 26:22) to explain the serious gravity of the action that the Galatian Christians are considering. He repeats "again" that anyone who receives circumcision, thinking that such external performance has any spiritual benefit in the sight of God, will of necessity place himself in the debtor's prison condemned to the hard labor of the legal system of performance. Although it is not usually evident in English translation, the word for "benefit" in verse 2 and the word for "obligation" in verse 3 are derived from the same Greek root word having economic implications. If they "receive circumcision" as advocated by the Judaizers, Christ will accrue no value to them, but they will instead accrue the indebtedness of an impossible and futile obligation of subservience and slavery to the performance-system of the Law.

Romans 2:25 must be considered at this point, because it uses the same Greek economic word in conjunction with circumcision: "Circumcision is of value, if you practice the Law; but if you are a transgressor of the Law, your circumcision has become uncircumcision." Writing to those of Jewish background in Rome, Paul explains that if the operative system of righteousness before God were meritorious external action of keeping the Law, then the performance of receiving physical circumcision would "count, accrue, have benefit or value" for some advantage before God. But since no man can self-generatively enact or perform the character of God, therefore all men are transgressors of the Law, violating the character of God in sin. Thus the physical circumcision of Jewish peoples done in the context of the self-effort of Law performance is revealed to be but another example of the sinful, uncircumcision of the heart, revealing all men to be sinners before God.

The Romans statement is entirely consistent with what Paul is writing to the Galatians. Paul is not saying that if you choose to live by the Law, you are obliged to keep every detail of the Law. That has already been established as impossible (3:10,11; cf. James 2:10). What Paul is saying to the Galatian Christians is that the reception of circumcision constitutes one's "buying into" the "whole," complete package of an all-encompassing nomistic orientation of self-actuated performance that replaces Jesus Christ, repudiates freedom, and relegates one to the enslaving obligation and condemnation of the Law, without any hope of righteousness (2:16).

5:4   To further amplify his point, Paul continues, *"You who are seeking to be justified by Law, you have been severed from Christ."* The collective group of people in Galatia who sought to become more righteous by engaging in the system of legal performance standards, as advocated by the Judaizers, needed to be aware of the severe consequences of such a choice. Paul had previously pointed out that no one is justified or made righteous by the works of the Law (2:16; 3:11; cf. Rom. 3:20). Here he restates the premise of verse 2 more inclusively by referring to any attempt to be righteous by legal performance (which includes circumcision), and explains the consequences more severely. He wants to make it clear that any attempt to add human works of performance to the reality of the Person and work of Jesus Christ is a complete repudiation of the "finished work" of Jesus Christ. Law performance is not an enhancement of the Christian life, but an estrangement from Christ.

Some might attempt to infer from verse 2 that legalistic acts of performance simply diminish the experiential benefits of the Christian life. This verse denies that possibility by explaining that any works of self-effort regarded as meritoriously righteous before God, create an alienated separation from Christ Himself. Again, this is based on the impossibility of detaching the presence of the Being of Jesus Christ from His "finished work" and the grace-dynamic of His functional work. Any attempt to detract from His all-sufficient function in our Christian lives, is to detach from His Being, from whence comes His function. The Being and the doing of Jesus Christ, His presence and His function, are inseparably united in the ontological dynamic of His life. He offers no benefits, blessings, gifts, or spiritual commodities apart from Himself. He is our righteousness (I Cor. 1:30), or there is no righteousness, and He is not present.

And yet, the preponderance of interpretive comment on this statement of Paul seeks to lessen the severity of its impact in order to preserve static presuppositions of permanence. Over and over again the commentators indicate that the Christian seeking to be made righteous by works is merely severed, estranged or alienated from the sphere of Christ's sanctifying activity, voiding and nullifying what Christ wants to do experientially and behaviorally in their life. Paul's statement is clear – the person who is "banking on" righteousness by works is severed and separated from the Being of Christ, from whence comes all His function.

Additional clarification is gained from Paul's further explanation of the consequences of such a choice of alleged works-righteousness: *"You have fallen from grace."* Severed from His Being, such an apostatizing person falls outside of the dynamic of Christ's activity. Christianity – the Christian life – is derived solely from God's grace activity in Christ, or not at all! Later in his epistle to the Romans, Paul would use the same Greek word for "falling out" of relationship with God, noting that the people of old covenant Israel experienced God's severity when they refused to stand firm in faith and were cut off.

Grace is the singularity of God's action in Jesus Christ (Jn. 1:17). It is the dynamic expression of divine activity which is singularly served in the "only begotten Son" (Jn. 3:16,18), Jesus Christ. Grace is not a static condition of redemptive efficacy, or just a threshold function of regenerative sufficiency. Grace is everything God does in and through Jesus Christ. When any man thinks that his own actions can make him righteous, then he is refusing God's grace-activity in Christ.

The dynamic efficacy of God's grace in Jesus Christ must not be statically boxed in epistemological formulations of fixed states of being. Traditional religious expressions of "once in grace, always in grace," or "once saved, always saved," misunderstand the dynamic nature of God's salvific grace in Christ, and lead to meaningless theological arguments about "eternal salvation" and "eternal security," as well as diminishing the consequences of misrepresentative behavior in the Christian. They fail (or refuse) to take into account the severity of the consequences of severance from Christ and His grace-activity that Paul explicitly explains in this verse.

5:5 In contrast to the Judaizers and those subscribing to their attempts to be made righteous by legalistic performance of the Law, Paul inclusively declares that *"we through the Spirit, by faith, are waiting for the hope of righteousness."* "We," genuine Christians who are receptive to God's grace in Christ for all function in the Christian life, are receptive in faith to the grace activity of God by His Holy Spirit. Having received the indwelling Spirit of Christ (3:2), Christians have the dynamic provision of the power of the Spirit (3:5), in order to walk by the Spirit (5:16) and manifest the "fruit of the Spirit" (5:22). By faith we are receptive to God's activity through His Spirit, anticipating and looking forward with confident expectation to the expression of Christ's righteous character in our Christian behavior. Having "Christ in us, the hope of glory" (Col. 1:27), we have the anticipatory expectation that the Righteous One (Acts 3:14; 7:52; I Jn. 2:1), Jesus Christ will express His righteous character in our behavior to the glory of God. The anticipated expectation of righteousness should not be objectified into merely or primarily a futuristic hope of arriving at an heavenly state of perfect righteousness with God. Right now, in the present, the Christian can expect that the indwelling Being of the Righteous One, Jesus Christ, will actively express His righteous character in our behavior by His grace. Of course, if we fail to "fix our eyes on Jesus" (Heb. 12:2) in order to derive all from Him by faith, and instead focus introspectively on our fleshliness with a sin-consciousness that masochistically attempts to suppress such or "die to self," then we are not expectantly anticipating the expression of Christ's righteous character in our behavior, but have reverted back to performance evaluation and expectation.

5:6 Since the expectant hope of all righteousness is from Jesus Christ alone, received by faith, then *"for those in Christ Jesus neither circumcision nor uncircumcision means anything, but faith working through love."* For those who are

Christians, "in Christ Jesus" (3:28), having received His Spirit in spiritual union with their spirit (Rom. 8:9; I Cor. 6:17), and abiding (Jn. 15:4-7) in the dynamic activity of Christ as "Christ-ones," the physical actions, the external rites and ritualistic performances have no meritorious significance. The Christian life is not the behavioral performance of "doing this" or "not doing that," whether eating or drinking (Rom. 14:17; I Cor. 8:8) or circumcision. What one does to the male penis is spiritually irrelevant, having no validity or force referent to righteousness. As noted above, this verse can serve as an antidote to an overly broad interpretation of verse 2 which might imply that anyone having received circumcision cannot be a Christian. The physical criteria of circumcision or uncircumcision are irrelevant when it comes to spiritual righteousness. As Paul will write later in this epistle, "Neither is circumcision anything, nor uncircumcision, but a new creation" (6:15) in Christ Jesus (cf. II Cor. 5:17). And when one becomes a "new man" in Christ, there is "no distinction between circumcised or uncircumcised, but Christ is all, and in all" (Col. 3:11).

What does have validity and meaning for righteousness in the Christian is not the physical criteria, but the spiritual criteria of "faith working through love." Faith is not just consent or assent to propositional statements of a belief-system, but is the receptivity of God's activity in Jesus Christ to dynamically energize His righteous character in loving Christian behavior. When the Christian is available by faith to allow God to "work according to His good pleasure" (Phil. 2:13), working according to the power of His Spirit within us (Eph. 3:20), God then willingly works out His character of righteousness and love. Without such outworking of His character, it cannot be legitimately maintained that there is any presence of Christ or faith (cf. James 2:17,18,26). "God is love" (I Jn. 4:8,16), and this other-oriented feature of His character is "poured out within our hearts by the Holy Spirit He has given to us" (Rom. 5:5), but the absence of such evidences that we do not know God

(I Jn. 4:8). The importance of this loving expression of God's righteous character will be further amplified later in this letter, when Paul writes of "serving one another in love" (5:13,14) by the "fruit of the Spirit" (5:22,23).

5:7 Paul now commences an impassioned appeal (7-12) to the Galatian Christians that is somewhat disjointed, and even coarse, due to the intensity of his passion for righteousness in Christ. *"You were running well,"* Paul writes, employing an athletic metaphor that he was fond of using (2:2; I Cor. 9:26; Phil. 3:14; II Tim. 4:7). After Paul had left the region of Galatia, he had apparently received reports that the Christians there were progressing and maturing in the process of allowing the Christ-life to be lived out through them by God's grace, without thinking that their self-effort of performance had any benefit before God. Paul's knowledge of their progress does not necessarily imply that he had returned to Galatia to observe such.

"What happened to your progress?" *"Who hindered you from obeying the truth?"* This rhetorical question (cf. 3:1) was not a search for the specific identity (names and addresses) of those who were interfering and preventing the progress of the Galatian Christians, but was likely an exposure of the diabolic hinderer behind all such religious diversion. Paul knew the general identity of the Judaizers who had infiltrated the Galatian churches, and there may have been one in particular who was the ringleader of the false-teachers, but the singular "who" can also refer to the spiritual adversary who "thwarts" the actions of Christians (I Thess 2:18), and "disguises himself in the false, religious agents who present themselves as servants of righteousness" (II Cor. 11:13-15).

The Galatians were "running well," progressing in the grace-expression of Christ, but someone "cut in" on them and tripped them up by persuading them against simple obedience to the Lordship of Jesus Christ. "Truth" is not merely propositional data, but is personified in Jesus Christ, who is the Truth (Jn. 14:6) that sets us free (Jn. 8:32,36) to function as God intends. The "truth of the gospel" (2:5,14) is Christ, but the Galatians were obstructed by someone persuading them against the single reality of allowing the Spirit of Christ to live out His life in them.

5:8 Religious legalists can be very persuasive as they use their "persuasive words of wisdom" (I Cor. 2:4), but Paul notes that *"This persuasion did not come from Him who calls you."* "God called you by the grace of Christ" (1:6), Paul said earlier, and now you have been persuaded to desert Him. God is constantly "calling" us by the impulse of His Spirit to be receptive to His activity in and through us, and to participate in the freedom that is ours in Jesus Christ (5:13). Whatever He calls us to, "He also will bring to pass" (I Thess. 5:24), for His calling is an effectual calling that provides His divine dynamic to "perfect, confirm, strengthen and establish us" (I Pet. 5:10). But if we resist this grace provision of God in Christ, then the antithetical persuasion of diabolic hindrance will attempt to counter God's work in the Christian. We either derive the character of our behavior from God (*ek theos*), or we derive character from Satan (*ek diabolos*). "Whatever is not of faith, is sin" (Rom. 14:23).

5:9 Employing another metaphor that was probably in the form of a proverbial saying, Paul warns the Galatian Christians about tolerating the Judaizing intruders, by saying, *"A little leaven leavens the whole lump of dough."* The persuasive action of the infiltrating false-teachers is likened to the pervasive, penetrating and permeating action of leaven. The fermentative process of leaven working in the dough was often identified with the contaminative and corruptive process of evil. The tiniest portion of leaven begins the process that will eventually permeate the entire lump, and in like manner the slightest form of perversion advocating legalistic performance or preferential priority can corrupt the presentation of the gospel of grace in Jesus Christ. Christians must be spiritually discerning about the subtle and pervasive influences that deny or fail to present the singularity of God's grace in Jesus Christ for everything in the Christian life. Sometimes in our quest to be tolerant, non-judgmental and non-discriminatory, we become undiscriminating in an epidemic of tolerance that fails to detect the insidious humanistic and diabolic premises that are contrary to God's grace, allowing the church to be infected with relativistic pluralism that denies the singularity of Christ with disastrous consequences. Paul's objective in using this proverbial metaphor was obviously to encourage the Christians of Galatia to take action to terminate the persuasive and pervasive influence of the Judaizers. In his letter to the Corinthians, Paul also used the same proverb to address the infectious situation of an incestuous relationship that was being tolerated in the local church. He wrote: "Do you not know that a little leaven leavens the whole lump? Clean out the old leaven, that you may be a new lump" (I Cor. 5:6,7). Likewise, Paul was advocating that the Galatians "clean out" the leavening influence of the Judaizers, just as he had indirectly advised them to "cast out the bondwoman" (4:30). In contemporary terms we might use a correlative statement such as, "A little cancer can kill the whole body," evidencing the necessity of taking action to excise the contaminative and corruptive influence of the cancerous cells.

5:10 Paul was still optimistic that such action could be effective in the churches of Galatia. ***"I have confidence in you in the Lord, that you will adopt no other view."*** Paul is persuaded that the Galatian Christians are genuinely "in the Lord," and "confident that He who began a good work in them would perfect it until the day of Christ Jesus" (Phil. 1:6). Thus persuaded of the preserving work of Christ in their lives, Paul was confident that God's grace would cause the Galatians to be spiritually discerning (cf. Phil. 3:15) and allow the Lord to "direct their hearts" (II Thess. 3:4,5), so that they would form opinions and "set their minds" (Col. 3:2), not on the false premises of the Judaizers, but on the singular gospel of grace and liberty in Jesus Christ. Adopting such thinking would allow them to "stand firm in their Christian freedom" (5:1), and take the action necessary to expel the Judaizing agitators.

Paul was also persuaded and convinced that *"the one who is disturbing you shall bear his judgment, whoever he is."* Paul's use of a singular subject, "the one," could refer to the collective whole of the Judaizing contingent that had invaded the churches of Galatia, for he had previously referred to a plurality of disturbing persons (1:7), and would do so again in three sentences when he wrote of "those who are troubling you" (5:12). On the other hand, as noted in verse 7, there may have been a singular ringleader among the false-teachers who was more prominent that the others. Regardless, whether individually or collectively as one, Paul was convinced that anyone who would distort the gospel (1:7) of Christ would have to face the condemnatory judgment of God's divine retribution of damnation (cf. 1:8,9). In that "those who believe in Christ are not judged" (Jn. 3:18), Paul must not have considered these false teachers to be Christians, having previously referred to their kind as "false brethren" (2:4). In Paul's mind such a cursed destiny awaited anyone, "whoever he is," without exception, who would purposefully pervert the gospel of the singular sufficiency of Jesus Christ and the living out of His life by the grace of God.

5:11 This statement of Paul may seem somewhat disconnected and interjected as a *non sequitur* of personal complaint, but in the intensity of his concern Paul may have failed to carry through his thoughts in careful logical transitions. Even so, the theme of circumcision (5:2,3,6), being the culminating act of accepting and identifying with the legalistic system of the Judaizers in contrariety to the gospel of grace, was the issue that Paul was addressing as antithetical to Christian freedom, and the flashpoint that had him so incensed with righteous indignation.

"But I, brethren, if I still preach circumcision, why am I still persecuted?" Apparently the claim had been made by the Judaizers that Paul still advocated the rite of circumcision as he necessarily had when he was involved in the Jewish religion. Perhaps they were attempting to imply that Paul, based on his Jewish heritage, was sympathetic with their emphasis on male circumcision, and that because of his brief ministry in Galatia he neglected to explain the importance of such. Then again, they may have charged that Paul "still preached circumcision," but did so inconsistently by advocating such for Jews but not for Gentiles, similar to the later occasion when one of the Galatian young men, Timothy, was circumcised as a cultural and religious accommodation of sociological convenience and expedience (Acts 16:3). These were false and illogical claims made by the Judaizers. The gospel that Paul preached (2:2) was Christ (I Cor. 1:23) alone, and did not include circumcision, for it was even reported that he told the Jews "not to circumcise their children, nor to walk according to the customs of the Law of Moses" (Acts 21:21). Paul reasons with an "if...then" logical syllogism: "If I still preach circumcision (which is not the case), then why (it would be completely illogical) do I continue to be persecuted by the Jewish religionists for the very reason that I have repudiated their legalistic customs (including circumcision), and by the Judaizing faction of "the party of the circumcision" (2:12) because I refuse to allow circumcision as a supplement to the grace of God in Jesus Christ?" Such an argument is contrary to reason, Paul maintains. The Judaizing faction was a persecutive group, Paul had already implied (4:29), but they themselves avoided persecution at the hands of the Jewish religionists by advocating circumcision (6:12).

Paul continues with another "if...then" syllogism that takes his argument to the core of the redemptive and restorative message of the gospel. "If (as is not the case) I still preach the necessity of circumcision, ***then*** (as a logical consequence) ***the stumbling-block of the cross has been abolished."*** Paul's preaching of "Christ crucified" was a scandalous stumbling-block to the Jewish peoples (I Cor. 1:23; Isa. 8:14;28:16; cf. Rom. 9:33; I Pet. 2:8), not only because they could not conceive of a crucified Messiah in place of their expected triumphant, nationalistic deliverer, but even more so because the crucifixion of Christ on the cross was proclaimed by Christians to be the singular basis of redemption and the "power of God" (I Cor. 1:18) for salvation unto righteousness. As such it was the abrogation of the old covenant Law as having any benefit of righteousness (2:16,21; 3:11), for the "new covenant in His blood (His death)" (Lk. 22:20; I Cor. 11:25), allowed the Law of God to be dynamically enacted in men's hearts by the indwelling presence of the life of Christ Himself. When Jesus declared "It is finished!" (Jn. 19:30) from the cross, He was proclaiming that He was doing and would do everything that needed to be done before God. As the representative Man, He accomplished and completed all the performance required on behalf of all men. There is nothing more man can do, apart from simply receiving God's grace in Christ by faith. There is absolutely no basis for any pride of performance-righteousness before God, as religious legalists inevitably advocate. Therefore, the "finished work" of Jesus Christ, set in motion at His death, is the scandalous stumbling-block for all Jews, Judaizers and religionists. The performance of circumcision or any other deed has no benefit before God. So Paul's argument is, "If (as is not the case) I preach the necessity of the performance of circumcision, then the stumbling-block of the cross (which is the declaration that there is no performance that man can do that has any benefit before God) would be voided, nullified, wiped out, and abolished." Impossible! Unthinkable! If so, "Christ died needlessly" (2:21), in an unfortunate, meaningless martyrdom.

5:12   The thought of the cross being a meaningless event of history, which is where the Judaizers' teaching logically leads, is so abhorrent to Paul that he reacts with a very human mutilation-wish for his Judaizing detractors. *"Would that those who are troubling you would even mutilate themselves."* Paul would be the first to admit that he was not perfect (Phil. 3:12), and this was not the most loving solution that Paul could have wished for his enemies (cf. Matt. 5:44; Lk. 6:35). But Paul was so appalled by the thought that Christ's work was all in vain, the logical conclusion of the Judaizers' teaching, that he reverts to the sarcastic irony of hyperbolic overstatement. He had no use for these religious bloodhounds, whom he elsewhere describes as "dogs, and evil workers of the false circumcision" (Phil. 3:2).

"Those Judaizers who are stirring you Galatian Christians up with their unsettling and destabilizing advocacy of circumcision; I could wish that those knife-happy proponents of cutting off male foreskins would just go all the way and cut off their entire organ; that the knife would slip and they would emasculate themselves in a total castration." Now, admittedly, there have been some translations and commentaries that have attempted to interpret these words in a figurative manner in order to avoid such a "delicate" sexual subject, suggesting that Paul simply wanted the Judaizers to "cut it out," to cease and desist from their advocacy of circumcision. Not likely! There is little doubt that Paul was suggesting a physical "cutting off" (cf. Mk. 9:43,45; Jn. 18:10,26) of the Judaizers' genitalia.

Some correlative cultural background information might be pertinent to Paul's thinking. In Jewish thought, it was clearly stated that "no one who is emasculated, or has his male organ cut off, shall enter the assembly of the Lord" (Deut. 23:1). It has been suggested that Paul was thinking that if the Judaizers were "cut off" genitally, they would be "cut off" from God's people, self-emasculated and self-excommunicated, and thus so totally discredited that they could no longer trouble Christian people with their false-teaching. Speculation, at best! Another observation notes that in the religion of the Greek goddess, Cybele, which was practiced in the Galatian region, the pagan priests ceremoniously emasculated themselves by self-castration, allegedly as an act of self-defeating devotion. Some have suggested that Paul was indicating that if the Judaizers wanted to really be religious, they should go all the way and make the "radical cut" like the priests of Cybele. Not very convincing!

As might be expected, Paul has been charged with being coarse, crude and vulgar for making the very earthy comment in this verse. Many have questioned whether he was being vindictive, vengeful, malicious, cruel and unloving. But we must not forget that Paul was passionately determined to defend the integrity, purity and singularity of the gospel of Jesus Christ against those who were equally determined to desecrate and destroy that gospel by their performance supplements. In a similar manner, Jesus Himself said that "whoever causes one of these little ones who believe in Me to stumble, it is better for him that a heavy millstone be hung around his neck, and that he be drowned in the depth of the sea" (Matt. 18:6; Mk. 9:42; Lk. 17:1,2).

Paul was so desirous that the Christians of Galatia should understand that they "were called to freedom" (5:13), that it was for Christian freedom that Christ endured everything, including death on a cross, to "set us free" (5:1), he was willing to defend that freedom by any means to encourage them to "keep standing firm" (5:1) in Christ alone. He is very forceful in drawing the "either/or," "all or nothing" alternatives of the singularity of Jesus Christ. There comes a time when if we are unwilling to draw the line between truth and error, between the freedom of grace in Jesus Christ and the bondage of religious performance, then there will be no lines of demarcation, and anything goes in the religion of relativistic pluralism in which man's reason and self-effort reign supreme, deified as the gods of humanism.

The "stumbling-block of the cross" (5:11), the thesis that man cannot do what is necessary before God, is indeed scandalous today in light of the prevailing humanistic theses of human potential and self-help. Christian religion adapts itself into evangelical humanism when it advocates that performance of any kind – moralistic behavior, keeping the Ten Commandments, commitment, dedication, ecclesiastical programs, etc. – have any efficacy in the sight of God. Then, as Paul says so clearly, "the stumbling block of the cross has been abolished" (5:11); and God forbid, "Christ died needlessly" (2:21).

When Christians attempt to add anything to the "finished work" of Jesus Christ and the dynamic of Christ's life functioning in their lives by the grace of God, then they ever so subtly negate the benefit of Christ. In Paul's day, in Galatia, the addition-issue was circumcision and the observance of the Mosaic Law. Today, the supplemental issues are different, of course. If we were to take Paul's statement in verse 2, "If you receive circumcision, Christ will be of no benefit to you," and rewrite the statement by inserting contemporary performance-issues, we might be able to see more clearly how this presently applies. "If you insist that a Christian believer believe in a particular form of baptism, ...speaking in tongues, ...a doctrine of "once saved, always saved," ...a particular millennial theory, ...two conflicting inner natures, etc., then Christ will be of no benefit to you." "If you insist that a Christian refrain from drinking alcohol, smoking tobacco, wearing certain clothing, going to movies, dancing, etc., then Christ will be of no benefit to you." "If you insist that a Christian be a contributing member of a particular kind of institutional church, attending three times a week, participating in the programs, tithing a certain percentage of their income, and you regard such as essential to Christian salvation, fellowship, or righteousness, then Christ will be of no benefit to you." This little exercise begins to expose some of our religious tendencies to add performances to the singular efficacy of God's grace in Jesus Christ.

Paul simply wanted Christians to "stand firm in freedom" by deriving all from Jesus Christ alone, apart from any supplemental additions of human performance. The "finished work" of Jesus Christ is the singular sufficiency of the Christian life, as God's grace-dynamic energizes His righteous character received by faith. There is absolutely nothing that can be added to Jesus Christ by man's performance in order to effect Christian living. To supplement is to supplant.

ENDNOTES

1   Betz, Hans Dieter, *Galatians. Hermeneia – A Critical and Historical Commentary on the Bible*. Philadelphia: Fortress Press. 1979. pg. 255.
2   George, Timothy, *The New American Commentary, Vol. 30, Galatians*. Broadman and Holman Publishers. 1994. pg. 355.

Freedom to Love By the Spirit

Galatians 5:13-26

Emphasis on freedom is always susceptible to being misunderstood and pushed beyond its contextual limitations. Having asserted "the liberty which we have in Christ Jesus" (2:4), identified Christians with Sarah, the "free woman" (4:22,23,30,31), and declared that "it was for freedom that Christ set us free" (5:1), Paul perceptively cautions the Galatian Christians about the misuse of liberty. As we attempt to reconstruct the situation in the Galatian churches by reading between the lines of Paul's correspondence, it may be that Paul was not only advising the Galatians with a precaution of the propensity of men to push freedom to an extreme, but also reacting to reports that behavior among the Christians of Galatia had dissipated into misrepresentative and unloving expressions. This does not necessarily mean, however, (as some have suggested) that Paul is now countering a distinct group of antagonists who are antinomian, in contrast to the Judaizing legalists addressed previously in the letter.

As noted previously (cf. comments on 5:1), Christian freedom entails both a freedom *from* diabolic tyranny and legalistic slavery, as well as a freedom *to* function as God intends by the dynamic of God's grace. By the work of Christ the Christian is free *from* sin (Rom. 6:14), Law (2:19) and elemental powers (3:3,9); free *from* the legalistic and moralistic expectations of behavioral conformity to rules and regulations; and free *from* the self-effort of performance productivity of "works" to please or appease God. By His "finished work" (Jn. 19:30) on the cross, Jesus Christ "set us free" (5:1) and delivered us *from* misused humanity, and by His resurrection from the dead Jesus Christ has graced us with the directed freedom *to* receive the functional dynamic of His own life and character. Every Christian person has the volitional freedom *to* make the choices to be receptive to the expression of God's character (instead of being a "slave to sin" - cf. Jn. 8:34,35; Rom. 6:6), and the teleological freedom *to* be man as God intended by deriving and manifesting God's character in Christian behavior unto the glory of God.

It must be recognized, though, that freedom is never absolute freedom. Freedom is not freedom *from* all constraint or restraint, and freedom *to* do anything one wants to do. Man does not have the inherent capability and power to do so, and God in His omnipotence exercises His power only in the consistent context of His own character and the self-limitation He has imposed on Himself to respect man's choices. Freedom is always freedom in context; never an unlimited absolute. God's freedom is in the context of His own character and stated self-limitation, while man's freedom is in the context of his choices of spiritual derivation. Though the Christian person may be volitionally free *to* sin, within the context of his being indwelt by the Spirit of Christ he is not teleologically free *to* misrepresent the character of Christ in self-oriented, self-indulgent, self-assertive, sinful behavior that does not manifest the love of Christ, who is the basis of his identity as a "Christ-one," i.e. Christian. Such understanding is foundational to Paul's explanation of Christian freedom and his caution to avoid allowing freedom to be misused in unloving behavior.

Paul's keen logical mind recognized that his argument for freedom could be pushed beyond its intent; that his argument against nomistic legalism could be inordinately extended into an argument for antinomian libertinism. He recognized the same tendency when writing at a later date to the Romans:

"Shall we continue in sin that grace may increase? May it never be!" (Rom. 6:1). In denying the legalism that quenches liberty, the pendulum can swing to the opposite extreme of a license that misuses liberty. Neither extreme will produce loving behavior, so Paul finds it necessary to emphasize the contextualized liberty that we have under the Lordship of the living Lord Jesus to manifest His character of love in our interpersonal relationships – the freedom to love by the Spirit.

5:13 In contrast to the Judaizing agitators who were attempting to put the Galatians under a "yoke of slavery" (5:1), and upon whom Paul had just expressed his anatomical mutilation-wish (5:12) that would excise them from their devious deeds, Paul reminds the young Galatian Christians that *"you were called to freedom, brethren."* Still regarding them as Christian "brethren," in contrast to the "false brethren" (2:4) who advocated bondage to the Law, Paul reiterates (cf. 5:1) the freedom in Christ that God has called Christians to participate in. This was not just Paul's proclamatory calling for freedom, but God's calling to the freedom of sanctification (I Thess. 4:7), with the corollary provision of His effectual calling wherein, "Faithful is He who calls you; He will bring it to pass" (I Thess. 5:24). Paul wanted the Galatians to understand the behavioral implications of Christian freedom, wherein they were free to be functional humanity, free to be man as God intended, free to let Christ reign as Lord in their lives, and free to express the character of God in their behavior.

The precautionary check against abuse of such freedom is addressed by, *"only do not turn your freedom into an opportunity for the flesh."* Preemptively, Paul recognizes the tendency of man to selfishly push freedom into improper latitudes of laxity and license. Later Paul would tell the Corinthians to "take care lest this liberty of yours become a stumbling-block" (I Cor. 8:9). Peter would likewise write, "Do not use your freedom as a covering for evil" (I Pet. 2:16). The Greek word that

5:13

Paul used for "opportunity" (*aphormen*) implies that freedom can be misused as a "starting-point, a spring-board, a stimulus, an occasion" (cf. I Tim. 5:14) for the self-indulgence of the "flesh." Though "flesh" can be employed to refer to the physicality of "flesh and blood" (cf. 2:20) or the broad spectrum of created humanity (cf. 2:16), Paul seems to be using "flesh" here to refer to the patterned propensities of selfishness and sinfulness that remain within the desires of a Christian's soul (cf. Rom. 7:15-21). The Christian is not "in the flesh" (Rom. 8:9) as an enslaved state of behavioral orientation (cf. 5:24), but he can still walk "according to the flesh" (Rom. 8:12,13) by reverting to the self-orientation of self-effort (cf. 3:3), self-assertion, self-promotion, self-gratification, (cf. I Jn. 2:16), etc.

Such self-orientation and self-focus is antithetical to the ***"love by which we are to serve one another."*** Instead of being self-oriented, divine love is unselfish and other-oriented. "God is love" (I Jn. 4:8,16), and the freedom to express His character as Christians is the freedom to seek the highest good of others apart from selfish narcissistic concerns. The ultimate example of such was Jesus' love for us in giving Himself for us (cf. 2:20). By His spiritual indwelling in us as Christians we have the dynamic provision whereby we can be receptive in faith to His working through us in love (cf. 5:6). The presence of Christ within the Christian is not only for our own spiritual benefit, but also for His loving beneficence toward others. It is always Christ in us for others! That we are free *from* enslavement to the Law, and free *to* love by serving (enslaving ourselves to) others, is not a self-contradictory irony. Remember, the contextualization of Christian liberty is in our subordination and submission to the Lordship of Jesus Christ as He expresses His love toward others. Jesus' love was evidenced in His "taking the form of a bond-servant" (Phil. 2:7) willing to die for others (all men). In like manner, servanthood love is the evidence of Christian discipleship (Jn. 13:35). Writing later to the Corinthians, Paul explained, "Though I am free from all, I have made myself a slave to all, that I might win the more" (I Cor. 9:19). It is instructive to note Paul's "one another" phrases in the ensuing context (5:13, 15 twice, 26 twice; 6:2), for it reveals that our Christian freedom is not to be conceived only individualistically, but in the other-oriented dynamic of Christ's loving character expressed in the deference of interdependent loving fellowship among Christians, and in interpersonal relationships beyond the Christian fellowship.

5:14 *"For,"* to explain more fully, *"the whole Law is fulfilled in one word, in that, 'You shall love your neighbor as yourself.'"* While the Judaizers were advocating that the Galatian Christians should fulfill the Law by being "under the Law" (3:23; 4:4,5,21; 5:18) and "keeping the whole Law" (5:3) by performing the demands of the Law, such as circumcision and religious observances, Paul is indicating that the entire objective of the Law is fulfilled by God's grace exhibiting His character of love in Christian behavior. Jesus had explained in His Sermon on the Mount that He had not come to denigrate the Law, "but to fulfill the Law" (Matt. 5:17) in the dynamic of His own Being. Later, to a Pharisaic lawyer, Jesus explained that the greatest commandment is to "love the Lord, your God," and the second is to "love your neighbor as yourself," and "on these two commandments depend the whole Law and the Prophets" (Matt. 22:36-40). Jesus was not repudiating or rejecting the Mosaic Law. It had served its purpose in the old covenant, part of which was to proclaim the character of God. But the inscribed Law of Moses had no dynamic provision to empower the character of God. The empowering dynamic of God was made available only by the indwelling presence of the Spirit of the risen Lord Jesus in receptive Christians, whereby the "law of Christ" (6:2) completes and consummates the old covenant Law by fulfilling and bringing it to fruition in love. Jesus is indeed the "one word" (*logos* - cf. Jn. 1:14) in and by Whom the whole law, the "royal law" (James 2:8), the "perfect

5:14

law, the law of liberty" (James 1:25) is fulfilled as He expresses His divine love to others. To the Romans Paul therefore wrote that the commandments are "summed up in the saying, "You shall love your neighbor as yourself" (Rom. 13:9), and "love is the fulfillment of the Law" (Rom. 13:8,10). This is not merely a reductionism that implies that it is easier to be receptive to God's character by faith than to attempt to keep the commandments, but is an explanation of the dynamic consummation of the Law in the Person and work of Jesus Christ.

Paul's quotation of Leviticus 19:18, "You shall love your neighbor as yourself," is one of several quotations that establishes this phrase as the most cited verse of the Old Testament Pentateuch within the New Testament Scriptures (cf. Matt. 5:43; 19:19; 22:34-40; Mk. 7:31; 12:33; Lk. 10:27; Jn. 13:24; Rom. 13:9; Gal. 5:14; James 2:8). The Jewish lawyer asked Jesus, "Who is my neighbor?" (Lk. 10:29), and in the parable of the wounded traveler Jesus explained that one's neighbor is anyone we come in contact with who has a personal need, evidencing that this love is not some vague, ethereal sentiment or feeling for the well-being of others, but is a practical, down-to-earth expression of ministry to mankind. That we are to "love our neighbor *as ourselves*" recognizes that there is a natural concern for ourselves, an almost instinctual sense of self-preservation, but it is not necessarily an inculcation to "self-love" as advocated by contemporary pop-psychology for the development of self-esteem, self-worth, self-value, self-image, etc. Self-orientation, as previously indicated, is antithetical to the other-orientation of God's love in Christ. To love others "as ourselves" is to seek the best interests of others as instinctively, unhesitantly, and spontaneously as we are concerned about our own best interest, and that can only be accomplished as "the love of God is shed abroad in our hearts by the Holy Spirit whom He has given to us" (Rom. 5:5).

5:15 In contrariety to such expression of God's love, Paul advised the Galatians, *"But if you bite and devour one another, take care lest you be consumed by one another."* The conjunction "but" can indicate an existing condition, in which case it might be translated "since." Perhaps Paul had received word that the Galatian Christians, under the influence of the legalistic Judaizers, were becoming quarrelsome and contentious, engaging in selfish infighting and internecine conflicts. Neither legalism or license will ever produce unity and love since they derive their motivation from the same self-oriented and rejective root of satanic character.

The three words that Paul uses to describe this unloving behavior were all used in the Greek language to describe savage, animalistic behavior indicative of a pack of wild animals as they nip, rip and slaughter other animals. When a group of people engages in power-struggles that entail back-biting, cutting each other down, chewing each other up, and eating each other alive like a bunch of social cannibals, the sense of community is destroyed in the absence of love. "Watch out, beware" of such behavior, Paul warns the Galatians. He will subsequently describe the divisions, dissensions and factions that are "works of the flesh" (5:19-21), and are often indicative of religious communities which fail to understand the freedom to love by the Spirit.

5:16 *"But"* in contrast to such behaviors, *"I* (Paul) *say,"* as an apostle, and in contrast to the religious false-teachers, *"walk by the Spirit."* As in 4:1, Paul is introducing an important contrastual statement by his pronouncement, "But I say...". Consistent with his theme of the liberty of love under the Lordship of Christ, Paul encourages the Galatian Christians to recognize their responsibility ("walk" is an imperative verb) to conduct their lives under the controlling influence and empowering of the Spirit of Christ. Step by step as we walk through life, the Christian is to be "led by the Spirit" (5:18; Rom. 8:14), "keep in step with the Spirit" (5:25), and "be filled with the Spirit" (Eph. 5:18) as the operational and controlling impetus of the Christian life, whereby we manifest the character-fruit of the Spirit (5:22,23). Later, to the Colossians, Paul would write, "Walk in a manner worthy of the Lord, bearing fruit in every good work" (Col. 1:10). But we must ever be mindful that the generative strength for doing so is not human potential, natural talent, nor the procedural precepts of religious rules or moral mandates. The dynamic to function in the freedom of Christian love is "by the Spirit." The divine energizing and enabling of God's Spirit within the Christian's spirit (cf. Rom. 8:16) is the provision and resource of Christian behavior, rather than external constraint and conformity of law.

The consequence of choosing by faith to "walk by the Spirit," will be that *"you will not carry out the desire of the flesh."* The conjunctive "and" is consequential, while the duplicated negative in the Greek is an emphatic disavowal indicating that while "walking in the Spirit," one will most definitely and assuredly not, by any means, enact and accomplish "the desire of the flesh." The fleshly patterns and propensities to selfishness and sinfulness in the soul of a Christian will be thwarted from their objectification in being "acted out" in the manifestations of misrepresentative behavior whenever the Christian is faithfully and receptively "walking by the Spirit." The self-seeking "desire of the flesh" will be superseded by the other-oriented love of God's Spirit. The supremacy of the power of God's Spirit is intrinsic to Paul's argument, for he is convinced without a shadow of a doubt that the action of God in man will supersede, overcome, and swallow up the negative and selfish expressions of fleshliness. John would later concur by writing, "Greater is He who is in you, than he who is in the world" (I Jn. 4:4). The responsibility of the Christian is maintained in the recognition that a choice not to be receptive in faith to "walk by the Spirit," will inevitably involve bringing to fruition the self-seeking desire of the flesh. "Whatever is not of faith, is sin" (Rom. 14:23).

As the tendency of religion is always to advocate human performance of action or abstention, the interpretation of this verse in Christian religion has often been misconstrued. In a rather dyslexic rendering of Paul's statement, religious teachers have often reversed the phrases to indicate, "Do not carry out the desire of the flesh, and you will be walking in the Spirit." By the abstention of suppression, or the self-denial of self-seeking desire, it is thought that "walking in the Spirit" is defined by what one does not do. "Don't do this and don't do that, and you will by consequence be 'spiritual' and walking in the Spirit." Not so! Paul's argument throughout the epistle to the Galatians is that man's performances of "doing" or "not doing" are not the basis of the Christian gospel, but Christianity is the dynamic of God's grace functioning in the Christian by the presence of the Spirit of Christ unto the expression of His divine character.

5:17 Continuing his explanation of the interaction of "Spirit" and "flesh," Paul writes, *"For the flesh sets its desire against the Spirit, and the Spirit against the flesh."* The self-seeking desire of the patterns of our "flesh" is set against the other-directed, loving desire of the Spirit of Christ. The Spirit is obviously personified in the triune Godhead, and Paul seems to personify the patterning of the "flesh" as capable of "setting its desire" against the Spirit, cognizant of course of the personal source of all evil in the satanic Evil One (cf. I Jn. 3:8,10). Contrary to much religious inculcation, it is not the Christian who is obliged to fight against and suppress the "flesh" by "dying to self" or "mortifying one's desires," but it is the Spirit of Christ who sets His desire against the flesh as we are receptive to such in faith. Once again the performance-orientation of religion is avoided by the grace provision of God in Christ.

5:17

When Paul further explains that *"these"* (flesh and Spirit) *"are in opposition to one another,"* he is noting the behavioral conflict between the patterned selfishness of our soul and the desire of God's Spirit to manifest divine character in our behavior. Having its root in the cosmic conflict of God and Satan, this adversarial conflict of behavioral motivation is a spiritual warfare between mutually antithetical and irreconcilable spiritual sources. Paul would later deal with the same behavioral conflict in Romans 7:14 – 8:13. The two conflicting motivations are not to be regarded as equal antagonists constituting a dualistic equality (like the *Yin-Yang* dualism of Eastern philosophy) ending in a frustrating stalemate of ethical dualism. In the previous verse we already noted the supremacy of the Spirit's power in the Christian. But despite the superior power of the Spirit of God in the Christian, the "flesh" patterning is not eradicated from the soul in a form of perfectionism that denies the behavioral conflict. It must also be noted that the conflict is between "flesh" and Spirit, not between an "old man" and a "new man" (cf. Eph. 4:22,24; Col. 3:9,10), not between an "old sinful nature" and a "new godly nature" (cf. Eph. 2:2; II Pet. 1:4), even though some versions of the Bible mistranslate these words in such a way as to create ambiguity of terminology and schizophrenic misunderstanding of Christian identity.

The adversarial opposition of "flesh" and Spirit creates a behavioral situation *"so that you may not do the things that you please."* This is an extremely difficult phrase which has been interpreted in many different ways, depending on the placement of the two subjunctive verbs "will" and "do," whether one or both is to be negated, and whether the phrase is contingent on the impulse and impetus of the "flesh" or the Spirit. Some of the variable options of interpretation are represented in the following interpretive translations: "The opposition of flesh and Spirit creates a consecutive or consequential situation so that...

(1) ...by the Spirit you might do the things you might not want to do in the desire of the flesh."
(2) ...by the flesh you might do the things you might not want to do in your spiritual intents."
(3) ...by the Spirit you might not do the things you might want to do in the flesh."
(4) ...by the flesh you might not do the things you might want to do by the Spirit."
(5) ...by the Spirit you might desire and will to overcome the things you should not do in the flesh."
(6) ...by the flesh you might desire and will to do the things you might do in the Spirit."
(7) ...by the Spirit you might not desire and decide to do the things you might do in the flesh."
(8) ...by the flesh you might not want to do the things you should do in the Spirit."

These are but a few of the interpretive options. Whatever translation and interpretation one arrives at must be subjected to the evaluation of whether it impinges upon the sovereignty and supremacy of the Spirit, or upon the freedom of man's volitional choice. The last choice (8) seems to pass these tests, and also serves as the basis of the contrastual "but" with which Paul begins the next sentence.

5:18 *"But if you are led by the Spirit, you are not under the Law."* Again, this is not the "if" of possibility, but the "if" of fulfilled condition, meaning "since, as is the case, you are Christians who are led by the Spirit, then you are not under the Law." Later, to the Romans Paul would write, "All who are being led by the Spirit, these are sons of God" (Rom. 8:14). All genuine Christians are indwelt by the Spirit of God and Christ, the Holy Spirit (Rom. 8:9), and the divine presence of the Spirit within our spirit (Rom. 8:16) becomes the operational provision of God's grace to dynamically direct, guide and lead them that they might discern what God wants to do in their

5:18

lives. This is not to imply that the Spirit constrains or compels us to act in a manner that impinges upon volitional freedom apart from the responsibility to be receptive and available to the leading of the Spirit. Nor is this to say that the Christian always and inevitably follows the leading of the Spirit without choices that misrepresent the character of the One who lives in him (I Jn. 1:8). But since we are, as Christians, led by the Spirit to walk according to the Spirit (5:16,25) in the teleological freedom to express the love-character of the Spirit (5:22), which is the essential fulfillment of the Law (5:14), then we are not subjected under the behavioral performance standards of the Mosaic Law. "The requirement of the Law is fulfilled in us, who do not walk according to the flesh, but according to the Spirit" (Rom. 8:4).

Paul was continually cognizant throughout the writing of this epistle that the infiltrating Judaizers were advocating that the Galatian Christians subject themselves "under the Law" and submit to the keeping of the performance-standards of the Law. He had already established that righteousness does not come by the works of the Law (2:16,21; 3:11,21), that the curse of inadequate performance is upon all who attempt to keep the Law (3:10), that Christians have been redeemed from such a curse by the work of Christ (3:13: 4:5), as the jurisdiction of the Law has been terminated (3:19), and we are no longer under the Law (3:23-25). But perhaps the Judaizers were insisting that the only way to keep the sinful desires of the "flesh" under control was to submit to the legislative restraints of the Law in the "dos" and the "don'ts" that attempt to suppress their external expression. If so, they were ignorant of the fact (as all religion is) that external constraints can never rule out inner behavioral tendencies of self-orientation. The self-effort of legal performance will never overcome the self-seeking desire of the flesh. Paul explained to the Colossians that the regulations of "do not handle, do not taste, do not touch; matters which have, to be sure, the appearance of wisdom in self-made religion and self-abasement and severe treatment of the body, have no value against fleshly indulgence" (Col. 2:21-23). Paul wanted the Galatian Christians to know that the external performance of the regulations of the Law, functioning "under the Law," might mask the desires of the flesh, but they could never prevent or overcome those desires (cf. Rom. 7:7-13). Only the fulfillment of the Law (5:14) in the gospel of God's grace in Jesus Christ provides the inner dynamic of the Spirit, freeing mankind to express the character of God's love under the Lordship of Christ. In fulfillment of Jeremiah's prophecy (Jere. 31:31-34), "the law is written in our hearts" (Heb. 8:10; 10:16) in the ontological dynamic of the "law of Christ" (6:2), allowing us to be "led by the Spirit" in love.

5:19   Paul now begins to set forth the contrast of "the deeds of the flesh" (19-21) and "the fruit of the Spirit" (22,23). These are not simply contrasting lists of moral vices and virtues as were found in the Greek moralists centuries prior to Jesus Christ, and which continue to be expressed in philosophy and religion to the present. In Paul's mind the desires and the deeds, the attitudes and the actions, always had to be traced back to polarized spiritual sources in God or Satan. The self-seeking desire of the flesh was indicative of an evil and diabolic character of self-orientation conveying self-aspiration, self-gratification and self-promotion (cf. I Jn. 2:16) based on a fallacious premise of self-potential to perform and produce for the betterment of man by the self-effort "works" or "deeds" of the flesh. The other-directed fruit of the Spirit is expressive of the love-character of God (cf. I Jn. 4:8,16). The Christian, by the receipt of the Spirit of Christ in faith, is thereby volitionally free to choose to receive and derive character from either God or Satan in the midst of his behavior. In this sense the Christian is the only one who is really volitionally free to choose the receptive derivation of character in his behavior, since the unregenerate are "slaves of sin" (Jn. 8:34,35; Rom. 6:6,17).

5:19

Paul's point in listing these "works of the flesh" is still in the context of asserting that the teleological freedom of the Christian to fulfill God's objective of expressing His character within His creation to His own glory, could never be used as an excuse or pretext for exhibiting such behaviors as here mentioned (cf. 5:13). As noted in reference to the savage behaviors mentioned in 5:15, these actions may have already been reported among the Galatian congregations after the arrival of the Judaizing religionists.

Paul commences his list by indicating, *"Now the works of the flesh are evident."* Referring to them as "works" of the flesh connects them to the self-effort performance "works of the Law" (2:16; 3:2,5,10), as well as with "works of darkness" (Rom. 13:12; Eph. 5:11). Interestingly enough, these behavioral expressions of the patterned selfishness and sinfulness in man's soul will be evidenced in the context of both legalism and license – in both of the extremes that disallow the Christian liberty to love by the Spirit under the Lordship of Jesus Christ. These selfish behaviors are so patently obvious and plain for all to see, even though the latent spiritual source and character is often not identified in a consistent theodicy.

"Immorality" is derived from the Greek word (*pornos*) for "prostitute," which is the root of the English word "porno". It refers to any sexual activity outside of God's intended context of marriage between one man and one woman. It is broader that just premarital fornication, as translated in some versions of the New Testament (cf. KJV).

"Impurity" expands the concept of sexual irregularity beyond the sexual acts themselves to any act and attitude that is defiling, unclean, or indecent; to anything other than the pure, clean and proper use of our physical bodies as the purity of God's character is expressed in us.

"Sensuality" denotes a lack of constraint whereby our passions, impulses and senses are given free rein to engage in wantonness, debauchery, excess and immoderation. Without

constraint there may be a shameless loss of public decency as well as dehumanizing exploitation of others.

5:20 *"Idolatry"* is the inordinate devotion or worship of someone or something other than God, by attributing ultimate worth to such an object. The sexual sins previously mentioned were often integrated with religious idolatry in the pagan worship of Cybele, Diana, Aphrodite, Baal, etc.

"Sorcery" is a translation of the Greek word from which we get the English word "pharmaceutics." Throughout human history drugs have been utilized in religious activities as the medicine-men and magicians have mixed up strange potions in witchcraft and occult activities.

"Enmities" refers to hatred of one's perceived enemies, and engaging in hostile antagonism with them.

"Strife" translates a Greek word that also identified the goddess *Eris,* the goddess of contentiousness and quarrelsomeness that leads to war. Actions of agitation and provocation that stir up trouble, discord and wrangling are indicated by this word.

"Jealousy" is a translation of the same word from which we get the English word "zealous." It is the boiling fervency of ungratefulness and resentment concerning what others have or do.

"Outbursts of anger" comes from the root of the Greek word meaning "to kill." Uncontrolled fits of passion and rage wherein one's fury and temper are so acute that it could lead to life-threatening action are implied by this word.

"Disputes" are rivalries and altercations caused by mercenary motives when a person attempts to manipulate and use another person for his own personal gain at the expense of the other.

"Dissensions" are any occasion when people refuse to stand together in unity, and instead stand against one another in disunity and divisiveness.

"Factions" translates the Greek word from which we get the English word "heresies." In its broadest meaning it refers to the sectarian and partisan attitude of wanting to choose up sides in order to engage in conflict.

5:21 ***"Envyings"*** is similar to "jealousy," for it refers to the grudging attitude that cannot tolerate another's success or prosperity, and regards the other as their rival.

"Drunkenness" is the Greek word that we now refer to as the drug "meth." It refers to the over-indulgence that leads to being intoxicated and controlled by another substance.

"Carousings" is derived from the Greek word *komos,* the name of the Greek god of revelry. The quest for and involvement in the uninhibited excess of cavorting and partying is implied by this word.

Paul concludes the list by adding ***"and things like these,"*** to explain that this is not an exhaustive listing of selfish behaviors, but comprises a few of the behaviors that are representative of the "works of the flesh." We must avoid the systematizing tendency of attempting to arbitrarily place the behaviors mentioned by Paul into classifications and categorizations that tend to be self-limiting. Paul simply lists these actions without any implied grouping.

Having listed these behaviors, Paul says directly to the Galatian recipients of his letter, ***"I forewarn you just as I have forewarned you, that those who practice such things shall not inherit the kingdom of God."*** "Just as I cautioned and forewarned you when I was present with you and preaching the gospel for the first time (cf. Acts 13:14 – 14:24), I tell you again in advance, forewarning you of God's judgment, that those persons who continue to behave in these ways, and keep on practicing these actions in an unconcerned and habituated pattern of behavior, failing and refusing to exercise their teleological freedom to express the character of God in the restored purpose of humanity in Christ, they evidence they have not received the "first-fruits of the Spirit" (Rom. 8:23), the "pledge of our inheritance" (II Cor. 1:22; Eph. 1:14) in the indwelling presence of Jesus Christ, and thus will not participate in the future consummation and continuum of Christ's reign in the eternal kingdom." That Paul had previously spoken about the "kingdom of God" to those in southern Galatia is documented by Luke's report of Acts 14:22 where Paul advised that "through many tribulations we must enter the kingdom of God." The kingdom should not be limited to a precise millennial period in the future in a particular realm of location or place. The reign of Christ as Lord and King has already been established (cf. Lk. 17:20,21; Rom 14:17; Col. 1:13), though it is not yet consummated in its unhindered expression (cf. I Cor. 15:24; Eph. 5:5; II Tim. 4:18). Paul had previously explained that the inheritance of God was not based on legal performance (3:18) or on Judaic ethnicity (3:29), but on the reception of the Spirit of Christ (4:6,7), and his emphasis here is that if there is no evidence of Christ's indwelling reign in one's life by the Spirit, evidenced by His character in Christian behavior, then there is no reason to expect that the Lordship reign of Christ will commence and be realized at a time and place beyond this life, whereupon the judgment of God (Heb. 9:27) upon unbelief shall be enacted.

5:22 In contrast to the "works of the flesh," those activities that express selfish character that is contrary to the character of God, Paul writes, ***"But the fruit of the Spirit is..."***. Whereas "works" of the flesh imply a self-oriented performance, the "fruit" of the Spirit implies a consistent expression and manifestation of the essential nature of the root-source. The spiritual root-source is the divine Spirit of God, so the "fruit of the Spirit" is the consistent expression of the character of God. The character-fruit that Paul mentions here is incapable of being generated, produced or "worked up" by the self-effort of man, and is not intrinsic to the natural temperaments of man.

5:22

Only God can produce and express His godly character. The power of divine character-fructification is only by His divine enabling. The Christian has received the personal presence of the Spirit of Christ (cf. Rom. 8:9), and since His divine character is inherent in His Being, we have been invested with the complete provision and resource of the character of Christ (and therefore do not need to be constantly praying to receive such). Our volitional freedom as Christians allows for the teleological freedom to allow Jesus Christ to manifest His character in our behavior, evidencing that we are Christian disciples (Jn. 15:8) wherein Christ as the vine (Jn. 15:5) produces the character-fruit that indicates that we are rooted in and deriving from Him (cf. Matt. 7:16,20; 12:33).

That Paul uses the singular "fruit" instead of a plural "fruits" would seem to indicate that these comprise a singular cluster of character "in Christ," and that they are not to be isolated particularly in separated bins of independent and detached consideration. They should be viewed conjunctively as a holistic consideration of Christ's character. The character of Christ is not limited to the characteristics that Paul lists here, though, for this list, like the previous list, is not exhaustive. Elsewhere Paul refers to the "fruit of righteousness which comes through Jesus Christ" (Phil. 1:11), and "the fruit of light which consists in all goodness and righteousness and truth" (Eph. 5:9).

"Love" is the first divine character trait mentioned, and may be the most comprehensive so as to be inclusive of all others. We have previously noted (5:13,14) that "God is love" (I Jn. 4:8,16). It is the essence of His Being to be self-giving and other-directed. Because it is His ultimate teleological objective to have His divine character exhibited in the behavior of His created human beings, Paul can thus say that "the whole Law is fulfilled in love" (5:14). We Christians have received the presence and character of God in Christ, and "the love of God has been poured within our hearts through the Holy Spirit who was given to us" (Rom. 5:5). Thus we have the divine provision

to "love in the Spirit" (Col. 1:18) with the "love of the Spirit" (Rom. 15:30). The love of God expressed through us will be unselfish, unconditional and non-selective, seeking the highest good of the other without self-seeking thought of reciprocal benefit. When expressed in the collective Christian community, such "love is the perfect bond of unity" (Col. 3:14), contrary to the divisive "works of the flesh." Such expression of God's love serves as the distinguishing mark of Christian discipleship (Jn. 13:35).

"Joy", from the Greek word *chara*, is the celebration of God's grace-giving (*charis*) in Christ. The Christian who loves Christ and believes in Christ will "greatly rejoice with joy inexpressible and full of glory" (I Pet. 1:8). Jesus told His disciples that when they received the Spirit their "heart would rejoice, and no one would take that joy from them" (Jn. 16:22), and indeed they "were filled with joy and with the Holy Spirit" (Acts 13:52). The presence of Christ in the Christian is inconducive to an attitude of gloom and doom, or a demeanor that is sour and dour. John Wesley once said that "sour godliness is the devil's religion." Doleful "dill-pickle Christians" who are negative, pessimistic and melancholy misrepresent the character of Christ. But neither is joy to be regarded as but a temporary "happiness" dependent on current circumstances. The word "happiness" is derived from the old English word *hap*, meaning "chance," whereas the "joy of the Lord" is a settled permanence of appreciation of God's grace in the midst of, and despite, all circumstances. "Consider it all joy, my brethren, when you encounter various trials" (James 1:20).

"Peace" is also the character of the "God of peace" (Rom. 15:33; I Thess. 5:23) manifested in the "Prince of Peace" (Isa. 9:6), Jesus Christ. Subjectively the Christian experiences the "peace of God, which surpasses all comprehension, guarding his heart and mind in Christ Jesus" (Phil. 4:7), fulfilling Jesus' promise to His disciples, "My peace I give unto you." (Jn. 14:27). Such peace is not simply the absence of conflict,

struggles or problems, but is a divinely supplied security, serenity and tranquillity in the midst of situations – the assurance that God is in control, the positive perspective of the plenteous provision of the Person of Jesus Christ in the midst of any circumstance. When such internal peace is experienced by the Christian as he allows "the peace of Christ to rule in his heart" (Col. 3:15), the social implications of "Christ as our peace" (Eph. 2:14) can be applied to our interpersonal relationships as we become "peacemakers" (Matt. 5:9) seeking "peace with all men" (Heb. 12:14). The harmony and "unity of the Spirit in the bond of peace" (Eph. 4:3) allows the function of the kingdom of God to be "righteousness and peace and joy in the Holy Spirit" (Rom. 14:17).

"Patience" is likewise the character of "the Lord God who is merciful, gracious and patient" (Exod. 34:6; II Pet. 3:9). Jesus Christ "demonstrates His perfect patience" (I Tim. 1:16) towards each of us as He seeks to manifest His saving life in us. The Spirit within us then "directs our hearts into the love of God and into the patience of Christ" (II Thess. 3:5). The patience of Christ is not fatalistic resignation, passive acquiescence, or stoic endurance. Rather, the divine character of patience forbears in long-suffering especially in the midst of provocation. The patience of Christ in us is not quickly offended, irritated, or put off with people. We can only "be patient with all men" (I Thess. 5:14) and with one another as Christians (Eph. 4:2), when we "bear fruit in every good work, strengthened with God's power, for the attaining of all steadfastness and patience" (Col. 1:10,11). Christ's patience is also willing to wait for God's timetable, and His sufficiency in every situation. This is why "tribulation works patience" (Rom. 5:3; James 1:3), providing opportunities for the divine character of patience to be expressed.

"Kindness" is derived from "the kindness of God" (Rom. 11:22) whose "lovingkindness is everlasting" (Ps. 106:1). The "kindness of God our Savior and His love for mankind was

manifested in Christ Jesus" (Titus 3:4; Eph. 2:7). The Boy Scout motto, "Be Kind," attempts to inculcate a duty of kindness, but Christian kindness, rather than being occasional acts of duty, is a constant character-attitude that puts legs on love by seeing another's need and reaching out to assist them by God's direction and sufficiency. Christian kindness is more than polite civility and courteousness that passively exclaims, "Ain't it nice to be nice to nice people." The kindness of Christ is linked with compassion (Col. 3:12) and with tender-heartedness (Eph. 4:32). Kindness is sensitive and respectful of other's feelings, considerate of their perspective, thoughtful about taking the initiative to tenderly address the welfare of another.

"Goodness" is very similar to "kindness" as these words merge into one another in the description of God's loving character. "No one is good except God alone" (Mk. 10:18; Lk. 18:19), Jesus said, when He was addressed as "Good Teacher" by one who did not recognize His essential divinity and goodness. The recognition that "goodness" is of God is inherent even in the etymology of the English word; the words "good" and "God" are related. It is reported that, "Jesus always went about doing good" (Acts 10:38), deriving such character from God the Father. He explained that "the good man out of his good treasure brings forth what is good" (Matt. 12:35; Lk. 6:45). The "good treasure" of the Christian is the presence of Christ by the Spirit in our "earthen vessels" (II Cor. 4:7), wherein is the power to express His character of goodness. "The one doing good derives what he does out of God" (III Jn. 11). The concept of "goodness" has been so relativized in humanistic thought ever since "the tree of the knowledge of good and evil" (Gen. 2:9,17) that many consider it inconceivable or offensive to assert that absolute goodness can only be derived from the presence and activity of God. The "goodness" that is the fruit of the Spirit is not the relative goodness of "You're a good man, Charlie Brown," but the goodness of a Barnabas who was "full of the Holy Spirit and faith" (Acts 11:24). "Let

us not lose heart in doing good" (Gal. 6:9), Paul will later write.

"Faithfulness" is intrinsic to God's character. "He is faithful and cannot deny Himself" (II Tim. 2:13). He is faithful to His promises (Heb. 10:23); faithful to empower us against temptation (I Cor. 10:13) and protect us from the Evil One (II Thess. 3:3); faithful to forgive us our sins (I Jn. 1:9); and faithful to bring to pass by His dynamic of grace in Jesus Christ all that He has called us to and desires to do through us (I Thess. 5:24). Jesus Christ who is "faithful and true" (Rev. 19:11) and "faithful over His house" (Heb. 3:6), the church, expresses His character of dependability, reliability, and trustworthiness in the loyalty and discipline of Christian behavior that is receptive to His activity. Only thus can we be "faithful unto death" (Rev. 2:10) exhibiting the faithfulness of God.

5:23 *"Gentleness"* was identified as the character of Christ when He invited the "weary and heavy-laden" to come to Him for rest, for He was "gentle and humble of heart" (Matt. 11:29). Writing to the Corinthians, Paul referred to "the meekness and gentleness of Christ" (II Cor. 10:1), which did not require him to be self-assertive, demanding, or threatening. The character of Christ is not harsh, abrasive and forceful, engaging in manipulative pressure and retaliation. But neither is the character of Christ weak, withdrawing, and waffling, refusing to stand up to wrongdoing and injustice, like a wimp. "Meekness," as this word is sometimes translated, is not weakness! Gentleness is the firm and fair strength of God that avoids a show of force, if at all possible, desiring to be "considerate of all men" (Titus 3:1) and allow God to change things "in a spirit of gentleness" (Gal. 6:1). Jesus said, "Blessed are the gentle, for they (rather than the forceful) shall inherit the earth" (Matt. 5:5).

"Self-control" is a rather unfortunate and misleading rendering of the Greek word that Paul employed (which simply means "in control"), although it adequately renders the mean-

ing of the word as it was encouraged by the Greek moralists. In the context of the "fruit of the Spirit," being the expression of God's character, the translation of "self-control" creates an ambiguity with the humanistic thesis of being in autonomous control of oneself. God is obviously in autonomous control of Himself, but His intent within His derivative human creatures is to allow for His divine control and expression of character. God does not want us to be "out of control" in wanton subjection to the self-seeking desires of the flesh enacted in "the works of the flesh," but instead wants us to be "controlled within" by the Spirit of the risen Lord Jesus, allowing for a godly control of our being and behavior. The same word is connected with righteousness in Acts 24:25, and seems to imply an "inner discipline" in I Cor. 9:25. Dropping the prefix "self-", it is best to view this character trait as the godly control and management of our inner-being whereby we have stability and consistency in our lives.

Paul concludes his listing of these representative "fruit of the Spirit" by noting that *"against such things there is no law."* Generally speaking, there is no moral law that condemns behavioral attitudes such as these, for this kind of positive behavior would meet the demands of all ethical conformity. If the operational objective of law is to restrain ungodly behavior (I Tim. 1:9), then there is nothing in this kind of character that requires restraint. More specifically, Paul may have had in mind the Judaizing tendency to think that the Law could restrain the "works of the flesh" by man's determined self-effort of performance, and thereby produce positive character, attitudes and behavior. "Concerning these kinds of character," Paul might be saying, "there is no Law that can produce or generate the character of God's Love."

5:24 Reiterating the supremacy of the Spirit over the self-orientation of the "flesh," and relating such triumph to the "finished work" (cf. Jn. 19:30) of Christ at the crucifixion, Paul

5:24

wants to make clear that the flesh/Spirit conflict is not an egalitarian balance that ends in an experiential "no win" stalemate and stand-off. By way of logical conclusion in the chronological present, Paul declares, *"Now those who belong to Christ Jesus have crucified the flesh with its passions and desires."* All Christians "belong to Christ Jesus" (cf. 3:29), identified with Him as "Christ-ones," having "been crucified with Christ" (2:20), having "put on Christ" (3:27), and being "in Christ" (3:26,28). Paul is indicating that all genuine Christians participate in a victory over the "flesh" which the Law could never effect (cf. Col. 2:23), for such a victory could only be effected by identification with the death of Jesus Christ and the empowering of His Spirit.

This verse is one of the most difficult and enigmatic statements in Paul's epistle to the Galatians. Commentators have tended to "weasel" their way around the problems posed by this text, and their interpretations, for the most part, are inadequate and unsatisfactory. Sincere Christians have been baffled by Paul's statement; some have felt guilty that they must not have "crucified the flesh" since they still battle such and commit sins (I Jn. 1:8), leading some to doubt, therefore, whether they really "belong to Christ Jesus" and are really Christians; leading some to determine to engage with renewed self-effort in the performance procedures of "dying to the flesh," "dying to self," "denying oneself," etc. This in complete contradiction to the entire thesis of Paul in this epistle, as he advocates the grace and liberty of the gospel.

That Christians "have crucified the flesh" must be understood figuratively or metaphorically. It cannot mean that the patterns of selfish and sinful behavior in one's soul have been "put to death" or "killed" in the sense of being terminated, eliminated or obliterated. Such an interpretation would present a contradiction with Paul's assertion that "the flesh sets its desires against the Spirit, and the Spirit against the flesh." (5:17). The tense of the verb "have crucified" (aorist) indicates that the action took place decisively, deliberately, and definitely at a particular time, and with finality. The most obvious time for this to have transpired in all Christians would be the decisive repentance required in conversion (and illustrated in baptism). This negates all interpretations that would encourage a continuous experiential process of "mortifying the flesh" and "dying to self" through suppressionist techniques or religious disciplines (ex. prayer, fasting, repentance, etc.).

By way of figurative expression Paul indicates that the Christian has enacted some form of separation, severance or disconnection from the "flesh" patterning. The "flesh" is to be considered, regarded or reckoned (cf. Rom. 6:11; Col. 3:5) as dead, or not viable as an expression of our new identity (cf. II Cor. 5:17; Eph. 4:24; Col. 3:10) in Christ. Not wanting (volitional freedom) to misrepresent the character (contrary to teleological freedom) of the One with whom he is identified, the Christian is to remain dynamically receptive in faith to the superseding strength of the indwelling Spirit of Christ, in order to avoid and overcome the tempting draw of both legalistic and libertine motivations and occasions of the "flesh," with its ever-present self-oriented passions and cravings.

5:25 Though some consider this verse to be the beginning of a new paragraph, the connecting concepts with the previous verse (5:24) are too tight to warrant a separation of thought. The "flesh" and Spirit contrast is still being emphasized, as well as the death and life contrast of "crucifying the flesh" and "living by the Spirit." ***"If"*** (since this is the case for all genuine Christians) ***"we live by the Spirit, let us also walk by the Spirit."*** Having begun (3:3) to live by the Spirit at our initial conversion and regeneration when the "Spirit of life" (Rom. 8:2; I Cor. 15:45), the Spirit of Christ (Rom. 8:9), brought His "newness of life" (Rom. 6:4) into our spirit by His own presence (I Jn. 5:12), the consequential implications and objective of this new spiritual condition is not to progress by legalistic or libertine expressions of the "flesh" (3:3), but to allow the Spirit of Christ to exercise His Lordship in our lives in order to enable us to "line up, keep in step, and correspond" with a consistent expression of His character in the conduct of our lives. Having "passed out of death into life" (John 5:24; I Jn. 3:14) at regeneration, our sanctifying "walk by the Spirit" (cf. 5:16) should consistently and representatively express the character of the One who lives in us, and has become our life (Col. 3:4). We are to behave like who we have become, manifesting the godly character, the "fruit of the Spirit" (5:22,23) of the One with whom we have identified as "Christ-ones," i.e., Christians. This is accomplished only by faithful receptivity of His activity in our behavior, for "as we received Christ Jesus, so we are to walk in Him" (Col. 2:6), by faith.

5:26   When we "walk by the Spirit" (5:16,25) manifesting the "fruit of the Spirit" (5:22,23), *"Let us not become boastful, challenging one another, envying one another,"* for these are not consistent with the character of Christ. Instead, they are misrepresentative "works of the flesh" (5:19-21), as were possibly reported to Paul as occurring within the Galatian churches. Both legalism and license lead to the violation of our teleological freedom to be all that God intends us to be by the expression of His character, as they foster the self-effort and self-seeking of our "flesh" patterns. Instead of the humility that is the character of Christ (cf. Phil. 2:3-8) because it recognizes man's place in reference to God and accepts that it is not what we do but what He does that is of value, the "flesh" prompts the "empty conceit" (cf. Phil. 2:3) of pretentious, haughty, arrogant pride, a self-inflated sense of one's own importance, which religiously becomes "spiritual pride." Such boastful pride leads to competitive power-plays and challenges of provocation concerning belief-systems, morality standards, personal position, etc., as well as grudging resentment of another's success, prosperity or position. The "one another" phrases that

Paul employs indicates that he is emphasizing the interpersonal relationships that should exist among Christian peoples. The humility and acceptance, harmony and unity, that should be indicative of collective Christian behavior when Christians are "through love, serving one another" (5:13) and "bearing one another's burdens" (6:2), is so quickly perverted when they "bite, consume, and devour one another" (5:15), "challenge and envy one another" (5:26), manifesting the divisive "works of the flesh" (5:19-21) that misrepresent the Body of Christ. Paul will continue to consider the interactive relationships of Christians within the Church community in the verses that follow (6:1-10).

Contrary to the Judaizers' inevitable attempts to interpret Paul's gospel of grace and freedom as an opening for antinomian license, Paul explains in these verses that our teleological freedom is to lovingly serve one another as Christians by the dynamic empowering of the Spirit. Only thus are we free to function as God intended man to function, and unto His glory.

As important as the gospel of the indwelling life of Jesus Christ is, we must not develop an inordinate focus on "Christ in me" to the extent that it negates the other-oriented essence of God's love expressed as "Christ in me *for others*." It would be a self-oriented gospel that merely concerned itself with the benefits of Christ in me, apart from the beneficence of Christ in me, through me, unto others. If the consistent demonstration of "walking by the Spirit" (5:16,25) is not "Christ in me *for others*," then there is no validity in asserting "Christ in me," for the character of Christ is love (and the correlative "fruit of the Spirit" - 5:22,23), actively expressed for the sake of others. The consistent expression of the character of Christ in the Christian must be consummated in loving expression that "serves one another" (5:13). Jesus explicitly declared that He "did not come to be served" (Matt. 20:28), but was "among us as One who serves" (Lk. 22:27), and He continues to manifest the same unchangeable loving character of service to others in Christians today.

That the living Lord Jesus wants to manifest His character of love, and is competent to do so by His Spirit, is an important emphasis of this passage. We have noted that the action of the Spirit is the greater power that supersedes the propensities of the flesh (cf. 5:16). Dutch theologian, Herman Ridderbos, has explained that "the dominant viewpoint under which Paul views the Christian life is not the continuing onslaught of the flesh on the Christian, but the power of the Spirit which enables him to win the victory over sin."[1] This is consistent with Paul's statement to the Romans: "The law of the Spirit of life in Christ Jesus has set you free from the law of sin and of death" (Rom. 8:2). Much of the teaching within Christian religion has tended to emphasize the Christian's inability, his weakness, and the sinful tendencies of the "flesh," advocating sin-consciousness, brokenness, confessionism, and legalistic, suppressionistic encouragements to "die to self." When these emphases predominate, you can be sure that an old covenant religion of Christianized Judaism has been reinstated, and the Judaizers are just as active today as they were in Galatia. The new covenant emphasis of Paul's gospel of grace and liberty recognized the sufficiency of the "finished work" of Jesus Christ to overcome the power of sin and to cause us to be all that God intends by the manifestation of His life and character (cf. II Cor. 4:10,11). This is not a theology of passive perfectionism or transcendent triumphalism, but a recognition of *Christus Victor*[2] and the sufficiency of God by His Spirit in the Christian life and community.

Another applicable observation can be made by noting Paul's collective or corporate emphasis on "serving *one another*" (5:13), as contrasted with "biting and devouring *one another* and consuming *one another*" (5:15), or "challenging *one another* and envying *one another*" (5:26). These, in addition to the obviously interactive behaviors of the "works of the flesh"

(5:19-21) such as enmities, strife, jealousy, disputes, dissensions, factions, envyings, etc., indicate that misrepresentative character and behavior is often exhibited in the collective social context of religion. Whether or not Paul was reacting to reports of such in the Galatian churches, personal and historical observation makes it apparent that such attitudes and behaviors are rampant in religion, whether legalistic or libertinistic, whether conservative or liberal. Religion will never generate or engender love! Religion has long been the fertile ground of immorality, impurity, sensuality, idolatry, sorcery, drunkenness, carousing, etc. (5:19-21), as well as boasting, challenging, envying (5:26), and back-biting, devouring (5:15) behaviors. Only when Christians individually and collectively recognize their freedom to love and serve one another (5:13) by the dynamic grace of God's Spirit, the Spirit of Christ, will we fulfill God's intent and present a witness of God's character to the world around us.

ENDNOTES

1 Ridderbos, Herman, *Paul: An Outline of His Theology.* Grand Rapids: Wm. B. Eerdmans Pub. Co. 1975. pg. 272.
2 Aulén, Gustaf, *Christus Victor: An Historical Study of the Three Main Types of the Idea of the Atonement.* London: S.P.C.K. 1931.

The Community of the Concerned

Galatians 6:1-10

The logical flow of Paul's argument moves smoothly from 5:13 through 6:10, making it difficult to arbitrarily ascertain a break or transition in the argument. Some have placed the contextual break between 5:24 and 5:25, thus dividing the obvious flesh/Spirit contrast that Paul was still making. Others would begin a new paragraph at 5:26, which would be quite legitimate. But in this study, we will retain the traditional chapter division, beginning with 6:1, since there does not seem to be any compelling evidence to do otherwise.

There is no doubt that the contextual theme of freedom continues to flow into chapter 6 from chapter 5. Paul began by emphasizing the *emancipatory freedom* of the Christian (5:1-12), encouraging the Galatian Christians to stand firm in their freedom from religious slavery and the constraint of legalistic performance of Law. In order to stand firm in such freedom, Christians would need to exercise their *volitional freedom* of choice, choosing to act responsibly in the receptivity of God's activity by His Spirit, in contrast to the flesh (5:13-25). Freedom of choice was to be exercised in order to function in the *teleological freedom* of operating consistent with God's purposed objective and design by His ontological dynamic of grace, and not in the inconsistent expression of the self-serving character of the flesh (cf. 5:13,16). The volitional freedom of responsible choice and the teleological freedom to serve one another in love are important underlying premises for the understanding of Gal. 6:1-10.

The theme of 6:1-10 has its starting point in the statement of 5:13, "Serve one another through love." Whereas 5:16-26 primarily addressed the *means* of exercising the freedom to serve one another in love, i.e. "by the Spirit"; the thrust of 6:1-10 addresses the *manner* of serving one another in love within the collective Christian community. Paul has been leading up to this collective emphasis of evidencing God's character of love in Christian community by repeated "*one another*" phrases. Positively, he admonished Christians to "serve *one another* through love" (5:13). Negatively, he referred to "biting, devouring and consuming *one another*" (5:15), as well as "challenging and envying *one another*" (5:26). Both the "works of the flesh" (5:19-21) and the "fruit of the Spirit" (5:22,23) had implicit interrelational social connotations also. But now in this section (6:1-10), Paul specifically addresses the practical implications of "bearing *one another's* burdens" (6:2) in the Christian community of the concerned.

In a new covenant response to Cain's question, "Am I my brother's keeper?" Paul would answer with a categorical "Yes!" In the Church, the Body of Christ, every Christian has a responsibility to allow God's character of love to be expressed to others in "brother-keeping." Even beyond the Christian fellowship, Christians have the responsibility to "do good to all men" (6:10), manifesting God's character in "the community of the concerned."

6:1 Considering the Galatian Christians to be "brothers in Christ" (3:15; 4:12; 5:13) in contrast to "false brethren" (2:14), Paul addresses them as ***"brethren."*** Paul then postulates a situation wherein ***"even if a man is caught in some trespass,"*** that person is not to be judgmentally "written off" for their performance failure in a "cut and dried" rule-book religion based on the Law. Avoiding all forms of triumphalism and perfectionism, Paul realistically recognizes that a "man" (presumably a Christian person within the Christian community) might lapse into a violation of the established norm, i.e., might misrepresent the character of Christ as just explained by the "fruit of the Spirit" (5:22,23), by exhibiting one or more of the sinful, self-serving "works of the flesh" (5:19-21; cf. 5:15,26). Such a person might be "caught in," overtaken, discovered in behavior that is a misrepresentative trespass of the character of God. Whether the person was actually "caught in the act" (cf. Jn. 8:4) or merely discovered in a pattern of behavior that indicated lapses of faithful receptivity of Christ's life and character cannot be ascertained with certainty from the verb Paul used. The verb can imply that an individual was caught or detected in an act of sinning by the Christian community; or it can indicate that the individual was overtaken by the patterned self-seeking tendencies of his "flesh;" or even that the individual was overtaken by Satan, the tempter, to engage in the selfish "works of the flesh."

Regardless of how the person was caught or overtaken, Paul's admonition is: ***"You who are spiritual, restore such a one in a spirit of gentleness."*** The identification of those "who are spiritual" has had widely divergent interpretations. Was Paul using sarcastic irony to refer to "a group of 'Holy Joes' and 'Pious Pollys' who had formed themselves into a cadre of moral watchdogs and were self-righteously lording it over their less 'advanced' brothers and sisters"?[1] Was Paul referring to a group of elitist gnostics who regarded themselves as having reached a higher level of "spirituality"? The term "spiritual" is a very loose term that had varied meanings even in Biblical usage (cf. I Cor. 2:13–3:1). Does Paul refer to [1] all Christians who have "received the Spirit" (3:2) and "live by the Spirit" (5:25); [2] those Christians who had the indwelling Spirit of Christ and were attempting to "walk by the Spirit" (5:16,25), or [3] those whose lives were marked by the "fruit of the Spirit" (5:22,23)? Was Paul referring [4] to Christians who had reached a certain level of strength, "maturity," or "spirituality" (cf. Rom. 15:1), or is the term merely a contrastual designation referring to [5] those Christians desirous of "walking in the Spirit" who had caught the other person in the trespass or violation of "walking according to the flesh"? The broadest reference to all Christians seems preferable. This disallows all escapist excuses of, "Well, I'm not 'spiritual,' so this doesn't apply to me!" All Christians are responsible to engage in the restorational endeavors of Christian fellowship!

What a sad indictment upon the Church when someone can charge, "The Church is the only army in the world that shoots its wounded!" In contrast to Paul's admonition, there has been too much judgmental condemnation, unloving and insensitive criticism, and harsh, legalistic application of moral standards that have led to ostracism and excommunication of Christian brethren. The loving (5:13) process of restoration and rehabilitation should be artistically applied (the English word "artisan" is derived from the Greek word for "restore"), in order to mend (cf. Matt. 4:21; Mk. 1:19) and amend the severed Christian unity, allowing the Christian community to be "made complete" (I Cor. 1:10; II Cor. 13:11) in a united expression of divine character, as we encourage one another (Heb. 10:25) to God's teleological objective in our lives, individually and collectively. This can only be accomplished by the activity of the Spirit of Christ within Christians, manifesting His character of gentleness (5:23) toward others who may have lapsed or fallen in their Christian expression. This gentleness is obviously not conceited, condescending or censorious; nor rude, demanding or abrasive. But neither is it a weak leniency that overlooks the problem, saying "It's okay," or avoids confronting the issue. In a sensitive, considerate and courteous manner the issue of failure is addressed firmly and fairly, just as Paul was doing in this epistle as he attempted to restore the Galatian Christians.

When we engage in Christian restoration, Paul reminds us to be ***"looking to yourself, lest you too be tempted."*** Every

Christian is susceptible to the temptation of the satanic tempter (I Thess. 3:5). "Let him who thinks he stands take heed lest he fall. No temptation has overtaken you but such as is common to man." (I Cor. 10:12,13). Since we are all tempted not only to selfish, misrepresentative violations of God's character, as well as to proud, arrogant superiority that would respond with harsh, critical judgmentalism toward those who have fallen, we must all engage in honest self-evaluation, self-examination, and self-scrutiny that avoids all self-righteousness. When our brother is overtaken in a fault or failure, we must all recognize that "there, but for the grace of God, go I."

6:2   Paul seems to go beyond the response to an occasional lapse of our Christian brother, expanding the imperative to the constant responsibility of Christians to assist one another. ***"Bear one another's burdens,"*** he commands. The collective and mutual responsibility of the Christian community to manifest the other-oriented character of God's love is essential to the function of the Body of Christ, the Church. Writing to the Corinthians, Paul explained, "the members should have the same care for one another. And if one member suffers, all the members suffer with it; if one member is honored, all the members rejoice with it. Now you are Christ's body, and individually members of it" (I Cor. 12:25-27). The collective sense of the Body of Christ means that "we are in it together," spiritually connected to one another in Christ. "No man is an island!" So, when others are weighted down with burdens, whether they be failures, faults and falterings, or the heaviness of hardships, responsibilities and ordeals of suffering, we must recognize Christ's character of concern that reaches out to assist in carrying and bearing their burdens. Problems are part and parcel of human life on earth (whether they be physical, psychological, social, financial or otherwise), and the Christian is not exempt or immune from such burdens. But the mutuality of unity and responsibility in the Body of Christ is such that "another's problem is also our problem." We must avoid the self-orientation of excessive individualism, and engage in personal intercession unto the upbuilding of the whole as we "bear one another's burdens."

In such mutual responsibility of concern we *"thus fulfill the law of Christ."* In light of Paul's careful argument about Christian freedom from the Law's demands of performance (2:16,19,21; 3:2,10,11,12,13,18,19,21, 23,24; 4:5,21; 5:3,14,18), it strikes some as incongruous that Paul would now refer to the "law of Christ." Paul is not indicating that there is a moral law that is maintained from the Mosaic Law in Christian teaching. Nor is he positing a new locus of ethical standards in the propositional commandment expressions of Jesus, or His ethical example (cf. Jn. 13:34; 15:12). Nor is Paul referring to a corpus of tradition and teaching developed within the Christian religion pertaining to Christian ethics or morality. Consistent with the recognition that "Christ is the end of the Law." (Rom. 10:4), and the "fulfillment of the Law" (Matt. 5:17), Paul viewed the living Lord Jesus as the dynamic personification of the expression of the character of God, which was the essence of the Law. The Law was no longer codified in external, written principles, precepts, propositions and procedures, but was embodied in a Person, in Christ, the living *Torah*, the ontological *Nomos*. The Law is written in our hearts (Heb. 8:10;10:16) by the indwelling presence of Jesus Christ. What the old covenant Mosaic Law lacked, being external letters written on tablets of stone leading to condemnation (cf. II Cor. 3:3-11), is now provided in the new covenant "law of Christ," as the operational provision of the dynamic grace of God in Christ by the empowering of His Spirit allows and enables the full and complete expression of His character in receptive mankind. So, consistent with his earlier statement that "the whole Law is fulfilled in one word, 'love'" (5:14), and his later statements to the Romans, "he who loves his neighbor has fulfilled the Law" (Rom. 13:8), for "love is the fulfillment of the Law" (Rom.

13:10), Paul is indicating that the expression of the love of God whereby we "bear one another's burdens" is the "filling full," the "full expression," of God's intent in the Law, i.e., to express His loving character within His creation unto His own glory. Later Paul would describe his Christian liberty as being "under the law of Christ" (I Cor. 9:21), and James would write of "the perfect law of liberty" (James 1:25; 2:12) in the "fulfillment of the royal law" of love (James 2:8).

6:3 Contrary to the other-oriented concern of God's love in "bearing one another's burdens," Paul presents the other side of the coin. ***"For if anyone thinks he is something when he is nothing, he deceives himself."*** The self-seeking pride of "the boastful pride of life" (I Jn. 2:16) creates an inflated view of superiority over others and their problems, presenting itself in such "works of the flesh" as "enmities, strife, jealousies, envyings, etc." (5:19-21). Perhaps Paul is referring to someone who "thinks he is something" because when he compares himself with others, he considers himself to be more advanced, more "spiritual," and thus beyond, above, or "too good" to be concerned with others' petty problems and burdens. Such a "holier-than-thou" attitude is inevitably based on comparing oneself with other men, rather than with the character of Christ. Such a self-righteous opinion of one's self-importance and self-sufficiency is also usually formulated by considering one's own performance and "works," rather than what Christ has done and is doing through him; thinking that "being" is established by "doing," identity based on deeds. The Christian must understand that all of his identity, value, worth and spirituality is found in Christ, not in himself. In and of ourselves, we are nothing, and can do nothing of any consequence before God. "Apart from Me, you can do nothing," Jesus said (Jn. 15:5). Paul admitted that "nothing good dwells in me" (Rom. 7:18), but he could also affirm that "I am who I am by the grace of God" (I Cor. 15:10). There is no need to engage in the "worm-theology" of self-negation, self-depreciation, self-contempt or self-loathing. We need only recognize that as Christians, we are who we are, and do what we do, only on the basis of God's grace in the Person and work of Jesus Christ. Thus we will avoid the self-deception of a false opinion of ourselves, thinking ourselves to be what we aren't; and allow the character of humility and gentleness to be evidenced in our attitudes and actions. Love, and the recognition of its source in the character of God, always leads to humility. To the Romans, Paul would write, "By the grace of God given to me I say to every man among you not to think more highly of himself than he ought to think; but to think so as to have sound judgment, as God has allotted to each a measure of faith" (Rom. 12:3). To the Philippians he would write, "Do nothing from selfishness or empty conceit, but with humility of mind let each of you regard one another as more important than himself; do not look out for your own personal interests, but also for the interest of others" (Phil. 2:3,4).

6:4 Rather than "thinking he is something when he is nothing," *"let each one examine his own work."* Along with "looking to oneself" (6:1) in self-scrutiny and self-evaluation, Paul advises those who have a self-inflated opinion of themselves to engage in the self-examination of self-assessment or self-appraisal. The only problem is that such proud people seldom have the ability to be self-critical in an objective evaluation of themselves and their actions. Such requires the discernment and appraisal of the Spirit of God upon our lives (cf. I Cor. 2:13; 12:10). In the testing, proving and evaluating of what is being worked out in the behavior manifestations of our lives, Paul is asking Christians to ascertain whether they are doing the "good works which God prepared beforehand, that we should walk in them" (Eph. 2:10); whether they are deriving God's love from the Spirit within (Rom. 5:5). The criteria of our evaluation of our work is not comparison with others, not man-made criteria of ethical behavior, and not humanistic evaluation of statistical success, effectiveness or influence. The only criteria for examining the outward conduct of our Christian lives is to evaluate whether it is derived from Christ and expresses the character of Christ. We are accountable, not to others, not to outward standards, but only to Christ, allowing the dynamic "law of Christ" to express His character in all of our behavioral out-working.

Paul's call for self-examination should not be misconstrued as a mandate for introspective "navel-gazing" wherein one is preoccupied with taking his own "spiritual temperature or pulse." We are not called to engage in excessive "fruit-inspection" of our own behavioral activity, for such would be to focus on ourselves in self-orientation. Paul's purpose in calling for such self-examination was to expose that when our "being" and "doing" is evaluated in reference to Jesus Christ rather than in comparison with others, *"then"* the person with spiritual pride, ***"he will have the boast in regard to himself alone, and not in regard to another."*** In other words, the arrogant and self-confident Christian will recognize that his self-righteousness is but an empty boast full of "empty conceit" (Phil. 2:3). When we compare ourselves and our actions only with the character of Christ, then there is no ground for boasting; only ground for humility that recognizes our inability and His ability. The "fruit of the Spirit" (5:22,23) is never the result of our generative action and effort, but always the result of the divine action of the Spirit.

Paul's reference to self-righteous boasting may have been another allusion to the Judaizers and their proud confidence in Law-keeping, leading to the Pharisaic attitude that condescendingly asserts, "I thank God that I am not like other people" (cf. Lk. 18:11). Whether he was thinking of the Judaizers or not, Paul was definitely addressing the spiritual pride that evaluates oneself by making competitive comparisons to the "spirituality" of others by evaluating their faults. Later Paul would write to the Corinthians, "We are not bold to class or compare ourselves with some of those who commend themselves; but when they measure themselves by themselves, and compare themselves with themselves, they are without understanding. But we will not boast beyond measure, but within the measure of the sphere which God apportioned to us as a measure, to reach even as far as you" (II Cor. 10:12,13).

6:5 Concluding his argument about self-evaluation by self-comparison, Paul explains, *"For each one shall bear his own load."* It is difficult to determine what Paul had in mind as he wrote these words. Some have thought this phrase to be inconsistent with what Paul had written three verses earlier when he wrote, "Bear one another's burdens" (6:2). Contextually considered, they do not appear to be contradictory, but the intended meaning of this concluding admonition has been variously interpreted. Does Paul mean that each person will have to bear his own load of responsibility or guilt before God on the day of judgment, at which time his "work" (6:4) will be tested and determined to be either "gold, silver and precious stones" or "wood, hay and straw" (I Cor. 3:12-15; cf. Rom. 14:12)? Or does Paul mean to say that in contrast to personal evaluation by comparative consideration of other's standards or behavior, each Christian is responsible before God to be and to do what God wants to be and to do in him? (Both interpretations are viable since the Greek verb can be translated as either a future indicative or a present imperative.) The present tense of personal responsibility seems to better fit the context, but we are still left with several variables of identifying the "load" which we are to carry. Are we individually responsible for our unique "load" of self-oriented flesh-patterns, which by constantly allowing the Spirit to overcome (5:16) day-by-day, we are more aware of what it means to "bear one another's burdens" (6:2)? Or is the "load" we must bear (1) the load of responsibility before God for the misrepresentative expressions of the sinful and selfish "works of the flesh" (5:19-21), or (2) the load of responsibility for spiritual pride and boasting (6:3,4), or (3) the load of responsibility for self-examination (6:4), or (4) the load of responsibility for personal availability to Christ's sufficiency, for receptivity of His character in our behavior? Whatever the "load" is that we are responsible to bear individually, we can be sure that Paul is not advocating or commanding a self-effort performance, but is correlating personal responsibility in the context of the grace and liberty in Jesus Christ.

6:6 What appears to be an abrupt change of thought when Paul writes, *"And let the one who is taught the word share all good things with him who teaches,"* may be connected to what precedes as an example of what Paul meant by mutual burden-bearing (6:2), or may be a clarification of what could have been misconstrued by an overly broad interpretation of "bearing one's own load" (6:5). In the community of Christian concern, Paul was keen to have Christians realize that those receiving oral instruction and teaching had a responsibility to contribute to those who were taking the time to be faithful teachers of the gospel. The words for "taught" and "teaches" are Greek participles from which we get the English transliterations of "catechism" and "catechumen," meaning "instruction" and "one being instructed." The content of this instruction is "the word," which can be equivalent to "the gospel," but should not be understood simply as biblical information, proper exegetical conclusions based on Scripture, or a corpus of Christian doctrines or traditions. The gospel is the good news of the living Word who became flesh (Jn. 1:14) and exegeted God (Jn. 1:18) by visibly expressing Him perfectly. The content of valid Christian instruction is always Jesus Christ! Consistent with Jesus' own words when He said, "The worker is worthy of his support" (Matt. 10:10; Lk. 10:7), Paul wanted Christians to understand that their loving concern for others included contributing to those who teach. To the Corinthians, Paul wrote that "the Lord directed those who proclaim the gospel to get their living from the gospel" (I Cor. 9:14), explaining that, "If we sowed spiritual things in you, is it too much if we should reap material things from you?" (I Cor. 9:11). Those who contribute spiritual sustenance to the Body of Christ have a legitimate right to expect that others will contribute physical sustenance for their physical bodies (even though Paul refrained from accepting such in some situations in order to illustrate the free grace of God - cf. II Cor. 11:7-11). Note that in I Cor. 9:11 Paul employed the sowing and reaping concept to explain the legitimacy of remuneration for Christian teachers (as he also did in II Cor. 9:6), and the connection of those thoughts may have precipitated the use of that same analogy in the verses that follow.

6:7   Still pointing out the necessity of practical Christian concern for others, Paul states, ***"Do not be deceived, God is not mocked."*** Whether Paul was thinking of being self-deceived (as in 6:3), or being deceived by the Judaizing infiltrators, or being deceived by the diabolic Deceiver, Satan, is not clear, for the verb can be either middle or passive, allowing for the varying interpretations. The means of the deception is not essential, however, to understanding that God will not tolerate those who would snub or spurn (cf. Prov. 1:30) Him by "thumbing their nose" (cf. Ezek. 8:17) at Him in mockery or contempt. How might a Christian mock God in this way? Perhaps by thinking that since he is "off the hook" from the death-consequences of sin, and eternally preserved in Christ, that he can continue to engage in misrepresentative, sinful behavior without consequence. Perhaps by failing to take into account the "finished work" of Christ by the dynamic grace of God, the Christian counts on his own performance of "good works" to establish his "spirituality," thus making a mockery of all that God has made available at great expense in Jesus Christ. Perhaps by refusing to recognize his responsibility to the collective whole of the Body of Christ by being receptive to God's love in restoring his brother (6:1), bearing his brother's burden (6:2), and contributing to Christian teachers (6:6). God will not allow Himself, or the actions that derive out of His Being, to be mocked without consequence.

"For whatever a man sows, this he will also reap." This proverbial saying about the principle of consequence was employed by Aristotle, Cicero, and many others. Old Testament usages include Eliphaz' mistaken counsel of arguing backwards to explain Job's problems: "Those who sow trouble, harvest it" (Job 4:8). The wise author of the Proverbs collection wrote, "He who sows iniquity will reap vanity" (Prov. 22:8). The prophet Hosea intoned that "they who sow the wind, reap the whirlwind" (Hosea 8:7), whereas those who would "sow with a view to righteousness, reap in accordance with kindness" (Hosea 10:12). The proverb is based upon a basic law of agriculture that explains the principle of cause and effect, the consequences of previous action. It you sow wheat, you can expect to reap wheat, and the harvest can usually be expected to be in proportion to the planting. The concept is proverbially transferred to human behavior indicating that in the responsibility of our choices we can expect certain consequences.

6:8 To explain what he intended to illustrate with this proverb, Paul reintroduces the flesh/Spirit contrast (5:16-25), and integrates it with this principle of consequence. *"For the one who sows to his own flesh shall from the flesh reap corruption."* The Christian who continues to plant his behavior in the fleshly soil of selfishness, choosing to submit to the patterned desires of self-interest, self-gratification, and self-promotion (cf. I Jn. 2:16), will, as a consequence, reap a harvest of defilement and destruction. The question is whether Paul's use of the future consequence refers to the chronological time of an eventual future corruption of a decomposing physical corpse (cf. I Cor. 15:42-50; II Cor. 4:16-5:5) and everlasting destruction? Or does the future tense indicate the logical consequence of fleshly behaviors in the destructive and defiling corruption of the consistent expression of the character of Christ, and the unity of the Body of Christ? Some interpreters choose to maintain both in a double entendre.

Conversely, Paul explains, *"but the one who sows to the Spirit shall from the Spirit reap eternal life."* Those Christians who plant their behavior in submission and receptivity to the Spirit of Christ within them, being "led of the Spirit" (5:18), "walking by the Spirit" (5:16,25), and being "filled with the Spirit" (Eph. 5:18), to allow for the manifestation of the "fruit of the Spirit" (5:22,23) unto God's own glory, shall as a consequence harvest and experience eternal life. Once again, we must question whether Paul is referring to a chronological future consequence of heavenly benefit, or the logical consequence of the blessedness of Christ's life in the present, or a combination of the two. "Eternal life" is not just an extended commodity of perpetual duration that is acquired by a believer after physical death. The "life of the ages" is intrinsic to and invested in the living Person of the resurrected Lord Jesus Christ. Jesus Christ is eternal life (cf. Jn. 14:6), and those who receive the Spirit of Christ have eternal life (cf. Jn. 17:2,3; I Jn. 5:12,13). Eternal life is the qualitative expression of Christ's life in the "fruit of the Spirit" (5:22,23), as well as the quantitative extension and continuum of Christ's life in heavenly eternity. It would seem, though, that Paul's primary emphasis here in the context of advocating consistent behavioral expression of the character of Christ (5:13 – 6:10) was to explain to the Galatian Christians the consequential corruption of the unity of Christ's Body when Christians live according to the flesh, and the consequential collective harmony of the expression of Christ's life and character as Christians live according to the Spirit.

6:9 Paul therefore encourages the Galatian Christians, saying, *"And let us not lose heart in doing good."* Later to the Thessalonians, Paul would use essentially the same words, "do not grow weary of doing good" (II Thess. 3:13). Paul seems to be saying, "Don't get to the point where you despise doing good because you wonder whether it is worth it." Granted, the immediate consequences of "doing good," loving one another (5:13), bearing the "fruit of the Spirit" (5:22,23), fulfilling the "law of Christ" (6:2), and manifesting the goodness of God's character in godliness by "sowing to the Spirit (6:8), will not always be visibly advantageous or pleasant. Jesus "went about doing good" (Acts 10:38,39), and they put Him to death on a cross.

Despite the absence of visible consequences and observable "results," Paul explains that *"in due time we shall reap if we do not grow weary."* Whereas the farmer, the basis of this agricultural metaphor, has a reasonable expectancy of the time of harvest, the metaphor breaks down since the timing of the consequences for the Christian are indeterminate. In God's own time (cf. Gal. 4:4) the consequences of our actions will be revealed, whether in this life or the next. The future tense of the reaping or harvesting again allows for future chronological time or logical consequence. The Christian may experience a realized sense of fulfillment individually or collectively, but there will always be a delayed "not yet" of fulfillment and consequence as well. The contingent responsibility for such consequence of fulfillment is "if we do not grow weary." We must not become faint or fatigued. We must not slacken or become lax. We must not give up or quit when we do not see visible consequences. We need spiritual stamina and endurance which comes as a result of God's preservation and our perseverance. The promise of God that Paul relays to the Galatian Christians is that the principle of consequence is as sure as God's own faithfulness.

6:10   In logical conclusion to his practical exhortations about "serving one another through love" (5:13), Paul advises the Galatian Christians, ***"So then, while we have opportunity, let us do good to all men."*** While we still have time within God's "due time" (the Greek word is the same in vss. 9 and 10), we are responsible to use our time as an opportunity and occasion for availability and receptivity to God's active expression of His character in our behavior. To the Ephesians, Paul would write, "Make the most of your time, because the days are evil" (Eph. 5:16). There is a legitimate sense of *carpe diem*, seizing the day, not for humanistic advantage, but for the expression of God's character of goodness toward all men. Such expression of God's goodness can only be derived from God. "The one doing good derives what he does out of God" (III Jn. 11), for "God alone is good" (Lk. 18:19). The "doing of good" is the "fruit of the Spirit" (5:22), expressing God's love to others (5:13). The objects of such divine love expressed through the Christian are to be "all men" comprehensively and universally, regardless of race, gender, class, nation, dress, cleanliness, custom or other distinction. The manner of "doing good" may be inclusive of physical relief, social and psychological development, or spiritual evangelism and discipleship.

In particular, though not exclusive, application of "doing good to all men," Paul notes that Christians should do so ***"especially to those who are of the household of faith."*** This is not necessarily a prioritizing of the recipients of love, for all love is God's love (cf. I Jn. 4:8,16) and God's love is all-embracing (cf. Jn. 3:16). But Christians have a particular sense of responsibility and an especial connection of concern to those with whom they are united in spiritual commonality in the Body of Christ, with whom they are "one in Christ" (3:28) in the same spiritual family, in "the household of the faith." This designation of the "household of the faith" is a transference of identification of God's people and family from the Judaic "house of Israel" (Matt. 15:24; Heb. 8:10) as the "house of

God" (Heb. 10:21), to the "spiritual house" (I Pet. 2:5), "the household of God which is the Church of the living God" (I Tim. 3:15; cf. Eph. 2:19). In the community of the concerned, the Church, we have a special concern for those who are family members, and Paul exemplified this concern in receiving collections for the poorer saints in Judea (cf. II Cor. 9:6-9).

In this practical portion of his epistle, Paul indicates that consistent out-working of God's character of love and righteousness in the collective community of the concerned, the Church, will involve being (1) lovingly concerned about restoring the faltering, (2) lovingly concerned about remunerating the teachers, and (3) lovingly concerned about recognizing the consequences of our choices.

Concern for the restoration of the fallen and faltering is not a ministry that we leave to the "Salvation Army" and their ministry to derelicts and "down-and-outers." We all falter, fail and fall, lapsing into "works of the flesh" (5:19-21). "If we say we have no sin, we are deceiving ourselves, and the truth is not in us" (I Jn. 1:8). We are all vulnerable, and must be vigilant to "look to ourselves, lest we be tempted" (6:1). But the excuses for avoiding the responsibility of restoring our lapsed brethren seem to know no end. "I'm not qualified since I do not consider myself to be 'spiritual'," is one excuse. Are you a Christian who has the Spirit of Christ dwelling in you (Rom. 8:9), and are you available to the working of the Spirit in your life? If so, then you qualify as "spiritual." Another will beg-off, arguing that he does not have a degree in psychology, sociology or counseling, and might thus do more harm than good. Another will attempt to opt-out by claiming that he does not have a natural temperament of gentleness, failing to recognize that gentleness is a "fruit of the Spirit" (5:22,23). Others will assert that "bearing another's burdens" is akin to "minding other people's business" and "putting your nose where it doesn't belong." Ours is a humanistic society where everyone "does

6:10

his own thing," and is expected to "solve his own problems" in self-sufficiency, resisting involvement in other people's problems as they withdraw into their cocoon of isolationistic anonymity. The Church is to be radically different from such an individualistic and unconcerned society. The Church is to be a functional Body wherein every part is important to the whole; a family wherein every member is concerned for the other, and willing to administer God's love. It is not that we have all the answers condensed into easy formulas, tidy techniques or pat procedures; but we care enough to be concerned and to confront, and to love unconditionally for as long as the process of restoration might take. The failure to restore others in love evidences the self-oriented indifference that pushes people aside, hoping that they will work out their problems by themselves. Unfortunately, the organized church has often presented itself as a place for people who are perfect and have no problems, rather than as a spiritual hospital wherein everyone is in the process of being healed of their spiritual and behavioral problems.

Concern for the remuneration of Christian teachers has fallen prey to abuses, both by ministers and by Christian congregations.$_2$ Some Christian pastors and teachers have not been accountable to God, and have shirked their responsibilities in undisciplined laxity, causing some people to regard them as "cashing in" on a "cushy job" where "they only have to work one day out of the week." Reports of flagrant misappropriation of contributed funds by some ministers or evangelists serves to expose such ministerial abuses. On the other hand, congregations can abuse what are supposed to be "love gifts" of sharing with the teacher, by considering themselves to be the pastor's employer, and thus in a position to control what the pastor does, says, and preaches. "We pay the piper, so we call the tune!" Loving concern for the remuneration of Christian teachers must involve an understanding of God's spiritual giftedness of teaching (cf. Rom. 12:7; I Cor. 12:28,29; Eph. 4:11,12), as well as personal accountability and discipline on the part of the teacher to study, pray, and teach.

Concern for the recognition of the results and consequences of Christian choices is also much needed in our contemporary churches. Many have failed to recognize that their choices have consequences; they affect us, and they affect others! The unconcerned and nonchalant attitude that our choices do not make much difference, and that God will protect us from all the consequences of our stupid and irresponsible choices, certainly impinges upon the character and sovereignty of God. It is a contemptuous mockery of God that "plays God for a fool," and paints God as a "cosmic cure-all" Who does not take into account our responsibility of choice and faith. No wonder some regard Christians as "escapists" who can justify everything by reference to God's grace, love, sovereignty and omnipotence. Paul makes it very clear that there are consequences to our choices, both now and in the future. Only by consistent choices of faith, whereby we are receptive to God's activity, can we expect to manifest the divine character of the "fruit of the Spirit" (5:22,23), and participate in the unity and harmony of the new spiritual society of "the household of faith."

The implications and applications of these practical admonitions of Paul are probably innumerable, as we seek to "serve one another in love" (5:13) in the "community of the concerned."

ENDNOTES

1. George, Timothy, *Galatians. The New American Commentary* series. Broadman and Holman Publishers. 1994. pg. 410.
2. Stott, J.R.W., *The Message of Galatians*. The Bible Speaks Today series. London: Inter-Varsity Press. 1968. pgs. 167-169.

The Completeness of the Gospel of Grace

Galatians 6:11-18

As Paul began to conclude this pyrographic epistle to the Christians in the churches of Galatia, he took the stylus from the scribe who had been writing what he had been dictating, and penned the final words in his own handwriting. In a summarizing postscript the apostle recaps the central features of the gospel of grace that had been revealed to Him by Jesus Christ Himself. Though the concluding statements of some letters may be filled with a few pleasantries whereby the author "signs off" without any substantial content conveyed, such is not the case with this straightforward epistle of Paul. These words should not be disregarded as but closing courtesies. Rather, they are gorged with theological content as Paul provides a synopsis and recapitulation of the Christocentric gospel that had become the essence of his life, and this he wanted to preserve in its dynamic manifestation among the Galatians. H.D. Betz indicates that this autographic postscript is "most important for the interpretation of Galatians," for "it contains the interpretive clues to the understanding of Paul's major concerns in the letter as a whole and should be employed as the hermeneutical key to the intentions of the Apostle."[1] As a summarizing synopsis it certainly draws together several of the major themes of the epistle to affirm that the only gospel (cf. 1:6-9) is the vital indwelling dynamic of the life of the risen Lord Jesus Christ by His Spirit enacted by God's grace, serving as the complete realization and fulfillment of God's intent for mankind.

But this concluding paragraph of the letter to the Galatians is more than just a recap of the themes previously addressed. It is at the same time the culminating climax of Paul's argument which serves as a capstone, the final thrust and finishing touch of his thesis of the completeness of God's work in the "finished work" of Jesus Christ. This paragraph, written in Paul's own hand, delivers the knock-out punch to the arguments of the intrusive Judaizers.

The tone of this concluding unstylistic postscript is still somewhat terse and pointed. Written with the recognition of the dire consequences of allowing the living gospel of Jesus Christ to be constrained in the legalistic restrictions of religion, Paul's comments are curt, crisp and clipped. There are no personal greetings to or from individuals. There are no prayer requests. There is no doxological paean of praise. The severity of the situation in Galatia demands a straightforward concluding salvo.

6:11 Drawing attention to the graphic change in handwriting, Paul writes, **"See with what large letters I am writing to you with my own hand."** Apparently the remainder of the letter (6:11-18) was written in Paul's own handwriting, whereas the preceding portion was inscribed by an amanuensis, a practice often employed by Paul (cf. I Cor. 16:21; II Cor. 10:1; II Thess. 3:17; Col. 4:18). The interpretive question has always been whether the secretarial scribe had any latitude in drafting the wording of the letter, or whether it was a process of direct dictation of the words of Paul.

The enlarged size of the text in this autographic summary has received various explanations. While some have speculated that Paul had an inability for small detail creating an illegibility in his writing, perhaps caused by physical deformities or injuries resulting from his persecutions, the predominate speculation has been that Paul wrote in "large letters" due to faulty eyesight (cf. 4:13-15). It may simply be that Paul's personal inscription of these final words was to provide attestation of the genuineness of this letter, and invest it with the personal impact of his apostolic authority. The textual enlargement could have been utilized to emphasize and underscore the importance of Paul's conclusions, in like manner as we might employ block capital letters or bold print in our typographic printing today.

6:12 In a final exposure of the Judaizers' methods and motives, Paul indicates that *"those who desire to make a good showing in the flesh try to compel you to be circumcised."* In this obvious allusion to the legalistic infiltrators of the "circumcision party" (2:12), Paul reveals the compulsive pressure (cf. 2:3,14) of intimidating and threatening manipulation that the intruding religionists in Galatia were employing on the young Christians there. Their demand for physical male circumcision was based on a faulty theology that maintained that such action had essential saving significance in identifying Gentile Christians with ethnic Jews and their Judaic religion as the "people of God." Paul exposes their self-serving "desire to make a good showing in the flesh," perhaps employing a double entendre that referred to how the circumcision of the foreskin of the male flesh as a distinctive mark of identifying Gentile Christians with Jews served as an external criteria of performance whereby the Judaizers could "look good" and make a self-seeking "good impression" in the sight of their racially biased kin.

Paul proceeds to indicate that the self-serving motivations of the Judaizers' circumcision compulsion was *"simply that they may not be persecuted for the cross of Christ."* These ethnic Jews who claimed to accept Jesus as the promised Messiah still had an undue allegiance to their racial ancestry and religion. Paul's understanding of the "cross of Christ" demanded that the death and subsequent resurrection of Jesus serve as the singular basis of God's remedial and restorative action in mankind. When Jesus declared from the cross, "It is finished!" (John 19:30), it was a triumphant proclamation of the completed accomplishment of everything necessary to restore man to God's functional intent. There was nothing more that man needed to perform or accomplish, for Jesus Christ had accomplished everything required in the performance of His death and resurrection, allowing His saving life (Rom. 5:10) and righteousness (Rom. 5:16-21) to be appropriated by the reception of faith. The "cross of Christ" thus served as a denial of all Jewish privilege of race and religion, all efficacy of the old covenant, and all benefit of keeping the Law with its ritual requirements and works of performance for righteousness. Such an understanding of the "cross of Christ" was repudiated by the Judaizers as they sought to preserve their racial and religious affinities with the Jewish peoples who regarded themselves as especially chosen by God for superior privileges.

In the particular context of the Judaizers' proselytizing promulgation of circumcision of Gentile believers in Galatia, the advocacy of the identifying mark of the flesh in male circumcision as a necessary performance of righteousness served as a mitigating factor whereby they could avoid the persecution that would necessarily result from regarding the "cross of Christ" as the sole basis of righteousness and the rejection of all Jewish privilege. Where would such persecution come from? Some have suggested that the Roman government was the persecuting agency, allowing a protective acceptance of the Jewish religion in the empire, but intolerant of new religions (especially Christians who adamantly claimed allegiance to one Lord and King, Jesus Christ). By identifying with the religion of Judaism in their identifying mark of circumcision, the Judaizers could thus avoid Roman persecution, giving the impression that Christianity was but a new sect of Judaism. The more probable source of persecution was from the Jewish religionists themselves. It was the Jews, for example, who had physically persecuted Paul during his ministry in Galatia (cf. Acts 13:50;

14:19). Paul had referred to Jewish persecution of Christians earlier in the epistle (4:29), indicating that his continued persecution was a result of "the stumbling block of the cross" (5:11), i.e., his insistence that the "cross of Christ" was the sole basis of righteousness before God (cf. 2:21), which both Jews and Judaizers felt compelled to resist. Though the Jews of Galatia were not in agreement with the Judaizers acceptance of Jesus as the Messiah, their persecutive actions were mollified by the fact that the Judaizers were compelling Gentile converts to be circumcised with the identifying mark of Judaism, which Paul regarded as a repudiation of the significance of the "cross of Christ." So Paul implies that the Judaizers were "saving their own skins" by demanding the cutting off of Gentile foreskins in circumcision.

6:13 In continued assault upon the inconsistency of the opportunistic Judaizers, Paul alleges that ***"those who are circumcised do not even keep the Law themselves."*** The advocates of circumcision who demand this particular performance of the Law, know very well that they are unable to perform every detail of the Law's demands. The cursedness of inability (3:10), inadequacy, and insufficiency (cf. II Cor. 3:5), renders every person guilty (James 2:10) of violating the Law's commands. Legalistic inculcations will never overcome the fleshly, self-seeking desires of man (Col. 2:23), and man does not have within himself the ability to generate or produce divine character as demanded by the Law. Religion inevitably settles for the inconsistent and insincere pretensions of hypocrisy (2:13) wherein they "pick and choose" the rules and regulations they will espouse, making token efforts to abide by such in their public performance when others are observing (cf. Matt. 23:2-5). Such a religious system of behavioral compromise was being promulgated by the Judaizers, based on their eclectic attempt to espouse both the "finished work" of the "cross of

Christ" (6:12) in conjunction with the performance of Law, which Paul denies is a viable combination.

Further expanding the Judaizers' "desire to make a good showing in the flesh" (6:12), Paul notes that *"they desire to have you circumcised, that they may boast in your flesh."* The objectives of the Judaizers were not seeking the highest good and welfare of the Galatian Christians, i.e., loving concern; but were instead the self-serving motivations of proud self-aggrandizement (cf. 4:17), whereby they could claim "bragging rights" for having "won over" Gentile Christians by imposing upon them the physical, visible, external mark of Jewish religious identification. Religion, throughout the history of man, has focused on the externalities of visible, physical marks of identification, adjudging the success of their propagandizing endeavors by the statistical analysis of the number of converts and adherents they could persuade to conform to their patterns of behavior. People have been used as pawns and trophies in the religious process of allowing the "end" of proud, boastful evaluation of physical and statistical success to justify the pragmatic "means" of accumulating adherents.

Scot McKnight identifies four problems with the Judaizers: (1) their method is force - they "compel you to be circumcised," (2) their motive is fear - "that they may not be persecuted for the cross of Christ," (3) their consistency is flawed - "they do not keep the Law themselves," and (4) their goal is to flaunt - "that they may boast in your flesh."[2]

6:14 In contrast to such religious methodology and motivation, Paul exclaims, *"But may it never be that I should boast, except in the cross of our Lord Jesus Christ."* He adamantly and decisively rejects the proud, self-serving tactics and objectives of the Judaizing religionists. Paul would no longer boast in racial superiority, ritual enactment or religious performance (cf. Phil. 3:4-7), but only in the sufficiency of Jesus Christ as set in motion in His finished work on the cross. All boasting of racial and religious superiority is excluded, Paul would later write to the Romans, because all that we have and do as Christians is only received by faith, our receptivity of His activity, and not by any Law performance on our part (Rom. 3:27,28). So, "let him who boasts, boast in the Lord" (I Cor. 1:31; II Cor. 10:17), for "Christ has become to us righteousness and sanctification" (I Cor. 1:30).

To "boast in the cross" is not to take gory delight in an execution instrument, which is what the cross was. Nor is it an exalted remembrance of the historical event when Jesus was crucified on such a torturous execution instrument, dying a martyr's death.[3] Even the theological implications of the remedial work of Jesus Christ in taking the punitive consequences of death on a cross on behalf of mankind in order to redeem man are insufficient to explain Paul's boast. When Paul boasts "in the cross of our Lord Jesus Christ," he recognizes the "finished work" (Jn. 19:30) of Christ, complete and unrepeatable (*contra* circumcision), whereby Jesus Christ triumphantly and victoriously set in motion the resurrection power (cf. Rom. 1:4) and the Pentecostal outpouring of His Spirit (cf. Acts 2:4), allowing humanity to be restored to God's creational intent by the reinvestiture of God's life and character in man by the Spirit of Christ. This cosmically decisive action of vicariously taking humanity's death in order to restore the presence and function of divine life to man by the Spirit of the living Lord Jesus Himself was the basis of an entirely "new creation" (6:15) of a "new humanity" (Eph. 2:15) in the "kingdom of God" (Rom. 14:17), distinct and mutually antithetical to the fallen world-order of evil. In Paul's mind the cross became representative of the entirety of the personal, divine action of God in Christ which became the crux of the demarcation of mankind polarized in the world-system of evil and the kingdom of Christ, and Paul could revel that he was a personal participant in Christ's life in the newly created kingdom.

6:14

Paul continues to explain, then, that *"through"* this completed reality of the recreation of God's order represented by the cross, ***"the world has been crucified to me, and I to the world."*** Consistent with his statement at the beginning of the letter when he affirmed that "the Lord Jesus Christ gave Himself for our sins, that He might deliver us out of this present evil age" (1:3,4), Paul explains again that Christ's completed action effects a severance and disconnection between himself and the world-order of evil. Christ has triumphed over the world-powers (cf. Col. 2:15), and Paul, in identification with Christ, has been "delivered from the domain of darkness and transferred into the kingdom of God's beloved Son" (Col. 1:13). Metaphorically, Paul links the salvific action of Christ's crucifixion, resurrection and Pentecostal outpouring (all signified by "the cross") with the terminal cessation of his identification and enslavement by the "god of this world" (II Cor. 4:4) who "works in the sons of disobedience" (Eph. 2:2). The diabolic order wherein Satan is the spirit (I Cor. 2:12) that rules over the world of fallen mankind (Jn. 12:31; 14:30; 16:11) is no longer the context which Paul is identified with or controlled by. In his receptivity of "the Lord Jesus Christ," Paul has died to the ruling authority and jurisdiction of the world-system; and the "powers that be" in that self-oriented, sinful system recognize that Paul is "as good as dead" to the serving of their purposes. His reception of the Lordship of Jesus Christ renders Paul outside of the rightful control and claims of the world-order, as he is no longer "in bondage under the elemental things of the world" (4:3,9; Col. 2:8). In connection with his co-crucifixion with Christ (2:20) and crucifixion of the flesh (5:24), along with his having "died to the Law" (2:19), Paul could affirm a crucified relationship to the world-order that stands in opposition to the kingdom of Christ, recognizing it to be powerless, impotent and sterile, with no right or jurisdiction to rule over him. Paul could affirm, as John did later, that "greater is He who is in me, than he who is in the world" (I Jn. 4:4), and glory in the functional Lordship of the living Spirit of Christ in the newly created order of the Kingdom.

6:15 In light of the new spiritual realities in Christ Jesus, Paul goes on to explain that *"neither is circumcision anything, nor uncircumcision."* Such physical externalities are totally irrelevant to God's order and the expression of God's character of righteousness. Circumcising the male penis does not make one a "new man" spiritually, but only the presence and dynamic of Jesus Christ (Eph. 4:24; Col. 3:10). For the factious false teachers in Galatia, physical male circumcision was the primary focus, serving as the supreme mark of identification with God's people, and therefore as an essential basis of righteous behavior. They failed to recognize that the purpose of the cutting off of the male foreskin in the old covenant was only for the prefiguring of God's intent to cut away sin from the heart of man in Jesus Christ (Rom. 2:29; Phil. 3:3). Paul had previously explained that "in Christ Jesus neither circumcision nor uncircumcision means anything, but faith working through love" (5:6). The receptivity of God's activity whereby we derive righteous character from Jesus Christ, the Righteous One (Acts 3:14; 7:52; 22:14; I Jn. 2:1), is the essence of the kingdom of Christ (Rom. 14:17).

"If any man is in Christ, he is a new creature; the old things passed away; behold, new things have come" (II Cor. 5:17). "There is no distinction between circumcised and uncircumcised, but Christ is all, and in all" (Col. 3:11). Therefore, the physical issue of circumcision is not an issue, for the "finished work" of Christ signified by the "cross" has established *"a new creation,"* a newly created spiritual order wherein the living Lord Jesus reigns as King in His kingdom. Jesus Himself, by His Spirit, is the beginning and essence of this "new creation of God" (Rev. 3:14). The completed performance of Christ in His "finished work" of the "cross," whereby He has done everything necessary and continues to accomplish all as the dynamic of His own demands, is the basis of an entirely new order of functionally restored humanity. The old created order fell into the world-order of evil, but God in Christ has re-created the viability of His original intent by regenerating man (re-Genesis), re-breathing the life of God into man (cf. Gen. 2:7) by the "wind of the Spirit" (Acts 2:2). The "new creation" is comprised of "new men" (Eph. 4:24; Col. 3:10) who have become "new creatures" (II Cor. 5:17) by receiving "new life" (Rom. 6:4) by the "renewing of the Holy Spirit" (Titus 3:5), that within the "new way" (Heb. 10:20) of a "new covenant" (Heb. 8:8,13; 12:24) whereby they function in the collective community of a "new humanity" (Eph. 2:15) unto the objective that Christ "makes all things new" (Rev. 21:5) in Himself. Within the kingdom of Christ and within the Church, Christians comprise and function as the "People of God" (Titus 2:14; I Pet. 2:9), in fulfillment of the Abrahamic promises, by the dynamic of the presence of the Christic Creator (Jn. 1:3,10; I Cor. 8:6; Col. 1:16), and not by submitting to a ritualistic act of physical circumcision.

6:16 Reaching the crescendo of his composition, Paul issues a conditioned invitation to *"those who will walk by this rule."* To all Christians living in the new created order of the kingdom of Christ, Paul encourages them to conduct their lives in the context of Christ and by the criteria of Christ. This seems to be the intent of Paul's phrase, "walk by this rule." Paul is not laying down some new rule or regulation that must be performed behaviorally by Christians, for this would be contrary to the entire argument of this epistle. The verb "walk" is the same verb used earlier when he admonished the Galatians to "walk by the Spirit" (5:25), which means to "line up, keep in step, and walk in sequence, corresponding to the other in a disciplined order." The word translated "rule" is the word from which we transliterate the word "canon," originally referring to a cane reed used as a measuring stick, but employed in Christian theology to refer to the acceptable and normative collection of scriptures regarded as authentic by measuring up to certain criterion of revelation and inspiration. But Paul is not encouraging Christians to conduct themselves by the Book, by the canonical Bible, nor by authoritative ecclesiastical maxims, moral standards or rules. Contextually we must conclude that Paul is encouraging the Galatians to conduct themselves in accordance with the reality of "the cross of Christ" (6:12,14), i.e., walking in the context of His "finished work" by the all-sufficient dynamic of the Spirit, corresponding to the normative criteria of His character by the enabling power of God's grace.

The result of such a "walk" will be God's ***"peace and mercy upon them."*** Drawing from his Hebrew heritage, Paul employs the traditional Hebraic benedictory blessing of God's peace and mercy upon Israel in the old covenant (cf. Ps. 125:5; 145:8). Paul transfers that blessing from the Judaic peoples of the old covenant to the "new creation" of the new covenant "people of God" who "have received mercy" in Christ (I Pet. 2:10) and know the "peace of Christ ruling in their hearts" (Col. 3:15).

By this transference of blessing, Paul proceeds to climax his argument by identifying Christian people as the new and genuine ***"Israel of God."*** Throughout this epistle Paul had challenged the Judaizers and their retention of old covenant concepts, indicating that he had "died to the Law" (2:19), been "redeemed from the curse of the Law" (3:13), and repudiated the distinguishing mark of Jewish circumcision (5:6; 6:15). He explicitly noted that the "sons of Abraham" (3:7,29) and "children of Sarah" (4:31) were those who were receptive of Jesus Christ in faith, thereby receiving the promises (3:29) and blessing (3:9,14) of Abraham to become residents of the heavenly Jerusalem (4:26) in the "household of faith" (6:10). The capstone of Paul's argument, rejecting the Judaizers' argument of racial and religious privilege, is the re-identification of "the Israel of God," establishing Christians as God's chosen people.

6:17

Though Gentiles were "once excluded from Israel" (Eph. 2:12), they are now included in the spiritual Israel of God's people in whom "God rules" by the Lordship of Jesus Christ. The derivation of the Hebrew word "Israel" is usually understood to be from the two root words, *yisra* (meaning "to rule") and *El* (meaning God), thus referring to "God rules." "Israel" was not meant to be just a physical, national, racial and religious designation, but the Hebrew peoples were to be the physical prefiguring of a spiritual people amongst whom and in whom "God rules." This is the basis of Paul's later assertion that "they are not all Israel who are descended from Israel" (Rom. 9:6), meaning that Gentiles are now spiritually included in "the people in whom God rules" by having received Jesus Christ, "the hope of Israel" (Acts 28:20), the basis by which all Christians, "all Israel will be saved" (Rom. 11:26).

6:17 Having set the capstone of his argument, transferring all God's blessings to those in Christ as "the Israel of God," Paul writes, *"From now on let no one cause trouble for me."* Paul's desire was that this correspondence would suffice to overcome the troubling problem in Galatia. He could hope that his clear explanation of the completeness of God's action in Christ would be the end of the matter. The last thing Paul sought was additional confrontational conflict. He was not out to pick a fight! But since religionists will fight to the death for their ideological agendas, it is doubtful that the Judaizers would give up the fight, and it is unclear whether the Galatian Christians were sufficiently convinced of the singularity of Jesus Christ to stand up and oust the intruders from their churches.

"I've been beaten up enough, both physically and emotionally," Paul seems to say. *"For I bear on my body the brandmarks of Jesus."* Paul bore the scars of persecutive beatings and stonings (cf. II Cor. 11:23-28), some of them perhaps inflicted during his ministry in Galatia (Acts 13:50: 14:19). Later, to the Corinthians, he would write that he was "afflicted, persecuted, struck down; always carrying about in the body the dying of Jesus" (II Cor. 4:8-10), for the purpose that "the life of Jesus might be manifested." Paul was not complaining about such mistreatment, for he could rejoice (Col. 1:24) in "the fellowship of His sufferings" (Phil. 3:10) with Christ. Nor was he ashamed of such physical marks, for he viewed them as "brand-marks" identifying him as a slave of Christ. The Greek word for "brand-marks" was later transliterated in the word "stigmata," which was used to refer to the crucifixion marks of nail-pierced hands and pierced abdomens which allegedly appeared in certain devout followers of Christ, though regarded by others as nothing more than a strange phenomena of neuropathic bleedings. Some Roman Catholic commentators have speculated that Paul was referring to such stigmatic marks on his own body, but it is more likely that he was referring to the physical marks of persecution. It is possible that Paul was taking a parting shot at the Judaizers by telling the Galatian Christians that if they were seeking physical "brand-marks," let them be the marks of persecution for having defended the gospel of grace in Jesus Christ alone, rather than physical "brand-marks" of circumcision.

6:18 Paul's final statement of instruction to the Galatians is, *"The grace of our Lord Jesus Christ be with your spirit, brethren."* Concluding where he began, with a reference to God's grace (1:3,6), as he did in all of his letters, Paul directs them to the divine dynamic of Christ which is the essence of Christianity. Far more than just the "threshold factor" of the Christian life that "gets one in the door to participate in the redemptive benefits of Christ," grace is the essential and comprehensive action of God in Jesus Christ that becomes the entire *modus operandi* of the Christian life. This has been Paul's argument throughout the epistle – that the gospel is the good news of the indwelling action of the living Lord Jesus, rather than legalistic, performance-oriented religion, as advocated by the Judaizers. The Christocentric reality of the risen "Lord Jesus Christ" functioning within our spirit (individually and collectively), manifesting His divine life and character in our behavior, to the glory of God – that, my brothers in Christ, is what it means to be a Christian. *"Amen."* So be it! Let it become the reality in our lives!

In this final paragraph of this "explosive epistle," Paul explodes the last underlying premise of the Judaizers, the proud positing of their privilege as "God's chosen people," identified as "Israel" by racial, national and religious heritage. Paul performs the *coup de grace* to such thinking by declaring that the completed work of God in the "finished work" of Christ on the cross (6:12,14) makes all things new, the formation of a spiritual "new creation" (6:15) wherein Christians comprise the real community of "Israel" (6:16) allowing God to rule in them through the Lord Jesus Christ. External ritualistic performances of religion will never make us "God's People," nor effect God's righteousness, for this is only accomplished by the grace (6:18) of God in the "Lord Jesus Christ" (6:14,18).

It is not difficult to see why this epistle has had such an impact throughout Christian history. Properly understood, this epistle will always serve to subvert the inevitable tendency of man to allow the Christian gospel of grace to lapse into legalistic religious performance. The letter to the Galatians is a constant summons to recognize the complete realization and fulfillment of God's intent in Jesus Christ, allowing no supplements or additional requirements. Without a doubt, legalistic, performance-oriented Judaizing elements will always dog the Church of Jesus Christ, but this letter remains a clarion call to the singularity of Jesus Christ as the essence of the gospel. If, as we have conjectured, this is the earliest of the extant letters of the apostle Paul, then the revolutionary reinterpretations that Paul makes in this letter must be regarded as foundational to the interpretations of the remainder of the Pauline writings.

ENDNOTES

1. Betz, Hans Dieter, *Galatians: A Commentary on Paul's letter to the Churches of Galatia.* Hermeneia – A Critical and Historical Commentary on the Bible. Philadelphia: Fortress Press. 1979. pg. 313.
2. McKnight, Scot, *Galatians.* The NIV Application Commentary series. Grand Rapids: Zondervan Publishing House. 1995. pgs. 299-301.
3. Fowler, James A., *The Cross of Christ.* Fallbrook: CIY Publishing. 1992.

Addendum

Map # 1 285

Map # 2 286

Map # 3 287

Bibliography 289

Ethnic Kingdom of Galatia
c. 278 — 25 B.C.

Map # 2

Roman Province of Galatia
25 B.C. — A.D. 137

Roman Province of Galatia
After A.D. 137

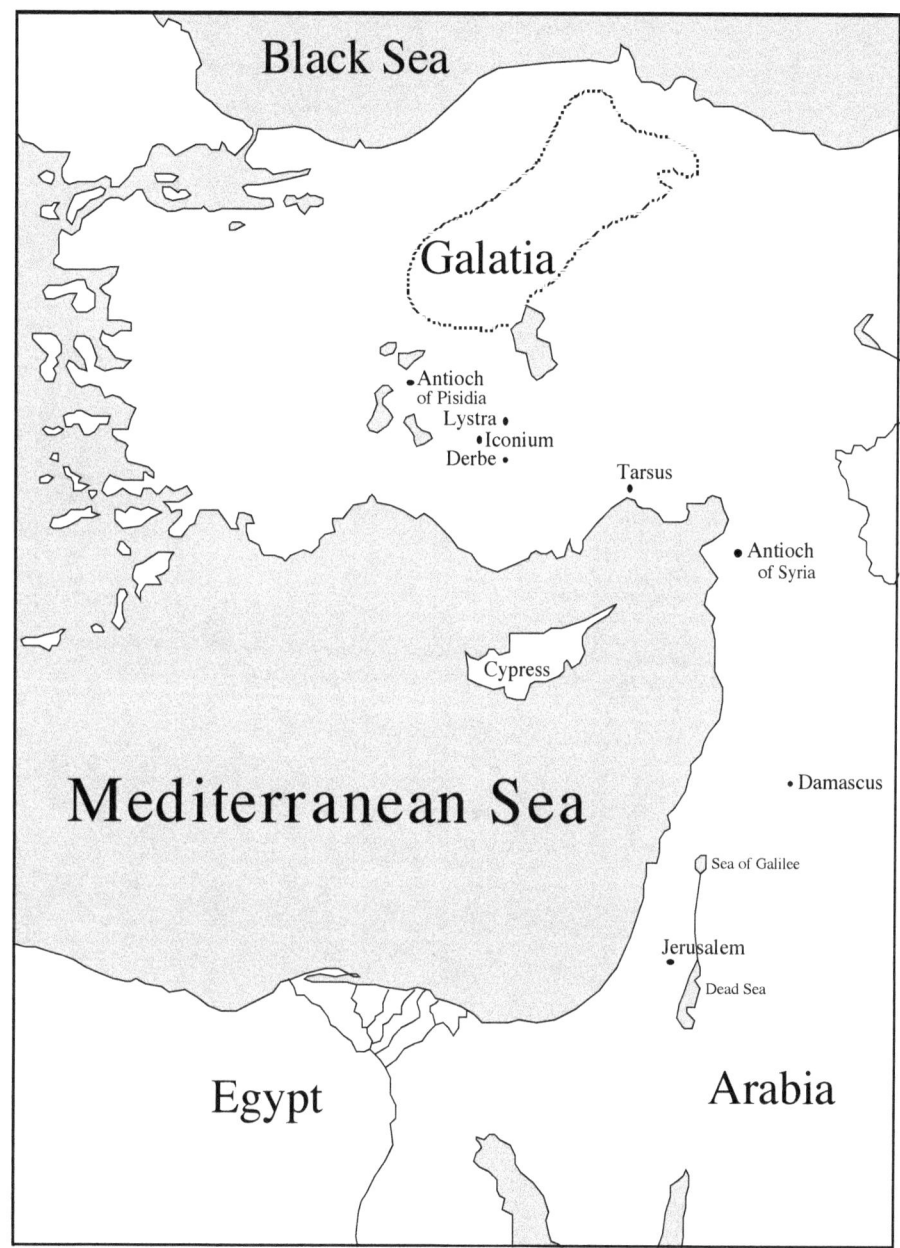

Bibliography

Acquinas, Thomas, *Commentary on Saint Paul's Epistle to the Galatians*. Acquinas Scripture Series Vol. 1. Albany: Magi Books, Inc., 1966.

Adeney, Walter F., *Thessalonians and Galatians*. The Century Bible series. Edinburgh: T.C. and E.C. Jack. n.d.

Andrews, Edgar H., *Free in Christ: The Message of Galatians*. Welwyn Commentary series. Durham: Evangelical Press. 1996.

Barclay, William, *The Letters to the Galatians and Ephesians*. The Daily Study Bible Series. Philadelphia: Westminster Press, 1958.

Barrett, C.K., *Freedom and Obligation: A Study of the Epistle to the Galatians*. London: SPCK, 1985.

Beet, Joseph Agar, *A Commentary on St. Paul's Epistle to the Galatians*. London: Hodder and Stoughton, 1885.

Betz, Hans Dieter, *Galatians: A Commentary on Paul's Letter to the Churches in Galatia*. Hermeneia—A Critical and Historical Commentary on the Bible. Philadephia: Fortress Press, 1979.

Bishop, George Sayles, *Grace in Galatians: A New and Concise Commentary on the Epistle*: Swengel: Reiner Publications. 1968.

Blunt, A.W.F., *The Epistle of Paul to the Galatians*. The Clarendon Bible. Oxford: Clarendon Press. 1925.

Boice, James Montgomery, *Galatians*. The Expositor's Bible Commentary, Vol. 10. Grand Rapids: Zondervan Publishing. 1976.

Bring, Ragnar, *Commentary on Galatians*. Philadelphia: Muhlenberg Press. 1961.

Brown, John, *An Exposition of Galatians*. Grand Rapids: Christian Classics. n.d.

Bruce, F.F., *The Epistle to the Galatians: A Commentary on the Greek Text*. The New International Greek Testament Commentary series. Grand Rapids: William B. Eerdmans Pub. Co., 1982

Burton, Ernest De Witt, *A Critical and Exegetical Commentary on the Epistle to the Galatians*. The International Critical Commentary series. Edinburgh: T&T Clark, 1971.

Bibliography

Calvin, John, *The Epistle of Paul the Apostle to the Galatians.* Calvin's Commentaries series. Grand Rapids: Wm. B. Eerdmans Pub. Co., 1965.

Clarke, Adam, *The New Testament: A Commentary and Critical Notes.* Nashville: Abingdon Press. n.d.

Cole, R.A., *The Epistle of Paul to the Galatians: An Introduction and Commentary.* London: The Tyndale Press. 1965.

Cosgrove, Charles H., *The Cross and the Spirit: A Study in the Argument and Theology of Galatians.* Macon: Mercer Univ. Press. 1988.

Cousar, Charles B., *Galatians.* Interpetation: A Bible Commentary for Teaching and Preaching. Atlanta: John Knox Press. 1982.

DeWolf, L. Harold, *Galatians: A Letter for Today.* Grand Rapids: William B. Eerdmans Pub. Co. 1971.

Duncan, George S., *The Epistle of Paul to the Galatians.* The Moffat New Testament Commentary. London: Hodder and Stoughton. 1966.

Dunn, James D.G., *The Epistle to the Galatians.* Black's New Testament Commentary. Peabody: Hendrickson Publishers. 1993.

Dunn, James D.G., *Jesus, Paul and the Law: Studies in Mark and Galatians.* Louisville: Westminster Press. 1990.

Dunn, James D.G., *The Theology of Paul's Letter to the Galatians.* New Testament Theology series. Cambridge: Cambridge Univ. Press. 1993.

Dunnam, Maxie D., *Galatians, Ephesians, Philippians, Colossians, Philemon.* The Communicator's Commentary. Waco: Word Books. 1982.

Eadie, John, *A Commentary on the Greek Text of the Epistle of Paul to the Galatians.* Grand Rapids: Baker Book House. 1979.

Ebeling, Gerhard, *The Truth of the Gospel: An Exposition of Galatians.* Philadelphia: Fortress Press. 1985.

Edwards, Mark J., *Galatians, Ephesians, Philippians.* Vol. VIII, Ancient Christian Commentary on Scripture series. Downers Grove: InterVarsity Press. 1999.

Findlay, G.G., *The Epistle to the Galatians.* The Expositor's Bible, vol. 5. Grand Rapids: Baker Book House. 1982.

Bibliography

Fung, Ronald Y.K., *The Epistle to the Galatians*. The New International Commentary on the New Testament. Grand Rapids: William B. Eerdmans. 1988.

Gelesnoff, Vladimir, *Paul's Epistle to the Galatians*. Canyon Country: Concordant Publishing Concern. 1977.

George, Timothy, *Galatians*. The New American Commentary, Vol. 30. Broadman and Holman Publishers. 1994.

Gibbon, J. Morgan, *The Epistle to the Galatians:* The Ancient Merchant Lecture for January 1895. London: James Clarke & Co. 1895.

Gill, John, *An Exposition of the New Testament*. Vol. VI. Grand Rapids: Baker Book House. 1980.

Guthrie, Donald, *Galatians*. The New Century Bible series. London: Oliphants. 1977.

Hansen, G. Walter, *Galatians*. The IVP New Testament Commentary Series. Downers Grove: InterVarsity Press. 1994.

Harrison, Norman B., *His Side Versus Our Side: Galatians – God's Greatest Antithesis*. Minneapolis: Harrison Service, Inc. 1940.

Hendriksen, William, *Exposition of Galatians*. New Testament Commentary series. Grand Rapids: Baker Book House. 1968.

Hubbard, David Allan, *Galatians: Gospel of Freedom*. Waco: Word Books. 1977.

Huttar, David K., *Galatians: The Gospel According to Paul*. The Deeper Life Commentary series. Camp Hill: Christian Publications, Inc. 2001.

Hogg, C.F. and Vine, W.E., *The Epistle to the Galatians, with Notes Exegetical and Expository*. Grand Rapids: Kregel Publications. 1921.

Koehler, Joh. Ph., *The Epistle of Paul to the Galatians*. Milwaukee: Northwestern Publishing House. 1957.

Krentz, Edgar, *Galatians*. Augsburg Commentary on the New Testament series. Minneapolis: Augsburg Publishing House. 1985.

Lange, John Peter, *Commentary on the Holy Scriptures*. Grand Rapids: Zondervan Publishing. n.d.

Lenski, R.C.H., *The Interpretation of St. Paul's Epistles to the Galatians, Ephesians and Philippians*. Minneapolis: Augsburg Publishing House. 1961.

Bibliography

Lightfoot, J.B., *The Epistle of St. Paul to the Galatians*. Grand Rapids: Zondervan Publishing. 1969.

Longenecker, Richard N., *Galatians*. Word Biblical Commentary, vol. 41. Dallas: Word Books. 1990.

Luhrmann, Dieter, *Galatians: A Continental Commentary*. Minneapolis: Fortress Press. 1992.

Luther, Martin, *A Commentary on Saint Paul's Epistle to the Galatians*. New York: Robert Carter & Brothers. 1860.

Machen, J. Gresham, *Machen's Notes on Galatians*. Philadelphia: Presbyterian and Reformed Pub. Co., 1973.

Martyn, J. Louis, *Galatians: A New Translation with Introduction and Commentary*. The Anchor Bible series, vol. 33a. New York: Doubleday. 1997.

McDonald, H.D., *Freedom in Faith: A Commentary on Paul's Epistle to the Galatians*. Old Tappan: Fleming H. Revell Co., 1973

McKnight, Scot, *Galatians*. The NIV Application Commentary. Grand Rapids: Zondervan Publishing. 1995.

Meyer, Heinrich August Wilhelm, *Critical and Exegetical Hand-Book to the Epistle to the Galatians*. Winona Lake: Alpha Publications. 1979.

Moore, David L., *Galatians: Grace Alone*. Schaumburg: Regular Baptist Press. 1979.

Morris, Leon, *Galatians: Paul's Charter of Christian Freedom*. Downers Grove: InterVarsity Press. 1996.

Nanos, Mark D., *The Irony of Galatians: Paul's Letter in First-century Context*. Minneapolis: Fortress Press. 2002.

Olshausen, Hermann, *Biblical Commentary on St. Paul's Epistles to the Galatians, Ephesians, Colossians, and Thessalonians*. Edinburgh: T&T Clark. 1864.

Perowne, E.H., *The Epistle to the Galatians*. The Cambridge Bible for Schools and Colleges. Cambridge: Cambridge Univ. Press. 1900.

Pettingill, William L., *By Grace Through Faith Plus Nothing: Simple Studies in Galatians*. Chicago: Van Kampen Press. 1938.

Quesnell, Quentin, *The Gospel of Christian Freedom*. New York: Herder and Herder. 1969.

Ramsay, William M., *A Historical Commentary on St. Paul's Epistle to the Galatians*. Grand Rapids: Baker Book House. 1965.

Bibliography

Ridderbos, Herman N., *The Epistle of Paul to the Churches of Galatia*. The New International Commentary on the New Testament. Grand Rapids: William B. Eerdmans. 1970.

Sadler, M.F., *The Epistles of St. Paul to the Galatians, Ephesians, and Philippians, with Notes Critical and Practical*. London: George Bell & Sons. 1892.

Silva, Moisés, *Explorations in Exegetical Method: Galatians as a Test Case*. Grand Rapids: Baker Books. 1996.

Smith, Ron & Penner, Rob, *Grace Simply Grace: Dealing with Condemnation and Legalism in the Christian Life*. Seattle: YWAM Press. 2002.

Stamm, Raymond T. and Blackwelder, Oscar Fisher, *The Epistle to the Galatians*. Interpreter's Bible, vol. 10. New York: Abingdon Press. 1953.

Stott, John R.W., *The Message of Galatians*. The Bible Speaks Today series. London: Inter-Varsity Press. 1968.

Tarazi, Paul Nadim, *Galatians: A Commentary*. Orthodox Biblical Studies series. Crestwood: St. Vladimir's Seminary Press. 1994.

Tenney, Merrill C., *Galatians: The Charter of Christian Liberty*. Grand Rapids: William B. Eerdmans. 1971.

Vos, Howard F., *Galatians: A Call to Liberty*. Everyman's Bible Commentary. Chicago: Moody Press. 1971.

Wallenkampf, Arnold Valentin, *Salvation Comes From the Lord*. Hagerstown: Review and Herald Publication Co. 1983.

Williams, A. Lukyn, *The Epistle of Paul the Apostle to the Galatians*. Cambridge Bible for Schools and Colleges. Cambridge: Cambridge Univ. Press. 1911.

Williams, A Lukyn, *The Epistle of Paul the Apostle to the Galatians*. Cambridge Greek Testament series. Cambridge: Cambridge Univ. Press. 1914.

Williams, Don, *Celebrate Your Freedom: An Inductive Bible Study on Galatians*. Waco: Word Books. 1975.

Wilson, Geoffrey B., *Galatians: A Digest of Reformed Comment*. Edinburgh: Banner of Truth Trust. 1973.

Witherington, Ben III, *Grace in Galatia: A Commentary on St. Paul's Letter to the Galatians*. Grand Rapids: Eerdmans Pub. Co. 1998.

Wood, Fred, *The Glory of Galatians*. Nashville: Broadman Press. 1972.

www.ingramcontent.com/pod-product-compliance
Lightning Source LLC
LaVergne TN
LVHW051622080426
835511LV00016B/2125